INTEGRATED POWER OF MANAGEMENT CONTROL SYSTEMS IN JAPAN

Japanese Management and International Studies
(ISSN: 2010-4448)

Editor-in-Chief: Kazuki Hamada *(Okayama Shoka University, Japan)*

Published

Vol. 21 *Integrated Power of Management Control Systems in Japan*
edited by Eri Yokota

Vol. 20 *Sustainability Management and Network Management*
edited by Kazuki Hamada, Johei Oshita & Hiroshi Ozawa

Vol. 18 *Management Accounting for Healthcare*
edited by Takami Matsuo & Yoshinobu Shima

Vol. 17 *Management Control Systems for Strategic Changes:
Applying to Dematurity and Transformation of Organizations*
edited by Shufuku Hiraoka & Akimichi Aoki

Vol. 16 *Sustainability Management and Business Strategy in Asia*
edited by Katsuhiko Kokubu & Yoshiyuki Nagasaka

Vol. 15 *Fixed Revenue Accounting: A New Management Accounting Framework*
edited by Kenichi Suzuki & Bruce Gurd

Vol. 14 *Holistic Business Process Management: Theory and Practice*
edited by Gunyung Lee, Masanobu Kosuga & Yoshiyuki Nagasaka

Vol. 13 *Management of Innovation Strategy in Japanese Companies*
edited by Kazuki Hamada & Shufuku Hiraoka

Vol. 12 *Lean Management of Global Supply Chain*
edited by Yasuhiro Monden & Yoshiteru Minagawa

Vol. 11 *Entrepreneurship in Asia: Social Enterprise, Network and Grassroots
Case Studies*
edited by Stephen Dun-Hou Tsai, Ted Yu-Chung Liu, Jersan Hu &
Shang-Jen Li

Vol. 10 *Management of Enterprise Crises in Japan*
edited by Yasuhiro Monden

Vol. 9 *Management of Service Businesses in Japan*
edited by Yasuhiro Monden, Noriyuki Imai, Takami Matsuo &
Naoya Yamaguchi

For the complete list of titles in this series, please go to
http://www.worldscientific.com/series/jmis

Japanese Management and International Studies – Vol. 21

INTEGRATED POWER OF MANAGEMENT CONTROL SYSTEMS IN JAPAN

editor

Eri Yokota
Keio University, Japan

NEW JERSEY • LONDON • SINGAPORE • BEIJING • SHANGHAI • TAIPEI • CHENNAI

Published by

World Scientific Publishing Co. Pte. Ltd.
5 Toh Tuck Link, Singapore 596224
USA office: 27 Warren Street, Suite 401-402, Hackensack, NJ 07601
UK office: 57 Shelton Street, Covent Garden, London WC2H 9HE

Library of Congress Cataloging-in-Publication Data
Names: Yokota, Eri, editor.
Title: Integrated power of management control systems in Japan /
  Eri Yokota, Keio University, Japan.
Description: New Jersey : World Scientific, [2025] | Series: Japanese management and
  international studies, 2010-4448 ; volume 21 | Includes bibliographical references and index. |
  Contents: volume 21. Japanese management and international studies.
Identifiers: LCCN 2024035241 | ISBN 9789811295645 (v. 21 ; hardcover) |
  ISBN 9789811295652 (v. 21 ; ebook) | ISBN 9789811295669 (v. 21 ; ebook other)
Subjects: LCSH: Management--Japan.
Classification: LCC HD70.J3 I558 2025 | DDC 658.00952--dc23/eng/20241107
LC record available at https://lccn.loc.gov/2024035241

British Library Cataloguing-in-Publication Data
A catalogue record for this book is available from the British Library.

Copyright © 2025 by World Scientific Publishing Co. Pte. Ltd.

All rights reserved. This book, or parts thereof, may not be reproduced in any form or by any means, electronic or mechanical, including photocopying, recording or any information storage and retrieval system now known or to be invented, without written permission from the publisher.

For photocopying of material in this volume, please pay a copying fee through the Copyright Clearance Center, Inc., 222 Rosewood Drive, Danvers, MA 01923, USA. In this case permission to photocopy is not required from the publisher.

For any available supplementary material, please visit
https://www.worldscientific.com/worldscibooks/10.1142/13914#t=suppl

Desk Editors: Kannan Krishnan/Pui Yee Lum

Typeset by Stallion Press
Email: enquiries@stallionpress.com

© 2025 World Scientific Publishing Company
https://doi.org/10.1142/9789811295652_fmatter

Japan Society of Organization and Accounting (JSOA)

President
Makoto Tomo, Seijo University, Japan

Vice Presidents
Kozo Suzuki, Tokyo Metropolitan Government, Japan
Naoya Yamaguchi, Aoyama Gakuin University, Japan

Directors
Akimichi Aoki, Senshu University, Japan
Gunyung Lee, Niigata University, Japan
Kazuki Hamada, Okayama Shoka University, Japan
Shufuku Hiraoka, Soka University, Japan
Noriko Hoshi, Hakuoh University, Japan
Masahiro Hosoda, Rikkyo University, Japan
Noriyuki Imai, International Professional University of Technology in Nagoya, Japan
Tomonori Inooka, Kokushikan University, Japan
Masanobu Kosuga, Kwansei Gakuin University, Japan
Takami Matsuo, Kobe University, Japan
Yoshiteru Minagawa, Nagoya Gakuin University, Japan
Yoshiyuki Nagasaka, Konan University, Japan
Hiroshi Obata, Meiji Gakuin University, Japan
Hiroshi Ozawa, Nagoya University, Japan
Yoshinobu Shima, Kindai University, Japan

Henry Aigbedo, Oakland University, USA
Mahmuda Akter, University of Dhaka, Bangladesh
Chao Hsiung Lee, National Chung Hsing University, Taiwan

Founder & Series Editor-in-Chief
Japanese Management and International Studies
Yasuhiro Monden, University of Tsukuba, Japan

Auditor
Mitsuru Kitagawa, North River Point, Japan

Assistant Managers
Satoshi Arimoto, Niigata University, Japan
Soichiro Higashi, Chiba Institute of Technology, Japan

Mission of JSOA and Editorial Information

For the purpose of making a contribution to the business and academic communities, the Japan Society of Organization and Accounting (JSOA), is committed to publishing Japanese Management and *International Studies* **(JMIS), which is a refereed annual publication with a specific theme for each volume**.

The series is designed to inform the world about research outcomes of the new "Japanese-style management system" developed in Japan. However, as the series title suggests, it also promotes "International Studies" on the managerial competencies of various countries that include Asian countries as well as Western countries under the globalized business activities.

Research topics included in this series are management of organizations in a broad sense (including the business group or inter-firm network) and the accounting for managing the organizations. More specifically, topics include business strategy, business models, organizational restoration, corporate finance, M&A, environmental management, operations management, managerial & financial accounting, manager performance evaluation, reward systems. The research approach is interdisciplinary, which includes case studies, theoretical studies, normative studies and empirical studies, but emphasizes real world business.

Our JSOA's board of directors has established an editorial board of international standing. In each volume, guest editors who are experts on the volume's special theme serve as the volume editors. The details of JSOA is shown in its by-laws contained in the home-page: http://jsoa.sakura.ne.jp/english/index.html.

© 2025 World Scientific Publishing Company
https://doi.org/10.1142/9789811295652_fmatter

Editorial Board

Japanese Management and International Studies (JMIS)

Editor-in-Chief
Kazuki Hamada, Okayama Shoka University, Japan

Managing Editors
Shufuku Hiraoka, Soka University, Japan
Noriko Hoshi, Hakuoh University, Japan
Tomonori Inooka, Kokushikan University, Japan
Gunyung Lee, Niigata University, Japan
Yasuhiro Monden, University of Tsukuba, Japan
Yoshiyuki Nagasaka, Konan University, Japan
Henry Aigbedo, Oakland University, USA
Mahmuda Akter, University of Dhaka, Bangladesh
Chao Hsiung Lee, National Chung Hsing University, Taiwan

Editorial Advisory Board
Takayuki Asada, Osaka University, Japan
Takahiro Fujimoto, University of Tokyo, Japan
Masanobu Kosuga, Kwansei Gakuin University, Japan
Yoshiteru Minagawa, Nagoya Gakuin University, Japan
Susumu Ueno, Konan University, Japan
Eri Yokota, Keio University, Japan
Péter Horváth, Horváth & Partners, Germany
Arnd Huchzermeier, WHU Koblenz, Germany
Christer Karlsson, Copenhagen Business School, Denmark

Rolf G. Larsson, Lund University, Sweden
Jose Antonio Dominguez Machuca, University of Sevilla, Spain
Luis E. Carretero Diaz, Universidad Complutense, Spain
Kenneth A. Merchant, University of Southern California, USA
Jimmy Y.T. Tsay, National Taiwan University, Taiwan
Stephen DunHou Tsai, National Sun Yat-Sen University, Taiwan
Yanghon Chung, KAIST, Korea
Mohammad Aghdassi, Tarbiat Modarres University, Iran
Mahfuzul Hoque, University of Dhaka, Bangladesh
Walid Zaramdini, Carthage University, Tunis

Prologue

Eri Yokota

Keio University, Tokyo, Japan

The frameworks and application of management control have been diversified both in Japan and overseas. The frameworks focus on formal financial and non-financial information, organizational culture and informal information, and management control processes and practices, thus broadening the scope of management control to include real-world operations. The scope of control has also been expanded from managers to employees which has ensured that the role of management control is not limited to goal alignment, but can be utilized in various ways, such as organizational transformation and integration.

In response to this trend, this book compiles studies by leading researchers in Japanese management control, in the context of the diversification of management control.

Japanese management control has not been operated according to the framework introduced in the US (Yokota, 1998). That is, management control systems have been constructed and operated in accordance with the management characteristics of post-war Japanese firms. It is certain that researchers who conduct their investigation in such a context continue to be influenced by the Japanese ways. However, even in such a situation, they sometimes try to generalize the theory, regardless of the region, observing not only their own country but also foreign countries; at other times, they try to construct a management control logic based on management styles peculiar to Japanese companies. Additionally, although the field of management control has developed with a focus on management accounting, some studies have examined it with respect to its relevance to issues currently faced by companies, such as environmental issues and digital transformation (DX).

By bringing together this literature, a new direction for future research with a global awareness of issues, from the distinctive management base of Japan, will be presented.

This book is organized as follows. The first two chapters present the actual situation of management control in Japan. Then more chapters discuss management control in the manufacturing industry, the use of performance evaluation, the ability to use management accounting systems, and a discussion of the hot topic of digital transformation. In addition, one chapter focuses on informal controls. The following two chapters discuss management control of Japanese firms overseas and management control of overseas firms in Japan. The final two chapters focus on the relationship between sustainability issues and management control.

In this way, this book develops a discussion of management control from a new perspective, with the main focus on Japanese firms.

Reference

Yokota, E. 1998. *Management and Psychology of Horizontal Organizations: Management Control in an Era of Change.* Keio University Press (in Japanese).

About the Editor

Eri Yokota is a Professor of Business and Commerce (from 2005) and Dean of the Graduate School of Business and Commerce (2021–2025), at Keio University in Japan. She was at Musashi University from 1995 to 2005. She received a doctorate degree from the Graduate School of Business Administration, Keio University. She is interested in research on management control systems, management accounting, and organizational behavior. Her books include *Management and Psychology of Flattened Organizations* (in Japanese, Keio University Press, 1998), Management Control (co-authorship in Japanese, Yuhikaku, 2014) and *Management Control of Japanese Companies* (in Japanese, Chuo-Keizaisha, 2022). She has also edited *Frontiers of Japanese Management Control Systems* (Springer).

Contents

Japan Society of Organization and Accounting (JSOA)		v
Editorial Board		ix
Prologue		xi
About the Editor		xiii

Chapter 1		The Role of Management Control Departments in Japanese Companies: Insights from a Questionnaire Survey	1
		Eri Yokota and Yudai Onitsuka	
	1.	Introduction	2
	2.	Survey Method and Sample Characteristics	3
	3.	Basic Information about the Companies Surveyed	3
	4.	The State of the Business Environment	6
	5.	Business Strategies and Mid-term Plans	7
	6.	The Current Roles of the Corporate Planning Department	9
	7.	Budget Management	17
	8.	Performance Management	19
	9.	MCS as a Package	24
	10.	Recognition of the Concept of Management Control	25
	11.	Conclusion	27
		References	27

Chapter 2	An Examination of the Differences between Management Control Tools in Japanese Companies	31
	Takeyoshi Senoo and Eri Yokota	
1.	Introduction	32
2.	Survey Method and Sample Characteristics	32
3.	Usage Rates of and Relationships between the Three Management Control Tools	34
4.	Analysis Results	35
	4.1. Emphasized performance measures	37
	4.1.1. Comparing medium-term management plans with budgeting	37
	4.1.2. Influence of PEU	39
	4.1.3. Summary	41
	4.2. Target levels	42
	4.2.1. Comparing medium-term management plans with budgeting; Influence of PEU	42
	4.2.2. Comparing budgeting with MBO and the influence of PEU	43
	4.2.3. Summary	45
	4.3. Reward link	45
	4.3.1. Comparing budgeting with MBO	45
	4.3.2. Influence of PEU	46
	4.3.3. Summary	47
5.	Conclusion	47
	References	48
Chapter 3	Configuration of Effective Management Accounting Systems in Manufacturing: An Exploration with QCA	51
	Kohei Arai	
1.	Introduction	51
2.	Effective Management Accounting Method in Manufacturing	52
	2.1. Job costing	52
	2.2. Standard cost of materials and labor (SCML)	53
	2.3. Profit management by process (PMP)	54
	2.4. Non-financial information	54
	2.5. Visualized performance measures (VLPM)	55

3.	Method		55
	3.1. Analytical method		55
	3.2. Sampling method		56
	3.3. Measurement items		57
	3.4. Calibration for QCA		60
4.	Result		60
5.	Discussion		63
6.	Conclusion		64
	References		64

Chapter 4   Japanese Management Accounting Mechanisms from the Perspective of the Management Control Package: Linkage of Target Costing, MPC System, and JIT Production System   67

Keita Iwasawa

1.	Introduction: The Present Conditions of the Innovation in Japan	68
2.	Research Question	69
	2.1. Prior research on the relationship between Japanese managerial accounting methods	69
	2.2. Changes accompanying systems implementation	70
	2.3. Research framework: Management control package	71
3.	Research Methodology	71
4.	Field Study	72
	4.1. Implementation of the MPC system	72
	4.1.1. Previous MPC system: Organizational structure and performance evaluation	72
	4.1.2. Challenges faced by Company X's MPC system: Inertness in behavior, culture, and personnel control	75
	4.2. Introduction of the JIT production system and changes in control	77
	4.3. Introduction of target costing and change in control	80
5.	Discussion	81
6.	Conclusion	83
	References	84

Chapter 5	Adapting Value-Based Management Practices to a Non-Anglo-Saxon Context: A Case Study of a Project to Implement ROIC Measures in a Japanese Company	87
	Keita Masuya	

1.	Introduction	88
2.	Analytical Framework	89
	2.1. VBM sophistication	90
	2.2. Japanese organizational context	91
	2.3. Technical, cultural, and political fit	93
3.	Method	93
4.	Case Study	94
	4.1. Developing a management accounting system focused on ROIC	94
	4.2. Fostering a culture of ROIC awareness	95
	4.3. Leveraging a ROIC measure in SBUs abroad	97
5.	Discussion	98
	5.1. Operations orientation and group dynamics	98
	5.2. Technical, cultural, and political fit as mediating variables	99
6.	Conclusion	101
	References	102

Chapter 6	The Effect of Management Accounting Capabilities on the Use of Management Accounting Systems	105
	Kazunori Fukushima	

1.	Introduction	106
2.	Literature Review and Research Framework	107
	2.1. Literature review	107
	2.2. Research framework	108
3.	Methods	109
	3.1. Data collection	109
	3.2. Definition of variables	110
4.	Results	114
5.	Discussion	116

6.	Conclusion	117
	References	119

Chapter 7 Influence of DX Promotion on Knowledge Sharing via Management Control Systems — 123

Haruo Otani

1.	Introduction	123
2.	Literature Review	125
	2.1. Research on MCS and knowledge sharing	125
	2.2. Research on MCS and DX	126
	2.3. Research on DX, MCS, and knowledge sharing	127
3.	Analytical Perspective of Knowledge Sharing via MCS in DX-Driven Organizations	129
4.	Kyocera's DX Promotion Case Study	131
5.	Discussion	134
6.	Conclusions and Limitations	135
	Acknowledgments	136
	References	137

Chapter 8 The Role of Informal Controls When Concurrently Used with Tight Formal MCS — 141

Koki Mori

1.	Introduction	141
2.	Literature Review and Theoretical Development	143
	2.1. Informal controls in management accounting studies	143
	2.2. Research question	144
3.	Research Method	146
4.	Case Analysis	147
	4.1. Traditional management of 3M Company	147
	4.2. Organizational change through the introduction of Six Sigma	149
	4.3. Findings from 3M Company case	152
5.	Conclusions	153
	References	155

| Chapter 9 | Management Control Systems of Japanese Overseas Subsidiaries | 159 |

Makoto Tomo

1. Introduction — 159
2. Changes in Global Group Management and Management Systems of Overseas Subsidiaries — 160
   - 2.1. Changes in global group management in HRM and management accounting — 160
   - 2.2. Management structure in overseas subsidiaries — 161
3. HRM and Management Accounting in Overseas Subsidiaries — 162
   - 3.1. Case study of advertising company A: Integration process (PMI) after in-out M&A — 163
   - 3.2. Case study of precision equipment manufacturer Company K — 164
   - 3.3. Case study of electrical equipment manufacturer Company B — 166
   - 3.4. Case study of automobile parts Manufacturer C — 167
4. Conclusion and Future Research — 168
   - 4.1. Conclusion — 168
   - 4.2. Future research — 171

   References — 172

| Chapter 10 | The Influences of Comprehensive Performance Management Systems on Subsidiaries: Comparative Analysis of Foreign Subsidiaries and Domestic Subsidiaries | 173 |

Yudai Onitsuka

1. Introduction — 174
2. Hypotheses — 175
3. Method — 178
   - 3.1. Data — 178
     - 3.1.1. Survey of foreign subsidiaries — 178
     - 3.1.2. Survey of domestic (Japanese) subsidiaries — 179

	3.2. Measures	180
4.	Results of Analyses	180
5.	Discussion	184
6.	Conclusion	185
	Appendix A	186
	Appendix B	189
	Acknowledgment	189
	References	190

Chapter 11 A Case Study on Enabling Control in Sustainability Management 193
Yan Li

1.	Introduction	194
2.	Literature Review	194
3.	Case Site and Data Collection	197
4.	Case Analysis	197
	4.1. Case background	198
	4.2. Outside activities to address the social problem	199
	4.3. Inside activities to integrate sustainability into business	201
	4.4. The presence of organizational barrier and its management	204
5.	Discussion and Conclusion	206
	References	208

Chapter 12 Establishment and Operation of Management Systems for Sustainability Development 211
Asako Kimura

1.	Introduction: Background of Japan	211
	1.1. Gender disparity	211
	1.2. Women's Advancement Promotion Act (WAPA)	213
2.	Literature Review	214
3.	Research Method	216

4. Case Study 216
   4.1. FlyAir overview and awareness of issues 216
   4.2. Management system for human resource development 217
   4.3. Management system Key Performance Indicators (KPIs) 218
5. Discussion and Conclusion 218
   Acknowledgements 220
   References 220

Index 223

© 2025 World Scientific Publishing Company
https://doi.org/10.1142/9789811295652_0001

Chapter 1

The Role of Management Control Departments in Japanese Companies: Insights from a Questionnaire Survey*

Eri Yokota[†] and Yudai Onitsuka[‡]

[†]*Keio University, Tokyo, Japan*
[‡]*Chiba University, Chiba, Japan*

Abstract

This chapter attempts to clarify the actual activities of the departments in charge of Management Control (MC) in Japanese firms. According to the results, the controller function, which is considered to be in charge of MC in Europe and the US, is still being performed by the "corporate planning department" in Japanese firms. This result is not significantly different from the result of a survey conducted 10 years ago, indicating that the management planning department, which is different from the accounting department, is still responsible for this function in Japanese firms. The specific roles of the corporate planning department are shown in the descriptive statistics in the areas of budgeting, performance evaluation, and planning.

---

*This chapter is a translation, revision and reprinted with permission from the Society of Business and Commerce, Keio University. *Mita Business Review*, 63(3), 83–108, 2020 (in Japanese). Some corrections and omissions have been made for this publication.

1. Introduction

The concept of Management Control (MC) has gained popularity in Japanese management accounting research over the last decade (Yokota *et al.*, 2020). Despite its origin in the US, Japanese companies aiming to integrate it into their operations may need to tailor it to suit the unique characteristics of the Japanese context (Goretzki and Strauss, 2018).

A notable difference between US and Japanese firms lies in the primary responsibility for MC tasks. In American companies, the position of management controller, closely linked with management accounting tasks, is prominent (Hiromoto, 1984). After World War II, the Japanese Ministry of International Trade and Industry (now the Ministry of Economy, Trade, and Industry) recommended that Japanese companies introduce the American controller system. However, owing to the limited capacity to manage planning alongside accounting and financial affairs, this recommendation did not take root (Kato, 2007). The responsibilities of controllers encompass accounting records, aiding in budget management, and overseeing financial reporting to external parties as well as internal management and financial accounting. Moreover, the emergence of the Chief Financial Officer (CFO), responsible for both financial and management accounting, has garnered attention in recent years. According to Kato (2007), Japanese companies have historically relied on their corporate planning departments to fulfill executive functions, effectively serving as the de facto decision-making body, leading to the inclusion of corporate management functions within this department.

This suggests that the role of a controller in American companies likely aligns with that of the corporate planning department in Japanese companies. Thus, if Japanese companies aim to incorporate such a role, it would naturally involve the corporate planning department. Consequently, this study conducted a questionnaire survey to explore the current status of MC in Japan. The survey focused on tasks performed by the corporate planning department, which is primarily responsible for MC, and the perceptions of MC held by department heads.

2. Survey Method and Sample Characteristics

This survey was conducted to investigate the current roles of corporate planning departments in charge of MC in Japanese companies, as well as the status of Management Control Systems (hereinafter "MCSs").

The questionnaire survey was posted to 2,002 heads of corporate planning departments at companies listed in the First Section of the Tokyo Stock Exchange as of November 2019. When deciding where to send the questionnaires, we referenced the corporate information database "eol" provided by Pronexus, identifying the departmental heads as far as possible. In cases where the head of the corporate planning department could not be identified through "eol," we referred to the company's website or sought another way to identify the management department likely to be well versed in business administration. If it was still not possible, we generically addressed the questionnaire to the "Head of the Corporate Planning Department" in November 2019.

The final response rate, including responses that arrived after the deadline, was 292 (14.59%). We then conducted tests to check for non-response bias. Firstly, goodness-of-fit was tested for industry distribution among the responding companies. The results showed that it matched the industry distribution of the First Section of the Tokyo Stock Exchange ($p > .10$). Next, a t-test was conducted regarding differences in company size (consolidated sales and number of employees) between responding companies and all companies to which the questionnaire was sent. The results did not indicate any significant differences ($p > .10$).

Table 1 shows the company responses by industry. Table 1 lists the responding companies that consented to have their names publicized and shows the questionnaire that we sent out.

3. Basic Information about the Companies Surveyed

We first looked at the responding companies' characteristics according to organizational structure, size, and financial performance trends. These characteristics are related to MC. MC is typically relevant in relatively big

Table 1. Responses by industry.

Industry	Company responses (%)		Industry	Company responses (%)	
Service	50	17.12	Warehousing and transportation	4	1.37
Trading companies	32	10.96	Banking	4	1.37
Electrical appliances	27	9.25	Railways and buses	3	1.03
Chemical	23	7.88	Precision machinery	3	1.03
Machinery	21	7.19	Ceramics	3	1.03
Construction	19	6.51	Communications	2	0.68
Food	17	5.82	Aquatic products	2	0.68
Retail	16	5.48	Insurance	2	0.68
Non-ferrous metal and metal products	13	4.45	Electricity	2	0.68
Other manufacturing	8	2.74	Securities	1	0.34
Iron and steel	6	2.05	Oil	1	0.34
Automobile and automobile parts	6	2.05	Pulp and paper	1	0.34
Medicine	5	1.71	Other transportation equipment	1	0.34
Other finance	5	1.71	Mining	1	0.34
Real estate	5	1.71	Textiles	1	0.34
Land transportation	4	1.37	Total	288[*]	100

Note: [*]Non-respondent companies = 4.

organizations that decentralize authority to business units (Anthony and Govindarajan, 2007).

Looking at the organizational structure of the responding companies in Table 2, 47.60% had business units (divisions). This is followed by companies organized by professional function and holding company systems. Considering that regional business units (divisions) only comprise 2.05%, most business units (divisions) are organized by industry rather than region.

With regard to the size of responding companies, Table 3 shows the maximum and minimum values, means, and standard deviations (SD) for sales and number of regular employees.

Table 2. Organizational structure on the business unit level.

	Responding companies	(%)
Business units (divisions)	139	47.60
Organized by professional functions	69	23.63
Holding company system	38	13.01
Matrix organization	22	7.53
Company system	9	3.08
Regional business units (divisions)	6	2.05
Other	4	1.37
No response	5	1.71
Total	292	100

Table 3. Organization size (sales, number of regular employees).

	Min	Max	Mean	Standard deviation
Sales (million yen)	21,697	6,960,000	408,888.528	92,059.701
Number of regular employees	81	144,628	8,468.570	17,401.741

Table 4. Trends in financial performance in the last 5 years.

	Min	Max	Mean	Standard deviation
Sales	1.000	7.000	4.872	1.138
Operating profit	1.000	7.000	4.638	1.459
Net profit	1.000	7.000	4.600	1.508
Other	1.000	7.000	4.624	1.227

Additionally, we asked about trends in financial performance in the last 5 years. Responses were scored on a 7-point scale (1 = "Declined greatly," 4 = "Unchanged," and 7 "Increased greatly"). Table 4 shows that the means for all the items, namely, sales, operating profit, net profit, and other, were higher than 4. Furthermore, looking at the SDs, net profit increased more consistently than sales (Table 4).

4. The State of the Business Environment

Since MC is a means to realize strategy, changes in the business environment are thought to affect strategy. As such, we asked the responding companies about various aspects of their business environments with regard to studies by Chenhall (2003), Ekholm and Wallin (2011), and Hoque (2004).

The results can be seen in Tables 5–7. Firstly, we asked several questions about how accurately they had been able to predict different changes in the business environment in the last 5 years on a 7-point scale (from

Table 5. Accuracy of predictions about the economic environment.

	Min	Max	Mean	Standard deviation
Actions of partners and suppliers	2.000	7.000	4.687	0.911
Customer preferences and demand	2.000	7.000	4.670	1.080
Trends among competitors	1.000	7.000	4.660	1.002
Other companies' products and services	2.000	7.000	4.591	0.962
Technology	2.000	7.000	4.561	0.999
Government regulations and policies	1.000	7.000	4.410	1.033
Economic situation	1.000	7.000	4.265	1.121

Table 6. Severity of competition.

	Min	Max	Mean	Standard deviation
Competition over human resources	2.000	7.000	5.784	0.951
Price competition	2.000	7.000	5.267	1.120
Quality competition	1.000	7.000	4.925	1.033
Competition over resources	1.000	7.000	4.091	1.453

Table 7. Environmental changes inside and outside the company.

	Min	Max	Mean	Standard deviation
Business environment	2.000	7.000	5.483	0.983
Economic environment	2.000	7.000	5.199	0.928
Technological environment	2.000	7.000	5.052	1.070

1 "not having predicted it at all" to 7 "having predicted exceedingly accurately"). Looking at Table 5, the means of all items exceed 4 and the standard deviations are around 1, so many responded that they were generally able to predict changes in the environment. Since no companies responded "not predicted at all" (=1) for "actions of partners and suppliers," "customer preferences and demands," "other companies' products and services," or "technology," we postulate that it was somewhat possible to make predictions about all items.

Moreover, we asked about the severity of four types of competition, also scored on a 7-point scale (from 1 "not severe at all" to 7 "exceedingly severe"). While resource competition had a mean close to 4, competition over human resources, price, and quality showed higher means, suggesting that the responding companies were facing severe competition (Table 6).

We also asked about how much the environment inside and outside the company had changed in the last 5 years, scored on a 7-point scale (from 1 "No change at all" to 7 "Considerable change"). The results are shown in Table 7. All means exceeded 5, with no companies responding "No change at all," revealing the general perception that the environment (and especially the business environment) had changed significantly.

5. Business Strategies and Mid-term Plans

As mentioned previously, MC is a means to realize the strategy. Therefore, we checked whether the companies had formulated business strategies and medium-term plans, and if they had, which department was responsible for these activities.

Firstly, Table 8 shows whether the companies had formulated business strategies, medium-term plans, visions, and various sub-systems of MC processes, such as budget, monitoring, performance management systems, personnel evaluation systems, and remuneration systems, as well as asking which department was responsible. These questions followed the MC framework of Anthony and Govindarajan (2007).

Table 8 shows that nearly all responding companies had formulated at least one of these elements. Moreover, looking at the responsible departments, remuneration systems and personnel evaluation systems were handled by personnel departments, while visions, business strategies, and

Table 8. Formulation and creation of strategy, vision, or other business management systems and responsible department.

	"Formulated or created" or not Yes	"Formulated or created" or not No	Responsible department[*] Corporate planning dept.	Responsible department[*] Personnel dept.	Responsible department[*] Accounting dept.	Responsible department[*] Other
Vision	278	13	236	3	1	35
Business strategy	279	11	244	0	1	31
Medium-term plan	273	17	256	0	2	12
Budget	288	3	154	0	104	20
Monitoring	275	14	191	7	47	18
Performance management system	277	12	122	14	105	25
Human resource evaluation system	279	8	7	274	0	2
Remuneration system	260	26	13	241	2	5

Note: [*]Multiple choices included.

medium-term plans (and other longer-term projects) were handled by corporate planning departments. Finally, budgets and performance management systems were often handled by either corporate planning departments or accounting departments, and monitored by corporate planning departments.

We asked four questions about business strategy, often handled by the corporate planning department, which were scored on a 7-point scale (from 1 "Does not apply at all" to 7 "Applies extremely well"). The highest score was given in response to the statement "a unified direction is shared by all employees at the company"; the statement that "a shared vision is more important [than a department-specific vision]" also had a high score. Meanwhile, the statement about working to meet demands from outside the company came closer to the neutral score (4), and the statement that a department-specific strategy was more important than a company-wide strategy fell below 4, although only marginally (Table 9).

When asking about the current status of medium-term plans according to a 7-point scale, we found that the score was highest for the statement that such plans were important for the sake of aligning company-wide and departmental direction, followed by the statement that "a unified direction

Table 9. Business strategy.

	Min	Max	Mean	Standard deviation
Permeation within the company	1.000	7.000	5.180	1.278
Shared vision is more important (than department-specific vision)	1.000	7.000	4.651	1.190
Demands from outside the company	1.000	7.000	4.280	1.726
Department-specific strategy is more important (than company-wide strategy)	1.000	7.000	3.917	1.397

Table 10. Medium-term plans.

	Min	Max	Mean	Standard deviation
It is important for the sake of aligning company-wide and departmental direction	1.000	7.000	5.586	1.243
Shared vision is more important (than department-specific vision)	1.000	7.000	5.034	1.445
Motivation for managers	1.000	7.000	4.681	1.326
An annual plan is more important	1.000	7.000	4.514	1.246
Demands from outside the company	1.000	7.000	4.388	1.788

is shared by all employees at the company." Meanwhile, the response about having formulated and presented a medium-term plan to meet demands from outside the company also scored above the neutral score. Moreover, the response that an annual plan is more important also exceeded the neutral score, suggesting that medium-term plans may encounter difficulties (Table 10).

6. The Current Roles of the Corporate Planning Department

Subsequently, we conducted an inquiry aimed at gaining insights into the dynamics of the corporate planning department, which we assumed to oversee MC.

First, we examined the department's scale based on employee count (full-time equivalents), the number of internal divisions, and annual staff turnover. The results indicate an average staff size of 16, with a standard deviation indicating a maximum average staff count of

Table 11. The corporate planning department.

	Min	Max	Mean	Standard deviation
Number of regular employees	0.000	492.000	16.010	34.781
Number of organizations in the department	0.000	46.000	2.500	3.222
Average number of yearly variations (persons/year)	0.000	25.000	2.161	3.195

approximately 50. On average, the department comprises 2.5 internal divisions, suggesting a moderate organizational size. Moreover, annual staff turnover averages approximately two individuals, indicating relatively frequent personnel movement for a smaller-scale entity (Table 11).

Second, we set a 7-point scale to measure the degree of involvement of the corporate planning department in various operational areas typically within its purview. The degree of collaboration ranged from 1 (where other departments primarily handle the task, with minimal support) to 7 (where the corporate planning department assumes primary responsibility, with minimal involvement from other departments), totaling 8 points. A comprehensive list of 34 tasks was set, drawing primarily from Kato (2007) and Kato et al. (2007), encompassing domains such as strategic management, group and global management, planning, budgeting, performance management, operations management, and human resource management.

Table 12 presents the 34 items listed in order of highest average value.

The results reveal that the following tasks were identified as particularly primarily tasks: formulating medium-term management plans, supporting the execution of top management's special orders, gathering comprehensive management information, collecting data for strategic planning, disseminating organizational management philosophy, examining group corporate strategies, formulating short-term plans, determining business domains, examining business portfolios, evaluating company-wide performance, formulating and managing company-wide budgets, allocating management resources, and managing the company's business portfolio. The average score for these tasks exceeded 4, indicating that the

Table 12. Descriptive statistics: The primary tasks of the corporate planning department.

	Min	Max	Mean	Standard deviation
Formulating medium-term plans	0.000 (7)	7.000	5.788	1.539
	1.000	7.000	5.932	1.253
Supporting the execution of top management special orders	0.000 (5)	7.000	5.545	1.570
	1.000	7.000	5.642	1.399
Collecting general management information	0.000 (4)	7.000	5.354	1.472
	1.000	7.000	5.429	1.338
Collecting information for devising a strategy	0.000 (2)	7.000	5.299	1.393
	1.000	7.000	5.336	1.326
Disseminating management philosophy in the organization	0.000 (15)	7.000	4.951	1.962
	1.000	7.000	5.223	1.624
Considering group company strategy	0.000 (13)	7.000	4.905	1.984
	1.000	7.000	5.140	1.708
Formulating short-term plans	0.000 (5)	7.000	4.769	1.963
	1.000	7.000	4.853	1.874
Deciding on business domains	0.000 (11)	7.000	4.710	1.902
	1.000	7.000	4.896	1.688
Considering business portfolios	0.000 (15)	7.000	4.628	1.964
	1.000	7.000	4.883	1.681
Evaluating company-wide performance	0.000 (24)	7.000	4.502	2.225
	1.000	7.000	4.913	1.838
Putting together and managing the company budget	0.000 (20)	7.000	4.371	2.298
	1.000	7.000	4.694	2.038
Distributing management resources	0.000 (12)	7.000	4.322	1.892
	1.000	7.000	4.509	1.700
Changing organizational structure and systems	0.000 (13)	7.000	4.269	2.109
	1.000	7.000	4.469	1.938
Deciding on the scope of responsibility and authority	0.000 (26)	7.000	4.150	2.310
	1.000	7.000	4.565	1.992
Considering systems to evaluate company-wide performance	0.000 (24)	7.000	4.148	2.224
	1.000	7.000	4.521	1.924

(*Continued*)

Table 12. (*Continued*)

	Min	Max	Mean	Standard deviation
Managing group companies	0.000 (21)	7.000	4.141	2.204
	1.000	7.000	4.471	1.939
Exploring and considering new businesses	0.000 (10)	7.000	4.076	1.983
	1.000	7.000	4.221	1.860
Considering systems for managing departmental performance	0.000 (28)	7.000	3.745	2.194
	1.000	7.000	4.145	1.914
Considering overseas business strategy	0.000 (20)	7.000	3.591	2.065
	1.000	7.000	3.869	1.876
Evaluating departmental performance	0.000 (41)	7.000	3.570	2.196
	1.000	7.000	4.167	1.770
Putting together and managing departmental budgets	0.000 (37)	7.000	3.232	2.204
	1.000	7.000	3.706	1.952
Managing overseas businesses	0.000 (40)	7.000	3.072	2.181
	1.000	7.000	3.591	1.921
Managing company morale and awareness	0.000 (66)	7.000	2.549	1.995
	1.000	7.000	3.314	1.624
Selecting managers for overseas businesses	0.000 (82)	7.000	2.418	2.322
	1.000	7.000	3.446	2.033
Promoting cost-cutting activities	0.000 (77)	7.000	2.151	1.976
	1.000	7.000	2.947	1.731
Collecting company-wide financial information and creating financial tables	0.000 (84)	7.000	2.063	2.075
	1.000	7.000	2.916	1.895
Collecting departmental financial information and creating financial tables	0.000 (96)	7.000	1.913	2.006
	1.000	7.000	2.870	1.813
Environmental management	0.000 (106)	7.000	1.817	2.044
	1.000	7.000	2.899	1.878
Assisting the selection of directors and executives	0.000 (136)	7.000	1.775	2.284
	1.000	7.000	3.396	2.114

Table 12. (Continued)

	Min	Max	Mean	Standard deviation
Supply chain management	0.000 (116)	7.000	1.343	1.637
	1.000	7.000	2.275	1.555
Quality management	0.000 (134)	7.000	1.227	1.652
	1.000	7.000	2.309	1.624
Employee education and training	0.000 (126)	7.000	1.158	1.543
	1.000	7.000	2.082	1.535
Considering personnel evaluation systems	0.000 (135)	7.000	1.116	1.565
	1.000	7.000	2.128	1.587
Deciding on salaries and bonuses	0.000 (167)	7.000	1.045	1.690
	1.000	7.000	2.513	1.784

Notes: *Lists minimum, maximum, mean, and standard deviation when including and excluding companies that responded "0."
*The number in brackets next to 0.000 minimum represents the number of companies that responded "0."

management department's predominant involvement in tasks requires a long-term perspective and encompasses the entire company.

Conversely, it can be inferred that the corporate planning department has limited involvement in operations, scoring below an average of 4, which indicates tasks primarily overseen by other departments with partial support from the corporate planning department. Notably, salary and bonus determination, personnel evaluation system assessment, employee education and training, environmental management, supply chain management, director and executive officer selection assistance, environmental management, and financial information collection and department preparation yielded lower average scores.

Third, Table 13 illustrates the departments with which the corporate planning department collaborates while executing its responsibilities. The listed items are arranged by mean value, highlighting departments with the most extensive collaboration. Numerous companies collaborate with functional and business divisions in tasks where the corporate planning department assumes a significant role. Additionally, regarding the dissemination of management philosophy throughout the organization, a

Table 13. Corporate planning department's contact points by task (number of responding companies).*

	Personnel dept.	Accounting dept.	Job function and business dept.	Other
Formulating medium-term plans	32	77	159	41
Supporting the execution of top management special orders	42	72	137	30
Collecting general management information	26	77	141	43
Collecting information for devising a strategy	23	56	192	23
Disseminating management philosophy in the organization	67	10	72	57
Considering group company strategy	8	25	143	38
Formulating short-term plans	25	115	163	27
Deciding on business domains	5	22	171	32
Considering business portfolios	4	39	153	29
Evaluating company-wide performance	28	121	55	29
Putting together and managing the company budget	10	162	80	21
Distributing management resources	51	76	124	34
Changing organizational structure and systems	146	9	77	34
Deciding on the scope of responsibility and authority	80	10	63	71
Considering systems to evaluate company-wide performance	7	134	62	64
Managing group companies	19	50	133	42
Exploring and considering new businesses	5	9	174	57

Table 13. (*Continued*)

	Personnel dept.	**Accounting dept.**	**Job function and business dept.**	**Other**
Considering systems for managing departmental performance	8	115	94	53
Considering overseas business strategy	2	13	178	42
Evaluating departmental performance	47	74	112	20
Putting together and managing departmental budgets	13	92	174	20
Managing overseas businesses	10	23	174	42
Managing company morale and awareness	170	2	49	43
Selecting managers for overseas businesses	102	6	114	35
Promoting cost-cutting activities	8	46	176	48
Collecting company-wide financial information and creating financial tables	4	242	16	4
Collecting departmental financial information and creating financial tables	3	215	46	7
Environmental management	9	1	134	88
Assisting the selection of directors and executives	120	1	13	70
Supply chain management	3	4	163	52
Quality management	2	1	166	63
Employee education and training	224	1	11	5
Considering personnel evaluation systems	227	0	2	3
Deciding on salaries and bonuses	201	6	8	13

Note: *Including multiple choices.

considerable number of firms exhibit robust cooperation with the human resource department, alongside functional and business departments.

Concurrently, the accounting department is highly involved in the formulation of short-term plans, evaluating company-wide performance, overseeing company-wide budgets, and devising systems for managing company-wide performance.

Table 14 illustrates the information exchange between the corporate planning department and other departments. We assigned a scale ranging from 0 (no exchange) to 7 (daily exchange) to quantify the frequency of exchanges. Notably, the items with the highest mean frequency

Table 14. Information exchanges between corporate planning departments and other departments.

	Min	Max	Mean	Standard deviation
Management, unofficial	0.000 (3)	7.000	5.858	1.319
	2.000	7.000	5.920	1.180
Accounting dept., unofficial	0.000 (4)	7.000	5.010	1.550
	1.000	7.000	5.081	1.440
Job function and business dept., unofficial	0.000 (5)	7.000	4.993	1.513
	2.000	7.000	5.081	1.373
Management, official	0.000 (7)	7.000	4.920	1.378
	1.000	7.000	5.043	1.153
Personnel dept., unofficial	0.000 (15)	7.000	4.142	1.794
	1.000	7.000	4.369	1.550
Job function and business dept., official	0.000 (14)	7.000	4.052	1.429
	1.000	7.000	4.258	1.125
Accounting dept., official	0.000 (24)	7.000	3.794	1.683
	1.000	7.000	4.141	1.283
Personnel dept., official	0.000 (40)	7.000	3.104	1.757
	1.000	7.000	3.602	1.334

Notes: *Lists minimum, maximum, mean, and standard deviation when including and excluding companies that responded "0."
*The number in brackets next to 0.000 minimum represents the number of companies that responded "0."

predominantly involve informal exchanges rather than formal meetings. Moreover, the frequent exchange of information with management, accounting departments, and professional/business units aligns with the findings from previous surveys.

7. Budget Management

The characteristics of budget management were ascertained using a 7-point scale, ranging from 1 (not at all true) to 7 (very true), across 20 items. This assessment drew upon the works of Sponem and Lambert (2016) and Seo (2017).

The items are illustrated in Table 15, arranged by mean value. Notably, items with mean values exceeding 4 indicate that budgets are formulated based on management strategies and mid-term management

Table 15. Characteristics of budgeting and budget management.

	Min	Max	Mean	Standard deviation
Department managers fully participate in budgeting	1.000	7.000	5.364	1.366
Action plans are developed based on the budget	1.000	7.000	5.295	1.165
Consistent with a mid-term management plan	1.000	7.000	5.261	1.465
Consistent with management strategy	1.000	7.000	5.186	1.399
Extreme importance is placed on the difference between monthly budget targets and actual results	1.000	7.000	4.866	1.443
Each department's budget is prepared, and the company-wide budget is prepared by adding up these budgets	1.000	7.000	4.801	1.712
Achieving budget targets requires considerable effort and skill	1.000	7.000	4.726	1.227

(*Continued*)

Table 15. (Continued)

	Min	Max	Mean	Standard deviation
Each department manager is required to report on actions taken	1.000	7.000	4.715	1.426
The appropriateness of budget targets and the need to revise them are reviewed during the term	1.000	7.000	4.610	1.612
General managers' compensation is linked to the achievement of budget targets	1.000	7.000	4.460	1.600
Strictly enforces performance forecasting outside of the budget	1.000	7.000	4.316	1.592
Budget targets are challenging levels that cannot be easily achieved	1.000	7.000	4.243	1.339
Remuneration for section managers is linked to the achievement of budget targets	1.000	7.000	4.172	1.586
Department managers are fully involved in budget preparation	1.000	7.000	4.038	1.557
Budget targets are usually achieved	1.000	7.000	3.808	1.254
Budget targets are regularly revised in response to changes in the internal and external environment	1.000	7.000	3.798	2.009
Company-wide budgets are prepared first, and then departmental budgets are prepared based on the company-wide budgets	1.000	7.000	3.601	1.940
New targets are added during the term in addition to the prior budget targets in response to changes in the internal and external environment	1.000	7.000	3.462	1.714
Budget targets are revised irregularly in response to changes in the internal and external environment	1.000	7.000	3.394	1.799

plans, with department heads actively involved in the process. Additionally, budgets are formulated to reflect each department's actual circumstances, and action plans are devised accordingly. Conversely, the mean value for revising budget targets or setting new targets in response to environmental changes falls below the median value of 4, suggesting a tendency for budget targets to be considered as "must achieve."

8. Performance Management

Performance management was clarified from several perspectives.

In this survey, the performance management system is defined as "a system for setting financial or non-financial indicators and measures (including Key Performance Indicators (KPIs), etc.) and using them to measure, monitor, analyze, and evaluate the activity processes and outcomes of each department." Subsequently, specific questions regarding this definition are presented.

First, we ascertained the quantity of financial and non-financial indicators in the performance management system. Table 16 shows that, on average, firms set about seven financial indicators and about nine daily financial indicators.

Second, we assumed the degree of significance assigned to specific evaluation indicators, utilizing a scale ranging from 0 (not set) to 7 (great importance). Sixteen specific indicators were set for measurement, drawing from Ittner et al. (2003) and Yokota et al. (2013). The results, depicted in Table 17, revealed that operating income received the highest average value, along with a ceiling effect. This was followed by sales, legal compliance, ordinary income, cost reduction, and product/service quality. While many indicators had average values exceeding 4, residual profit

Table 16. Number of performance indicators.

	Min	Max	Mean	Standard deviation
Financial indicators	0.000	100.000	7.153	10.903
Non-financial indicators	0.000	500.000	8.936	34.747

Table 17. Emphasis on individual indicators.

	Min	Max	Mean	Standard deviation
Operating income	0.000 (3)	7.000	6.462	1.033
	1.000	7.000	6.529	0.799
Net sales	0.000 (3)	7.000	5.836	1.485
	1.000	7.000	5.896	1.368
Legal compliance	0.000 (18)	7.000	5.716	1.844
	1.000	7.000	6.091	1.153
Ordinary income	0.000 (12)	7.000	5.490	1.825
	1.000	7.000	5.725	1.456
Cost reduction	0.000 (13)	7.000	5.205	1.649
	1.000	7.000	5.448	1.234
Product service quality	0.000 (23)	7.000	5.113	1.970
	1.000	7.000	5.552	1.330
Customer satisfaction	0.000 (29)	7.000	4.828	2.054
	1.000	7.000	5.363	1.346
Environment-related indicators	0.000 (23)	7.000	4.568	1.962
	1.000	7.000	4.959	1.494
New product service development	0.000 (30)	7.000	4.536	2.014
	1.000	7.000	5.057	1.370
Business process improvement	0.000 (28)	7.000	4.459	1.871
	1.000	7.000	4.932	1.238
Employee satisfaction	0.000(36)	7.000	4.264	2.111
	1.000	7.000	4.863	1.469
Manufacturing provision lead time and service provision efficiency	0.000 (37)	7.000	4.158	2.100
	1.000	7.000	4.761	1.472
Market share	0.000 (33)	7.000	4.100	2.137
	1.000	7.000	4.624	1.649
ROA	0.000 (63)	7.000	3.293	2.326
	1.000	7.000	4.207	1.749

Table 17. (Continued)

	Min	Max	Mean	Standard deviation
ROI	0.000 (72)	7.000	3.059	2.341
	1.000	7.000	4.074	1.775
Residual income	0.000 (105)	7.000	2.083	1.979
	1.000	7.000	3.279	1.495

Notes: Minimum value, mean value, and standard deviation are shown for companies that answered "0" and for companies that did not answer "0." The maximum value, mean value, and standard deviation are shown.
* The number in parentheses next to the minimum value of 0.000 indicates the number of firms that answered "0."

scored 2.083, Return on Investment (ROI) scored 3.059, and ROA scored 3.293. This shows that despite recent attention, these indicators are not necessarily considered crucial in a company's internal performance management system.

To assess the characteristics of the performance management system, we employed a 7-point scale (1 = not at all applicable, 7 = very applicable) for each item. Notably, we utilized nine items from (7) to (15) in Q6(D) to identify the characteristics of a comprehensive performance management system, incorporating diverse perspectives such as a balanced scorecard (BSC), as referenced in Hall (2008, 2011). Table 18 illustrates the average of these items, arranged by mean value.

The answers revealed the following: The companies' management and various departmental heads take a keen interest in daily and comprehensive performance evaluation systems, departmental activities and overall company objectives and goals are linked, and information about departmental performance is provided from diverse angles. Simultaneously, the low mean scores of the questions about defining various financial and non-financial indicators for all activities in the company probably suggest that this is not always done.

Next, referencing Henri (2006) and Simons (1995, 2000), we asked 17 questions about how performance management systems are utilized,

Table 18. Characteristics of comprehensive performance management systems.

	Min	Max	Mean	Standard deviation
Linking departmental activities with company-wide targets and goals	1.000	7.000	5.072	1.294
Mutually matching and linking departmental performance with company-wide strategy	1.000	7.000	4.805	1.390
Providing information about departmental performance from various angles	1.000	7.000	4.345	1.356
A series of financial and non-financial indicators concerning departmental activities	1.000	7.000	4.315	1.554
Providing important information for departmental activities	1.000	7.000	4.275	1.357
Showing the influence of departmental activities on the activities of the whole company and other departments	1.000	7.000	4.034	1.359
Clearly explaining and documenting all protocols and procedures	1.000	7.000	3.814	1.615
Providing wide-ranging information about a variety of fields	1.000	7.000	3.725	1.436
Defining various financial and non-financial indicators for all company activities	1.000	7.000	3.418	1.371

measured according to a 7-point scale (from 1 "Not utilized at all" to 7 "Always utilized"). The results are shown in Table 19 in order of mean size. All means exceeded the neutral score of 4, while some scored more than 5, meaning there was high utilization. These were checking progress, discussions between management and departments, conveying management intentions to departments, deciding on company-wide direction, dealing with matters where goals are not being met, and making departments aware of company-wide strategy.

Table 19. Usages of the performance management system.

	Min	Max	Mean	Standard deviation
Checking progress	1.000	7.000	5.595	1.249
Discussions between management and departments	1.000	7.000	5.341	1.338
Conveying management intentions to departments	1.000	7.000	5.254	1.361
Deciding on company-wide direction	1.000	7.000	5.173	1.381
Dealing with matters where goals are not being met	1.000	7.000	5.124	1.471
Making departments aware of company-wide strategy	1.000	7.000	5.114	1.425
Having departments check the direction and validity of their activities	1.000	7.000	4.983	1.312
Evaluating the appropriateness of departmental decisions and activities	1.000	7.000	4.887	1.348
Bringing departmental attention to company-wide issues	1.000	7.000	4.784	1.457
Making discussions within the company smoother	1.000	7.000	4.715	1.389
Supporting departmental decisions and activities	1.000	7.000	4.677	1.275
Continuous experimentation and discussion	1.000	7.000	4.491	1.345
Deciding on general manager-level salaries	1.000	7.000	4.309	1.602
Promoting departmental coordination and collaboration	1.000	7.000	4.234	1.402
Speeding up departmental responses to uncertain events	1.000	7.000	4.079	1.464
Bottom-up suggestions in the company, such as from departments to management	1.000	7.000	4.069	1.413
Deciding on section head-level salaries	1.000	7.000	4.062	1.570

9. MCS as a Package

Table 20 summarizes the relevant items to show whether budget and performance management systems are consistent with other systems with MC.

In their research on MCSs, Malmi and Brown (2008) developed the theory of "Management Control Systems as a Package" where multiple control systems exist and function in an organization and are mutually influential. According to Malmi and Brown (2008), it is important to consider the interconnectedness of accounting controls and systems since

Table 20. MCS as a package.

	Min	Max	Mean	Standard deviation
Departmental action plans are formulated based on and are consistent with budgets	1.000	7.000	5.295	1.165
(Budgets) are put together based on and are consistent with medium-term management plans	1.000	7.000	5.261	1.465
(Budgets) are put together based on and are consistent with business strategies	1.000	7.000	5.186	1.399
(Performance management systems) are designed based on and are consistent with medium-term management plans	1.000	7.000	5.096	1.526
(Performance management systems) are designed based on and are consistent with business strategies	1.000	7.000	5.048	1.386
Departmental action plans are formulated based on and are consistent with performance management systems	1.000	7.000	5.003	1.312
(Performance management systems) are designed based on and are consistent with budgets	1.000	7.000	5.630	1.244
(Budget management systems) are formulated based on and are consistent with performance management systems	1.000	7.000	4.324	1.754

they do not function independently, but concern other control systems in the organization. Accordingly, we measured variables that take into account MCS as a package. Specifically, the questionnaire measured the degree to which the budget and performance management systems are consistent with each other and with budget and planning. Five questions were asked about consistency with medium-term management plans, management strategies, action plans, budgets, and performance management systems. The results indicate means exceeding a neutral score of 4 for all items, so each sub-system was arguably designed consistently.

10. Recognition of the Concept of Management Control

Lastly, approximately five decades after the introduction of the MC concept, with almost 50 years having gone by since the term was first translated into Japanese, we confirmed the level of recognition by heads of corporate planning departments. We asked about their recognition of the word MC itself as well as its meaning. We investigated this by asking respondents to pick the most appropriate option.

To begin with, Table 21 shows how much they recognized the word MC itself. Just under 84% of the responding companies selected "I have heard of it but do not use it daily." Just under 10% answered, "I have never heard of it." These results suggest that the MC concept is somewhat familiar but not widely applied in Japanese companies. The process of directing the head of each department to achieve organizational objectives is a statement that relates to one of the key purposes of MC.

Table 21. Reactions to the concept of management control.

	Number of responding companies	(%)
I have heard of it but do not use it daily	245	83.90
I have never heard of it	29	9.93
It is a term frequently used in the company	12	4.11
Other	4	1.37
No response	2	0.68
Total	292	100

Table 22. Perceived meanings of MC.

	Number of responding companies	(%)
Setting targets and managing performance	78	25.24
Processes to direct departmental heads toward achieving organizational goals	64	20.71
PDCA cycles	63	20.39
Mechanisms to align company-wide and partial (departmental) goals	44	14.24
Business management systems	33	10.68
Processes utilizing sub-systems to implement strategy	11	3.56
Managing budgets and evaluating performance	9	2.91
Others	1	0.32
No response	6	1.94
Total	309*	100

Note: *Including multiple choices.

Taking this process further, we asked the respondents to select one of eight items describing the meaning of the word MC. As shown in Table 22, all options are possible definitions. For example, "setting targets and managing performance" and "managing budgets and evaluating performance" are examples of two key sub-systems under MC, while "processes utilizing sub-systems to implement a strategy" is a description that focuses on the process aspect of the ideas found in Anthony and Govindarajan (2007). Meanwhile, "business management systems" is a fairly big concept in Japanese. "Mechanisms to align company-wide and partial (departmental) goals" and "processes to direct departmental heads toward achieving organizational goals" describe MC objectives. "Plan-do-check-act (PDCA) cycles" is a definition from Tani (2013). Therefore, this question enabled us to check how practitioners define MC.

The results show that about 25% defined it as a general term of concrete systems, "setting targets and evaluating performance," while about 35% selected "processes to direct departmental heads toward achieving organizational goals" or "mechanisms to align company-wide and partial (departmental) goals," which have to do with aligning the whole organization and its parts.

11. Conclusion

This chapter presented a simple summary of the Fact-Finding Survey on Corporate Planning Departments in Japanese Companies that we conducted in 2019. The findings of this chapter can be broadly summarized as follows. In addition to tasks from a company-wide, long-term perspective, the corporate planning department in Japanese companies also connects with tasks related to accounting and human resources, performing tasks while exchanging information with the various sites. Although the heads of the corporate planning departments in Japanese companies do not use the word MC, we see that they consistently utilize the kinds of systems that it signifies.

This chapter has clarified the current status of MC in Japanese companies. Future studies should analyze in detail how the corporate planning department affects the management and performance of Japanese companies.

References

Anthony, R. N. and Govindarajan, V. (2007). *Management Control Systems* (12th edn.). McGraw-Hill.

Chenhall, R. H. (2003). Management control systems design within its organizational context: Findings from contingency-based research and directions for the future. *Accounting, Organizations and Society*, 28(2–3), 127–168.

Ekholm, B. and Wallin, J. (2011). The impact of uncertainty and strategy on the perceived usefulness of fixed and flexible budgets. *Journal of Business Finance & Accounting*, 38(1/2), 145–164.

Goretzki, L. and Strauss, E. (2018). *The Role of the Management Accountant: Local Variations and Global Influences*. London: Routledge.

Hall, M. (2008). The effect of comprehensive performance measurement systems on role clarity, psychological empowerment and managerial performance. *Accounting, Organizations and Society*, 33(2–3), 141–163.

Hall, M. (2011). Do comprehensive performance measurement systems help or hinder managers' mental model development? *Management Accounting Research*, 22(2), 68–83.

Henri, J. F. (2006). Organizational culture and performance measurement systems. *Accounting, Organization and Society*, 31(1), 77–103.

Hiromoto, T. (1984). The controller system and management accounting theory: A perspective on the history of the development of American management accounting theory. *Ikkyo Ronso*, 92, 303–325 (in Japanese).

Hoque, Z. (2004). A contingency model of the association between strategy, environmental uncertainty and performance measurement: Impact on organizational performance. *International Business Review*, 13(4), 485–502.

Ittner, C. D., Larcker, D. F. and Randall, T. (2003). Performance implications of strategic performance measurement in financial service firms. *Accounting, Organizations and Society*, 28(7–8), 715–741.

Kato, Y. (2007). The work of the "corporate planning department": What is it and what should be done? *Business Insight*, 15(4), 4–19 (in Japanese).

Kato, Y., Ishikawa, K., Oura, K. and Arai, Y. (2007). Fact-finding survey on corporate planning departments in Japanese companies: Analysis on the basis of a questionnaire survey. *Journal of Cost Accounting Research*, 31(1), 52–62.

Malmi, T. and Brown, D. A. (2008). Management control systems as a package: Opportunities, challenges and research directions. *Management Accounting Research*, 19(4): 287–300.

Senoo, T. 2017. Budgeting patterns in Japanese companies and their relationship to exploration and exploitation: An exploratory study. *The Journal of Cost Accounting Research*, 41(1), 38–50 (in Japanese).

Simons, R. (1995). *Levers of Control: How Managers Use Innovative Control Systems to Drive Strategic Renewal*. Boston, MA: Harvard Business School Press.

Simons, R. (2000). *Performance Measurement and Control Systems for Implementation Strategy*. Prentice Hall, Upper Saddle River, New Jersey, US.

Sponem, S. and Lambert C. (2016). Exploring differences in budget characteristics, roles and satisfaction: A configurational approach. *Management Accounting Research*, 30, 47–61.

Tani, T. (2013). *Essential Management Accounting* (3rd edn.). Chuo Keizai-sha (in Japanese), Tokyo, Japan.

Yokota, E., Senoo, T., Takahashi, S. and Goto, Y. (2013). Fact-finding survey on performance management systems in Japanese companies. *Mita Business Review*, 55(6), 67–87 (in Japanese).

Yokota, E., Otomasa, S., Sakaguchi, J., Kawai, T., Onishi, Y. and Senoo, T. (2020). Developments in Japanese management control research: A survey of 51 years of literature. *Accounting Progress*, 21, 17–31 (in Japanese).

Chapter 2

An Examination of the Differences between Management Control Tools in Japanese Companies*

Takeyoshi Senoo[†] and Eri Yokota[‡]

[†]*Chuo University, Tokyo, Japan*
[‡]*Keio University, Tokyo, Japan*

Abstract

In this chapter, we examined the differences between three management control tools (MCTs) (i.e., medium-term management plans, budgeting, and management by objectives (MBO)) in Japanese companies. Specifically, based on the results of a postal survey we conducted among companies listed in the first section of the Tokyo Stock Exchange (TSE), we compared the three MCTs using three critical factors in management control: (1) performance measures, (2) target levels, and (3) reward link. These three factors are the most important in the planning and evaluation stages of the management control process. We also examined the influence of perceived environmental uncertainty (PEU), a key contingency variable that affects management control and MCTs.

---

*This chapter is an edited version of the following paper (with added analysis): Senoo, T. and Yokota, E. (2024). A survey of management control tools in Japanese companies: Focusing on medium-term management plans, budgeting, and management by objectives. *Mita Business Review*, 66(6), 77–99 (in Japanese).

1. Introduction

In the literature on management accounting, the most important theme is management control (Grabner and Moers, 2013; Yokota, 2022, 2023), which has a number of definitions. Yokota and Kaneko (2014) define it as follows: "a concept intended to guide management behavior toward the accomplishment of organizational goals (strategies) based on information supply, primarily numerical information" (Yokota and Kaneko, 2014, p. i).

While there are several tools that can be used for management control, the main tool is budgeting (Yokota, 2023). In this chapter, we refer to these tools as management control tools (MCTs). Most large companies in Japan use the following MCTs: medium-term management plans, budgeting, and management by objectives (MBO) (Sakurai, 2019; Sawabe et al., 2008).

These three MCTs correlate, producing complementary effects (Hayashi, 2005). However, little is known about how these differ from one another.

We therefore set the following research question to address in this chapter: What are the differences between the MCTs used by Japanese companies? To address this question, we compared the three MCTs using three critical factors in management control: (1) performance measures, (2) target levels, and (3) reward link. These three factors are the most important in the planning and evaluation stages of the management control process (Ferreira and Otley, 2009; Otley, 1999; Yokota, 2022; Yokota and Kaneko, 2014). We also examined the influence of perceived environmental uncertainty (PEU), a key contingency variable that affects Management control and MCTs (Chenhall, 2007; Gordon and Narayanan, 1984). Specifically, we analyzed the results of a postal survey we conducted among companies listed in the first section of the Tokyo Stock Exchange (TSE).

2. Survey Method and Sample Characteristics

Described further is the 2018 Fact-finding Survey on Management Control Systems in Japanese Companies used to collect data for this research. It was conducted among 2,080 companies listed in the first section of the TSE. We addressed each survey form to the person responsible for management control in the company and requested that the survey be completed and returned by June 5, 2018. We sampled companies on the first section of the TSE on the basis that such companies are representative of large Japanese companies. We obtained the postal addresses from "Employee/Manager Information File" in the D-Vision series published by Diamond Inc. In selecting the participants, we prioritized the company's corporate planning division head or director (or equivalent rank). If we found no such person, we selected whoever was in charge of the company's accounting and finance division. If we found neither person, we visited the company's website and identified the person in charge of management control. If we still failed to identify the person, we addressed the form to "the person in charge of management control."

Ultimately, 365 companies returned the survey form (17.5% response rate), and some were returned after the indicated deadline. To check for a non-response bias, we conducted three tests with a 5% significance level. For these tests, we used data from Nikkei NEEDS-FinancialQUEST. For the first test, we compared the distribution of industry types between the companies that responded and those that did not. The industrial types we used were the major groups delineated by the Securities Identification Code Committee. We conducted a chi-squared test to measure goodness of fit. The results indicated that the distribution of industry types among the responding companies was consistent with that of companies listed in the first section of the TSE ($\chi^2 = 31.059$, $p = 0.514$).

For the second test, we compared the responding and non-responding companies in terms of company size (measured by sales and number of employees). In this comparison, we referred to the consolidated data as some of the companies were purely holding companies. If the company in question had no consolidated subsidiaries, we used non-consolidated data instead. Instead of sales revenue, we used ordinary income if the company in question was in the major group titled "Banks" and operating revenue if the company was in the major group titled "Securities and Commodities Futures." We subjected the two group samples to an independent samples t-test. The results demonstrated no statistically significant difference between the groups in either sales ($t = -0.594$, $p = 0.552$) or number of employees ($t = 1.698$, $p = 0.092$). For the third test, we compared the responses of companies that returned the survey form within the indicated deadline (there were 235 such companies) with those that did so after the deadline (130 companies). We found no statistically significant difference in either mean score or usage rate. In view of the results of the three tests, we concluded that our sample was free of any significant non-response bias.

In the tables given in this chapter, "n" means number of valid responses, "SD" means standard deviation, "min" means minimum, and "max" means maximum. Number of valid responses varies because some companies answered only some of the questions.

3. Usage Rates of and Relationships between the Three Management Control Tools

Outlined further are the responses concerning the definitions and usage rates of the three MCTs. The survey defined a medium-term management plan as a business plan lasting one to six years. This MCT was used by 95.1% of the respondents (346 of the 364 companies with valid responses). The survey defined budgeting as follows: "formulation of a budget for a certain period (within one year) in the future from a comprehensive perspective of the company, and the use of this as a means to guide and coordinate daily activities of each department, in addition to a variance analysis between the budget and the actual results; it is a comprehensive management control method based on numbers to take appropriate improvement measures based on the analysis, and is a specific means of corporate profit management" (Miki *et al.*, 2003, p. 130) This MCT was used by 98.4% of the respondents (359 of the 365 companies with valid responses). The survey defined MBO as follows: "A management control tool for achieving organizational objectives; it involves integrating the organization's objectives with the objectives of individuals so that each employee manages the objectives by himself" (Kinugasa, 2015, pp. 91–92). This MCT was used by 88.7% of the respondents (322 of the 363 companies with valid responses). While the survey items for the other two MCTs (medium-term management plans and budgeting) pertained to the organization, the survey item for MBO pertained to the managers' major organizational units within the organization (such as business units and operating companies). The survey results revealed that most large companies in Japan use all three MCTs: medium-term management plans, budgeting, and MBO.

Outlined as follows are the relationships between the MCTs. Table 1 illustrates the relationship between budgeting and medium-term

Table 1. Relationship between budgeting and medium-term management plans.

	n	%
Budgeting is related to some extent to medium-term management plans (e.g., the medium-term management plan is incorporated into the budgeting policy).	180	50.6
We align budget targets with key quantitative targets in the medium-term management plan (e.g., profit, sales)	147	41.3
We prepare budgets independently from the medium-term management plan (or we do not use medium-term management plans).	29	8.1
Total	356	100.0

Table 2. Relationship between MBO and budgeting.

	n	%
MBO is related to some extent to budgeting.	174	54.5
MBO is essential for budgeting.	122	38.2
We practice MBO separately from budgeting (or we do not use budgeting).	23	7.2
Total	319	100.0

management plans. A total of 91.9% of the companies said that their budgeting and medium-term planning are related at least to some extent.

Table 2 illustrates the relationship between MBO and budgeting. A total of 92.8% of the companies said that MBO and budgeting are related, at least to some extent.

Thus, the survey results reveal that the three MCTs are interconnected in most large companies in Japan.

4. Analysis Results

As stated in Section 1, we compared the three MCTs with respect to three critical factors in management control: performance measures, target levels, and reward links. However, due to space constraints in the survey form, we did not compare all three MCTs in each factor; instead, for a given factor, we compared medium-term management plans with budgeting and budgeting with MBOs.

Of the contingency variables affecting management control and MCTs, the literature has focused on PEU (Chenhall, 2007; Gordon and Narayanan, 1984). Accordingly, we compared the MCTs in terms of how PEU affected them.

PEU is a multidimensional concept, but the dimension we were interested in was environmental predictability. To measure this, we used the scale developed by Gordon and Narayanan (1984), which asks respondents about two aspects of the business environment: market activities of competitors and customer demands. For both these items, respondents rate the perceived predictability of that item over the past three years using a scale from 1 to 7, where 1 is "becoming less predictable," 4 is "neutral," and 7 is "becoming more predictable. We defined the mean score as the measurement score. Cronbach's alpha was 0.73, denoting that the items were internally consistent.

Setting 4.50 as the cut-off median for environmental predictability, we classified companies whose median fell short of this cut-off as companies with low environmental predictability (184 of the 361 companies with valid responses) and those whose median was above the cut-off as companies with high environmental predictability (177 of the 361 companies with valid responses).

We then checked for statistically significant differences between the MCTs and between the two groups of companies (high and low environmental predictability). For the former, we subjected the mean scores to a paired samples t-test. For the latter, we subjected the mean scores to an independent samples t-test. To test for differences in usage rate, we used McNemar's test on the former and a chi-squared test on the latter.

Of the companies with low environmental predictability, 92.9% (170 out of 183) used medium-term management plans, 98.4% (181 out of 184) used budgeting, and 88.5% (162 out of 183) used MBO. Of those with high environmental predictability, 97.2% (172 out of 177) used medium-term management plans, 98.3% (174 out of 177) used budgeting, and 88.7% (157 out of 177) used MBO. Medium-term management plans were the only MCT affected by environmental predictability: Companies with low environmental predictability (high PEU) were slightly less likely to use medium-term management plans, a trend that proved statistically significant at the 10% level ($\chi^2 = 3.468$, $p = 0.063$).

4.1. Emphasized performance measures

4.1.1. Comparing medium-term management plans with budgeting

Table 3 illustrates the performance measures that companies emphasize in their medium-term management plans and budgeting. Note that ordinary income is calculated in accordance with Japan's generally accepted accounting principles. None of the companies surveyed chose comprehensive income or residual income (which includes economic value added) as a performance measure. Of the companies who selected "other," ten companies used this "other" measure as a performance measure for medium-term management plans and eight as a performance measure for budgeting. We omitted these 18 companies from the table data.

For both medium-term management plans and budgeting, the amount of profit and sales dominated as the top performance measures, with operating income as the most emphasized performance measure. Relatively few companies favored profit rates such as return on equity (ROE), return on assets (ROA), or return on sales.

Table 3. Performance measures most emphasized for medium-term management plans and budgeting.

Medium-term management plans	n	%	Budgeting	n	%
Operating income	164	49.5	Operating income	197	56.0
Ordinary income	54	16.3	Ordinary income	66	18.8
Sales	39	11.8	Sales	39	11.1
ROE	24	7.3	Net income	18	5.1
Net income	19	5.7	Return on sales	16	4.5
Return on sales	18	5.4	ROE	6	1.7
ROA	3	0.9	ROA	2	0.6
Total	331	100.0		352	100.0

Table 4. Emphasis on performance measures for MBO.

	n	Mean	SD	Min	Max	Median
Budget achievement in the manager's division, department, or team	320	5.88	1.05	2	7	6
Budget achievement across the major organizational unit	320	5.62	1.14	1	7	6
Budget achievement across the whole company	320	4.85	1.49	1	7	5
Business process-related measures (e.g., quality, productivity)	320	5.22	1.13	1	7	5
Customer-related measures (e.g., market share, customer satisfaction)	320	4.73	1.23	1	7	5
Employee-related measures (e.g., employee satisfaction, number of ideas proposed)	320	4.32	1.25	1	7	4

However, we did observe a statistical difference between medium-term management plans and budgeting: For medium-term management plans, operating income was significantly less likely to be given top emphasis than other measures (χ^2 = 8.800, p = 0.003). Conversely, we observed a significantly large number of companies that placed maximum emphasis on ROE (binominal test: $p < 0.001$). For medium-term management plans, companies were significantly less likely, at the 10% significance level, to place maximum emphasis on ordinary income (binominal test: $p < 0.093$).

Table 4 illustrates the degree of emphasis placed on performance measures for MBO. The companies, as well as using financial measures such as degree of budget achievement, placed relatively high importance on non-financial measures, including business process-related measures (quality and productivity, for example). While the data are not illustrated in the table, the mean score for the three items pertaining to emphasis on budget achievement was 5.45, while that for the three items pertaining to non-financial measures was 4.76 (among 320 companies in each case). Cronbach's alpha was 0.68 for emphasis on budget achievement and 0.80 for emphasis on non-financial measures, suggesting that both items were internally consistent.

Table 5. Influence of environmental predictability in determining which performance measure for medium-term management plans is most emphasized.

Environmental predictability low	n	%	Environmental predictability high	n	%
Operating income	74	45.1	Operating income	89	54.6
Ordinary income	27	16.5	Ordinary income	26	16.0
Sales	21	12.8	Sales	17	10.4
Net income	14	8.5	ROE	11	6.7
ROE	11	6.7	Return on sales	10	6.1
Return on sales	8	4.9	Net income	6	3.7
ROA	2	1.2	ROA	3	0.6
Total	157	100.0		162	100.0

Table 6. Influence of environmental predictability in determining which performance measure for budgeting is most emphasized.

Environmental predictability low	n	%	Environmental predictability high	n	%
Operating income	93	52.0	Operating income	103	60.9
Ordinary income	37	20.7	Ordinary income	27	16.0
Sales	24	13.4	Sales	15	8.9
Net income	7	3.9	Net income	11	6.5
Return on sales	7	3.9	Return on sales	8	4.7
ROE	5	2.8	ROE	1	0.6
ROA	1	0.6	ROA	1	0.6
Total	178	100.0		166	100.0

4.1.2. Influence of PEU

Table 5 illustrates an inter-group comparison (companies with low environmental predictability versus those with high environmental predictability) for the most emphasized performance measure for medium-term management plans. Compared to those with high environmental predictability, companies with low environmental predictability (high

Table 7. Influence of environmental predictability in determining which performance measure for MBO is most emphasized.

	Environmental predictability low			Environmental predictability high		
	n	Mean	SD	n	Mean	SD
Budget achievement across the whole company	161	4.66	1.57	157	5.04	1.38
Budget achievement across major organizational unit	161	5.47	1.27	157	5.76	0.99
Budget achievement in the manager's division, department, or team	161	5.79	1.18	157	5.96	0.89
Business process-related measures (e.g., quality, productivity)	161	4.62	1.28	157	4.86	1.16
Customer-related measures (e.g., market share, customer satisfaction)	161	5.15	1.15	157	5.27	1.11
Employee-related measures (e.g., employee satisfaction, number of ideas proposed)	161	4.24	1.33	157	4.39	1.31

PEU) were significantly less likely, at the 10% significance level, to place maximum emphasis on operating income ($\chi^2 = 2.938$, $p = 0.087$).

Table 6 illustrates another inter-group comparison, this time for the most emphasized performance measure for budgeting. Compared to those with high environmental predictability, companies with low environmental predictability (high PEU) were significantly less likely, at the 10% significance level, to place maximum emphasis on operating income ($\chi^2 = 2.857$, $p = 0.091$).

For reference, Table 7 illustrates the inter-group comparison for the degree of emphasis placed on performance measures for MBO. While the data are not illustrated in the table, the following mean scores were observed: For emphasis on budget achievement as a performance measure for MBO, companies with low environmental predictability had a mean score of 5.30 (161 companies), while those with high environmental predictability had a mean score of 5.58 (158 companies). For emphasis on non-financial measures for MBO, companies with low environmental predictability had a mean score of 4.67 (161 companies), while those with high environmental predictability had a mean score of 4.84 (157 companies). Only in budget achievement did the intergroup difference prove statistically significant ($t = -2.605$, $p = 0.010$).

4.1.3. Summary

We compared companies' emphasized performance measures for medium-term management plans and budgeting, revealing that, for both MCTs, around half of the companies placed the most emphasis on operating income as the performance measure, but also that operating income was more likely to be given top emphasis in the case of budgeting. Few companies placed top emphasis on profit rates as a performance measure for either of the MCTs, but a relatively high number of companies placed top emphasis on ROE as a performance measure for medium-term management plans. As to why relatively few companies placed top emphasis on operating income as a performance measure for medium-term management plans while a fairly large number, by comparison, placed top emphasis on ROE as a performance measure for such, given that ROE emphasizes the level of gains from an investment, some companies may regard the medium-term management plans MCT as a more strategic MCT compared to the budgeting MCT.

As for the influence of environmental predictability, we found that companies with low environmental predictability (high PEU) were less likely than the other companies to place top emphasis on operating income as a performance measure for either medium-term management plans or budgeting. This trend (high PEU being associated with a

Table 8. Percentage considered achievable for most-emphasized medium-term management plans and budgeting.

Med-term	0%	10%	20%	30%	40%	50%	60%	70%	80%	90%	100%	Total
n	0	1	3	6	2	38	34	91	111	32	24	342
%	0.0	0.3	0.9	1.8	0.6	11.1	9.9	26.6	32.5	9.4	7.0	100.0
Budg	0%	10%	20%	30%	40%	50%	60%	70%	80%	90%	100%	Total
n	0	0	1	1	1	15	9	68	163	63	34	355
%	00	0.0	0.3	0.3	0.3	4.2	2.5	19.2	45.9	17.7	9.6	100.0

decreased likelihood of placing top emphasis on operating income as a performance measure for either medium-term management plans or budgeting) may be related to the difficulty these companies have in predicting their future operating performance. For reference, companies with low predictability placed less emphasis on budget achievement as a performance measure for MBO. This trend may be related to how companies with high predictability have greater confidence in their budgeting.

4.2. Target levels

4.2.1. Comparing medium-term management plans with budgeting; Influence of PEU

Table 8 illustrates what companies regarded as an achievable level of attainment for their most emphasized performance measure for medium-term management plans and budgeting. While the data are not illustrated in the table, we found that the percentage considered achievable for budgeting was significantly higher than that for medium-term management plans ($t = 9.894$, $p < 0.001$). Specifically, in the case of the most-emphasized performance measure for medium-term management plans, the mean percentage considered achievable was 72.5%, while the median percentage considered achievable was 70.0%. In the case of the most-emphasized performance measure for budgeting, the mean percentage considered achievable was 79.6%, while the median percentage considered achievable was 80.0%.

We analyzed the influence of environmental predictability on the percentage considered achievable for the most-emphasized performance measure for medium-term management plans and budgeting. While the data are not illustrated in the table, we found that companies with low environmental predictability (high PEU) envisaged a lower achievable level regardless of MCT, although the difference was only statistically significant at the 10% level in the case of medium-term management plans ($t = -1.740$, $p = 0.083$). Specifically, in the case of the most-emphasized performance measure for medium-term management plans, we observed a mean of 71.0% and a median of 70.0% among companies with low environmental predictability and a mean of 73.9% and a median of 70.0% among companies with high environmental predictability. In the case of the most-emphasized performance measure for budgeting, we observed a mean of 78.6% and a median of 80.0% among companies with low environmental predictability and a mean of 80.5% and a median of 80.0% among companies with high environmental predictability.

4.2.2. Comparing budgeting with MBO and the influence of PEU

For any given target level, the perceived difficulty of attaining that level would differ between companies. We, therefore, measured target difficulty for budgeting and MBO using a scale that we had adapted from one used by Anderson and Lillis (2011) and Van der Stede (2000), as illustrated in Table 9. The scale consisted of a series of statements to which respondents expressed a level of agreement on a seven-point scale (1: strongly disagree, 4: neutral, 7: strongly agree). The results are illustrated in Table 9. While the data are not illustrated in the table, we observed no statistically significant difference in mean target difficulty between budgeting and MBO: For budgeting, the mean target difficulty level by item was 4.09 (358 companies), and for MBO, it was 4.17 (320 companies). Both budgeting and MBO were internally consistent: Cronbach's alpha was 0.69 for budgeting and 0.79 for MBO.

However, as Table 9 illustrates, for one of the items, "targets incorporated in the budget (the managers' targets) are typically extremely difficult to reach," the mean target level for budgeting, at 3.05, was significantly lower than that for MBO, which was 3.40 ($t = -5.447$, $p < 0.001$).

Table 9. Target difficulty for budgeting and MBO.

	Budgeting			MBO		
	n	Mean	SD	n	Mean	SD
Budget targets (managers' targets) are generally set to be extremely demanding	359	4.56	1.22	320	4.46	1.20
Stretch budgets (stretch managers' targets) are the norm	359	4.66	1.23	320	4.65	1.22
Targets incorporated in the budget (the managers' targets) are typically extremely difficult to reach	358	3.05	1.33	320	3.40	1.23

Note: The parenthesized parts illustrate how the question reads for the case of MBO.

Table 10. Influence of environmental predictability on target difficulty for budgeting.

	Low environmental predictability			High environmental predictability		
	n	Mean	SD	n	Mean	SD
Budget targets are generally set to be extremely demanding	181	4.48	1.22	174	4.62	1.19
Stretch budgets are the norm	181	4.62	1.25	174	4.69	1.22
Targets incorporated in the budget are typically extremely difficult to reach	181	3.24	1.33	173	2.87	1.31

Table 11. Influence of environmental predictability on target difficulty for MBO.

	Low environmental predictability			High environmental predictability		
	n	Mean	SD	n	Mean	SD
Managers' targets are generally set to be extremely demanding	161	4.42	1.24	157	4.50	1.17
Stretch managers' targets are the norm	161	4.58	1.24	157	4.73	1.20
The managers' targets are typically extremely difficult to reach	161	3.47	1.21	157	3.32	1.26

Tables 10 and 11 illustrate the influence of environmental predictability on target difficulty level for budgeting and MBO. While the data are not illustrated in the tables, we observed no statistically significant difference in either MCT. In the case of budgeting, we observed a mean target difficulty level of 4.11 among companies with low environmental predictability (181 companies) and a mean target difficulty level of 4.06 among companies with high environmental predictability (173 companies). In the case of MBO, we observed a mean target difficulty of 4.16 among companies with low environmental predictability (161 companies) and a mean target difficulty of 4.18 among companies with high environmental predictability (157 companies). However, as Table 10 illustrates, for one of the items, "targets incorporated in the budget are typically extremely difficult to reach," the mean target difficulty level was significantly higher among companies with low environmental predictability (high PEU) than it was among the others ($t = 2.602, p = 0.010$).

4.2.3. Summary

We compared target levels for medium-term management plans and budgeting, revealing that the percentage of the target considered achievable was lower in the case of medium-term management plans than it was for budgeting. This result is consistent with the fact that medium-term management plans have a longer-term scope than budgeting does. When we used a target difficulty scale to compare budgeting with MBO in terms of target levels, we found that mean scores were lower for budgeting than they were for MBO in one of the scale items: "targets incorporated in the budget (the managers' targets) are typically extremely difficult to reach." This result suggests that companies are more likely to perceive budget targets, compared to targets for other MCTs, as targets to be achieved without fail.

When we analyzed the influence of PEU, we found that companies with low environmental predictability (high PEU) were less likely than other companies to perceive targets in the medium-term management plan as achievable. This result is unsurprising. On target difficulty for budgeting, low environmental predictability was associated with a lower mean score for the item "targets incorporated in the budget are typically extremely difficult to reach." In the previous paragraph, we suggested that companies are more likely to perceive budget targets, compared to targets for other MCTs, as targets to be achieved without fail; however, the aforementioned result suggests that this trend might be somewhat weaker among companies with high PEU.

4.3. Reward link

4.3.1. Comparing budgeting with MBO

Budgeting and MBO can be linked to reward systems. We therefore measured the degree to which managers' reward is linked with budgeting and MBO (reward link) using a scale adapted from that used in Anderson and Lillis (2011) and Van der Stede (2000), as illustrated in Table 12. The scale consisted of a series of statements to which

Table 12. Reward link with budgeting and with MBO.

	Budgeting			MBO		
	n	Mean	SD	n	Mean	SD
Compensation for managers is strongly linked to meeting budgets (their targets)	359	4.32	1.45	320	4.71	1.28
Financial rewards for managers greatly increase as performance exceeds budget (their) targets	359	4.38	1.44	319	4.66	1.23
The probability of job promotion increases for managers when performance exceeds budget (their) targets	359	4.46	1.14	318	4.77	1.09
Achieving budget (their) goals is an extremely important indication of the performance of managers	359	5.00	1.14	320	5.23	1.08

Note: The parenthesized parts illustrate how the question reads for the case of MBO.

respondents expressed a level of agreement on a seven-point scale (1: strongly disagree, 4: neutral, 7: strongly agree). While the data are not illustrated in the table, we observed that the mean score (expressing degree of reward link) for MBO was, at 4.84 (319 companies), significantly higher than that for budgeting, which was 4.45 (359 companies) ($t = 4.476, p < 0.001$). Both budgeting and MBO were internally consistent: Cronbach's alpha was 0.87 for the reward link with budgeting and 0.91 for the reward link with MBO.

4.3.2. *Influence of PEU*

While the data are not illustrated in the table, we observed no statistically significant difference between high and low environmental predictability in reward link for either budgeting or MBO. Specifically, in the case of budgeting, we observed a mean reward link score of 4.49 among companies with low environmental predictability (181 companies) and a mean reward link score of 4.57 among companies with high environmental predictability (173 companies). In the case of MBO, we observed a mean reward link score of 4.84 among companies with low environmental predictability (161 companies) and a mean reward link score of 4.83 among companies with high environmental predictability (157 companies).

4.3.3. Summary

When we compared the reward link between budgeting and MBO, we found that MBO has a higher reward link than budgeting. This result suggests that, of the two MCTs, MBO is linked more directly with rewards for managers. Additionally, PEU had no impact on the reward link for either budgeting or MBO.

5. Conclusion

We examined three MCTs that are commonly used by Japanese companies — medium-term management plans, budgeting, and MBO. We wanted to understand how these MCTs differ from each other in relation to three critical factors of management control: most-emphasized performance measure, target level, and reward link. In this analysis, we also considered the influence of PEU. Our analysis yielded the following findings.

Most-emphasized performance measure: When we compared the most-emphasized performance measure between medium-term management plans and budgeting, we found that ROE is more likely to be given top emphasis for medium-term management plans than it is for budgeting. This result suggests that, for some companies, the MCT for medium-term management plans is more strategic than the budgeting MCTs. For both MCTs, high PEU was associated with a decreased likelihood of placing top emphasis on operating income. This result may be related to the difficulty companies with high PEU experience in predicting future operating performance.

Target level: When we compared the target level for medium-term management plans with that for budgeting, we found that the percentage of the target considered achievable was lower for targets for medium-term management plans than it was for targets for budgeting. This result is unsurprising given that medium-term management plans have a longer-term scope than budgeting does. When we compared the target level for budgeting with that for MBO, we found that companies are more likely to perceive budget targets, compared to targets for other MCTs, as targets to be achieved without fail. Unsurprisingly, high PEU is associated with lower perceived achievability in targets for medium-term management plans. The results also suggest that high PEU diminishes the tendency to perceive budget targets as targets to be achieved without fail.

Reward link: When we compared the reward link between budgeting and MBO, we found that MBO has a higher reward link than budgeting does. This result suggests that, of the two MCTs, MBO is linked more directly with rewards for managers. PEU had no impact on the reward link for either budgeting or MBO.

While our study yielded the aforementioned findings, it had at least three limitations. First, we did not compare all three MCTs with all three factors in management control. Second, we considered only one component of PEU: environmental predictability. Third, we used only a univariate analysis. To address these limitations, we plan to conduct a more precise analysis in a future study.

References

Anderson, S. W. and Lillis, A. M. (2011). Corporate frugality: Theory, measurement and practice. *Contemporary Accounting Research*, 28(4), 1349–1387.

Chenhall, R. H. (2007). Theorizing Contingencies in Management Control Systems Research. In C. S. Chapman, A. G. Hopwood, and M. D. Shields (eds.), *Handbook of Management Accounting Research*, Vol. 1, Elsevier, 163–206.

Ferreira, A. and Otley, D. (2009). The design and use of performance management systems: An extended framework for analysis. *Management Accounting Research*, 20(4), 263–282.

Gordon, L. A. and Narayanan, V. K. (1984). Management accounting systems, perceived environmental uncertainty and organization structure: An empirical investigation. *Accounting, Organizations and Society*, 9(1), 33–47.

Grabner, I. and Moers, F. (2013). Management control as a system or a package? Conceptual and empirical issues. *Accounting, Organizations and Society*, 38(6–7), 407–419.

Hayashi, S. (2005). Strategy communication by integrating management systems: The interaction of long-term planning, budgets, and MBO. *Accounting Progress*, 6, 86–102 (in Japanese).

Kinugasa, Y. (2015). The convergence of "management by objectives" and "policy management (hoshin kanri)", and its complementarity based on their heterogeneousness. *The Journal of Cost Accounting Research*, 39(2), 91–102 (in Japanese).

Miki, R., Masuda, M., and Suzuki, K. (2003). Fact-finding survey of Japan's corporate budgeting system 2002 (1): Survey tabulation and its bird's eye analysis. *Financial and Cost Accounting*, 63(1), 125–151 (in Japanese).

Otley, D. (1999). Performance management: A framework for management control systems research. *Management Accounting Research*, 10(4), 363–382.

Sakurai, M. (2019). *Management Accounting*, 7th edition. Dobunkan (in Japanese).

Sawabe, N., Hirata, H., Ichihara, Y., Sonekatsu, S., Bando, K., and Yamamura, T. (2008). Survey of the current management accounting practices in Japan: A comparison of Tokyo Stock Exchange Listed companies and non-listed companies in Kansai region. *Melco Journal of Management Accounting Research*, 1(1), 81–93 (in Japanese).

Van der Stede, W. A. (2000). The relationship between two consequences of budgetary controls: Budgetary slack creation and managerial short-term orientation. *Accounting, Organizations and Society*, 25(6), 609–622.

Yokota, E. (2022). *Management Control in Japanese Companies*. Chuo-Keizaisha (in Japanese).

Yokota, E. (ed.) (2023). *Frontiers of Japanese Management Control Systems: Theoretical Ideas and Empirical Evidence*. Springer.

Yokota, E. and Kaneko, S. (2014). *Management Control: Considering the Direction of People Corporation through Eight Cases*. Yuhikaku (in Japanese).

© 2025 World Scientific Publishing Company
https://doi.org/10.1142/9789811295652_0003

Chapter 3

Configuration of Effective Management Accounting Systems in Manufacturing: An Exploration with QCA

Kohei Arai

Osaka Metropolitan University, Osaka, Japan

Abstract

Various cost accounting methods are widely recognized as key management accounting techniques in the manufacturing sector. These methods are expected to be highly effective when aligned with environmental factors, such as production systems. However, there has been little research on the compatibility between different production systems and cost accounting or management accounting systems, especially in terms of how they can be combined. Therefore, this study investigates the effective combinations of contextual factors, such as production systems, with cost accounting or management accounting systems using Qualitative Comparative Analysis (QCA).

1. Introduction

Traditionally, management accounting has developed around methods of control in manufacturing. For example, accounting systems for measuring financial information were implemented in the Waltham System, a very early form of production system, and many architects of the Industrial

Revolution in the United States, such as Andrew Carnegie, actively used cost accounting systems to develop their companies (Johnson, 1983; Porter, 1980; Swain, 2021).

During the 1990s, however, questions arose about the effectiveness of introducing standard costing in manufacturing. This is in response to arguments that the dysfunction of cost accounting has become apparent with the shift in production systems from mass to lean production. These arguments include the shift to management centered on non-financial information, such as quality information (e.g., Fullerton and Wempe, 2009) and the shift to management based on financial information centered on profit information from cost information (e.g., Arai *et al.*, 2013).

However, although some evidence on the effectiveness of individual systems has been presented, the question of how complementary and substitutable the systems are remains unresolved. Therefore, I investigate the effective configuration of management accounting systems in manufacturing.

In this study, the survey was sent to 670 factories, of which 181 samples responded (response rate: 27.0%). 146 samples with no missing items were analyzed using QCA, which identifies effective configurations using Boolean algebra. Consequently, effective configurations of use were identified for each of the following components: job costing, standard cost of materials and labor, profit management by process, visualized performance measures of non-financial information.

This chapter is structured as follows. The next section reviews the elements that are effective. Section 3 outlines the research methodology and sampling. Section 4 presents the results of the analysis, followed by a discussion of the contents in Section 5. Section 6 concludes the chapter by summarizing the findings of the study and identifying the research contributions and limitations.

2. Effective Management Accounting Method in Manufacturing

2.1. *Job costing*

It has often been argued that job costing, including the calculation of allocation of manufacturing overhead costs, provides useful information in manufacturing. For example, Hayashi (2009) argued that "the process costing theoretically cannot calculate costs by product" (p. 157), and that individual costing is effective because it aggregates costs by manufacturing order and links the actual product and the calculation results.

Researchers in cost and management accounting have made similar claims (e.g., Ogura, 2017), which are also supported by empirical evidence. Arai *et al.* (2009) showed through a multinomial logit analysis that the more cost information is used for budget control, variance analysis, and cost management, the higher the percentage of companies that adopt job costing. Based on the above, this study adopts job costing as one of the effective management systems in manufacturing for investigation.

2.2. Standard cost of materials and labor (SCML)

Standard costing has been an important management tool in Japanese companies (Fukushima, 2009). For example, Toyota Motor Corporation, a prime example of lean manufacturing, has promoted *kaizen* by using standard costing for variable costs (Yoshikawa, 2008).

However, surveys have shown that the actual management situation differs from what is assumed in Japanese textbooks. In the aforementioned case study of Toyota Motor Corporation, standard costs were budgeted costs and calculated in units such as by department or process (Yoshikawa, 2008, p. 433). In Shimizu's (2018) study of 200 listed companies, standard cost in about one-third of the companies did not have the character of "target as norm," and one-quarter of the companies only recognized the total amount of difference in the analysis of standard cost variance, rather than by expense item. In the analysis of manufacturing overhead cost variance, 63.4% of the companies only recognized the total amount of difference.

From these points, Fukushima (2009) suggests that "setting standards at the component or product level without setting detailed standard consumption or standard prices for each component or production process" or "implementing standard costing for highly important products or standard products" are the actual conditions for management by standard costing. I assume that this is the actual situation of management based on standard costing.

Considering the above discussion, it would be more appropriate to verify the effectiveness of standard costing not through a detailed analysis of differences but by examining whether standards are set for direct material costs and direct labor costs. In other words, in this study, we use the standard setting for each cost item, such as material and labor cost (SCML), to verify whether the standard is effective in manufacturing.

2.3. *Profit management by process (PMP)*

A management accounting system implemented in units smaller than the usual profit and loss calculation by factory process, as exemplified by amoeba management, is called a microprofit center (MPC) (Cooper, 1995). According to Otani (2012), MPCs include Kyocera's amoeba management, Higashimaru Shoyu's management, and Harima Kasei's line profit management. Kennedy and Brewer (2005) also argued for value stream costing in the context of lean accounting, arguing for the effectiveness of profit by department rather than costing by product.

Profit in such a small organization would provide information content to the field that is not available in cost information, namely the transmission of market information to the production department. This characteristic of profit information motivates the discovery and solution of problems, it is easy to share information across departments with a common scale, which promotes empowerment by fostering managers' profit consciousness (Otani, 2012, pp. 82–84). Using survey data from 61 companies, Yoshida and Fukushima (2010) demonstrated that the adoption of MPC influences business improvement in organizations with improved orientation. Based on the above, we consider profit management by process (PMP) to be an effective management system in manufacturing.

2.4. *Non-financial information*

Since Foster and Horngren (1988) pointed out that non-financial information such as time, quality, efficiency, and flexibility information is used more than cost information, there is evidence on the use of non-financial information in manufacturing. For instance, Banker et al. (1993) pointed out that the use of quality and efficiency information in manufacturing has increased with the spread of JIT production systems and TQM. In addition, Fullerton and Wempe (2009) show that the use of non-financial information in lean manufacturing leads to improved profits.

Why is non-financial information more effective than cost information in modern production systems such as lean production? The reasons are as follows: (1) cost accounting takes too much time (Johnson and Kaplan, 1987); (2) fixed overhead costs are allocated in cost accounting systems, making it easy to create waste due to overproduction (Arai, 2020); and (3) traditional cost information is complicated and difficult to understand, such as allocation, total cost accounting, and variance analysis (Maskell *et al.*, 2011, p. xxix). The use of non-financial information can be considered an effective management system in manufacturing and is used as an explanatory variable in this study.

2.5. *Visualized performance measures (VLPM)*

Whether financial or non-financial, its performance indicators will not be used for decision-making unless they are properly presented and communicated. Iwasawa (2020) identified "presentation quality" as a dimension of cost information quality and found that the degree of use and satisfaction with cost information increases when the information is presented in a concise and easy-to-read format. Cardinaels (2008) also showed that the presentation of available accounting information differs depending on the level of accounting knowledge of the decision makers. Laboratory experiments have shown that visualizations such as graphical formats are effective for decision-makers with low accounting knowledge. In addition, Fullerton *et al.* (2014) found that "visualized" performance measures were an essential component of performance improvement in a survey of 224 companies attending the Lean Accounting Summit in the United States. Based on the above discussion, we included visualized performance measures (VLPM) as an explanatory variable in this study.

3. Method

3.1. *Analytical method*

To answer the research question, "What is an effective management accounting system configuration?" in the previous section, we presented the following elements as candidates for configuration: job costing, standard cost of materials and labor, profit by process, non-financial information, and visualized performance measures. In this section, we discuss research methods to clarify the compatibility among these elements.

To investigate effective configurations, this study employs an analytical method called QCA (qualitative comparative method). QCA has become popular in recent years, as Fiss (2011) and others have published in the *Academy of Management Journal*, and its effectiveness is beginning to be recognized. In recent years, QCA has also been used in accounting research, as in (Bedford *et al.*, 2016), where QCA is used to develop hypotheses about the compatibility of strategy and MCS. QCA is a method typically used to test configurations of factors that lead to outcomes.

QCA works as follows (Rihoux and Ragin, 2008). First, for a given concept, a "membership score" is calculated that indicates the extent to which the sample belongs to that case. It takes the value 1 if it belongs completely to the concept and 0 if it does not belong completely. In QCA, the process of converting continuous variables into membership scores is called "calibration." Next, a "truth table" is created to clarify the consistency of the results for each configuration of elements. Here, the consistency score, which is the percentage of a given configuration that belongs to a set of outcomes, was used as a threshold. Many studies use 0.8 as the consistency score, and this study also uses this value. The work performed after creating the truth table is to verify the commonality of the truth table columns with respect to the outcomes according to a Boolean algebra algorithm.

3.2. Sampling method

QCA has the advantage of being able to conduct analyses with small sample sizes, but a certain number of sample sizes is required when conducting analyses that focus on configurations. In addition, measurement scales have been established in previous studies to measure concepts. Therefore, we conducted a survey by random sampling using a mailed questionnaire survey. The target of the analysis was assumed to be at the factory level rather than at the corporate level. This is because we believe that responding directly to factory accounting would be effective in clarifying management accounting practices in manufacturing.

The sampling procedure is as follows. First, 670 manufacturing factories in Gunma Prefecture as member companies of Gunma Economic Research

Table 1. Summary of samples.

	M	Q1	Q2	Q3	n
Annual Sales (Thousand Yen)	3,612,249	515,613	1,110,000	2,550,000	135
Number of Employee	103.2	33	55	100	175
Factory completion year	1980.0	1968	1981	1995	155

Note: M is the mean; Q1 is the first quartile; Q2 is the median; Q3 is the third quartile; and n is the sample size.

Institute, an affiliate of Gunma Bank. This is because the Gunma Economic Research Institute, as a research partner, has a certain influence in Gunma Prefecture, and a high response rate can be expected. A questionnaire was mailed to "accounting staff" in early June 2018, and responses were requested by the end of July. Postcard reminders were sent to 536 factory establishments, excluding 134 factories and business establishments that had responded by July or were informed that they could not respond (at this point, there were two factories whose names were anonymous, so the sample size was 136). As a result, questionnaires were returned by 44 factories in August (the sample size was 45 because there was one factory whose name was anonymous). The total sample size was 181 factories, for a response rate of 27.0%. The sample did not include multiple factories from the same company, as they all belonged to different companies. A summary of the sample is presented in Table 1. The breakdown of the sample by industry is 25 for metal products and transportation equipment; 15 for electrical equipment; 13 for food, chemicals, glass, and stone products; 10 for general machinery; 6 for non-ferrous metals and precision instruments; 4 for textiles and apparel; 3 for rubber products; and 12 for other.

3.3. Measurement items

First, regarding the implementation of job costing, participants were asked to select a cost accounting method using a self-administered questionnaire. In addition to job costing, we asked participants to select process costing and direct costing in a multiple-choice format for comparison purposes. Note that this is a dummy variable that takes the value of 1 if both variables are implemented.

Regarding the setting of standard cost for materials and labor (SCML), for each cost item we asked whether "budget figures (standard costs) are calculated for cost control" on a 5-point Likert scale (not at all (1) to completely measured according to (5)).

Profit management by process (PMP) was measured by whether profit calculations were performed by department and process. However, to accurately measure the use of the management system, we also measure whether budget figures were set for profits by process. Therefore, in this study, profit management by process is expressed as a dummy variable that takes the value of 1 if profit and loss calculations by department and process are performed and budget figures are set for them.

I simultaneously measured the use of (non)financial information and visualized performance measures (VLPM-FI, VLPM-NFI). In terms of visualization of (non)financial information, I used a translated version of the Visualized Performance Measures (VLPM) scale employed by Fullerton *et al.* (2014). In terms of financial information, we used the VLPM scale as a reference and replaced non-financial information with financial information. These are "Please answer your thoughts about the management accounting system used in your factory. For each item, please choose a number from 1 (strongly disagree) to 5 (strongly agree)."

To statistically control for the contingency of the production system, I used the lean production scale (LEAN) adopted by Fullerton *et al.* (2014). This scale has been adopted in recent management accounting research and is easier to answer because it refers to a specific management system than the scale proposed by Banker *et al.* (1993) and others. These are "Please answer about the production management methods used in your factory. For each item, please choose a number from 1 (not used at all) to 5 (used to a great extent)."

In addition, the size variable (SIZE) was also included as a contingency variable. I used the logarithmically transformed value of the number of employees in the factories as the size variable.

I used Fullerton *et al.*'s (2014) operational performance scale (OP) as the dependent variable. The Fullerton *et al.* (2014) operating performance scale measures the improvement in operating performance over the past three years, considering measures to avoid common method bias and measures such as "scrap reduction."

Measurement scales consist of multiple questions. For analysis, I use the average value of the Likert scale. Table 2 presents descriptive statistics

Table 2. Descriptive statistics of measurement items.

	M	SD	Q1	Q2	Q3
[SCML] Cronbach's α = 0.93, McDonald's ω = 0.94					
Standard Cost of Materials	3.16	1.58	1	3	5
Standard Cost of Labor	3.15	1.59	1	3	5
[VLPM-FI] Cronbach's α = 0.85, McDonald's ω = 0.86					
cost information	2.21	1.1	1	2	3
revenue information	2.24	1.2	1	2	3
capacity utilization information	2.48	1.18	1	2	3
[VLPM-NFI] Cronbach's α = 0.88, McDonald's ω = 0.88					
data workstations	2.72	1.23	2	3	3.25
aligned measures	3.17	1.13	2	3	4
visual boards	2.86	1.23	2	3	4
quality information availability	3.01	1.13	2	3	4
defect charts	2.62	1.25	2	3	4
data workstations	3.37	1.23	3	3	4
productivity information	3.13	1.17	2	3	4
visualized quality information	3.33	1.21	3	3	4
[LEAN] Cronbach's α = 0.78, McDonald's ω = 0.76					
standardization	3.28	1.19	3	3	4
cells	2.46	1.19	1	2.5	3
reduced setup	3.36	1.02	3	3	4
Kanban	2.39	1.22	1	2	3
one-piece flow	2.4	1.32	1	2	3
reduced lot size	2.85	1.19	2	3	4
5S	3.92	1.01	3	4	5
Kaizen	3.82	0.93	3	4	4

(*Continued*)

Table 2. (Continued)

	M	SD	Q1	Q2	Q3
[OP] Cronbach's α = 0.80, McDonald's ω = 0.80					
scrap	3.17	0.64	3	3	3
rework	3.14	0.64	3	3	3
setup times	3.44	0.6	3	3	4
queue time	3.33	0.61	3	3	4
lot sizes	3.07	0.68	3	3	3
cycle time	3.22	0.72	3	3	4

Note: n = 164. M is the mean; Q1 is the first quartile; Q2 is the median; and Q3 is the third quartile.

for these scales. Measurement reliability items, such as Cronbach's alpha and McDonald's ω, demonstrate reasonable values.

3.4. *Calibration for QCA*

In the case of Likert scales, it is necessary to perform a calibration to convert them into member scores ranging from 0 to 1. Since this is a 5-point Likert scale, the lower threshold was calibrated at 2 and the upper threshold was calibrated at 4, similar to Bedford *et al.* (2016). For OP, the lower threshold was set at 3 because we only need to calculate member scores on business performance improvement. Then, the upper threshold of OP was calibrated at 3.5 because setting the upper threshold at 4 would reduce the number of samples with high member scores due to the nature of the performance improvement concept. For the size variable, the lower limit was set at 33 employees in the first quartile and the upper limit was set at 100 employees in the third quartile. The size variable here is a variable whose members are relatively large factories.

4. Result

Table 3 presents the descriptive statistics and correlation coefficients of the variables analyzed prior to calibration. Correlation analysis cannot completely eliminate the influence of control variables, so the results

Table 3. Descriptive statistics of variables.

		M	SD	①	②	③	④	⑤	⑥	⑦	⑧	⑨
Direct Costing	①	0.09	0.29	1								
Process Costing	②	0.35	0.48	0.12	1							
Job Costing	③	0.29	0.46	−0.11	−0.22***	1						
SCML	④	0.30	0.42	0.11	0.16**	0.40***	1					
PMP	⑤	0.27	0.45	0.18**	0.23***	0.05	0.15*	1				
VLPM-FI	⑥	0.29	0.34	0.01	0.07	0.05	0.05	0.16**	1			
VLPM-NFI	⑦	0.53	0.33	0.11	0.09	0.18**	0.29***	0.19**	0.57***	1		
LEAN	⑧	0.53	0.32	0.16**	0.10	0.17**	0.27***	0.18**	0.30***	0.51***	1	
SIZE	⑨	0.48	0.41	0.05	0.19**	0.06	0.06	0.21**	0.10	0.26**	0.41***	1
OP	⑩	0.42	0.42	0.10	0.12	−0.01	0.18**	0.14*	0.16**	0.26***	0.32***	0.14*

Notes: n = 164. M is the mean; SD is the Standard Deviation. *, $p < 0.1$; **, $p < 0.05$; ***, $p < 0.01$.

should be interpreted with caution. However, it is worth noting that various management accounting systems are positively correlated with lean manufacturing implementation. In addition, SCML, VLPM-FI, VLPM-NFI, and LEAN are shown to correlate with business performance.

I use QCA to verify the configuration of factors that are expected to affect high business performance. Therefore, I create a truth table and explore configurations of sufficient conditions for high business performance. Specifically, following Rihoux and Ragin (2008), I created a truth table of configurations that would lead to high business performance with a consistency of 80% or higher, and then Boolean minimized the truth table to derive sufficient conditions. Table 4 shows the results of the

Table 4. Result of QCA.

	\multicolumn{8}{c}{High OP}
	1	2	3	4	5	6	7	8
Direct Costing	●		•					⊗
Process Costing					•	⊗		⊗
Job Costing		●	●	●		⊗	●	⊗
SCML	●	●						
PMP		●	●		●	●	●	●
VLPM-FI			●	●	●			
VLPM-NFI		•	•	•	•	●	●	●
LEAN				⊗		•	⊗	●
SIZE		•			⊗	•	•	•
Consistency	0.818	0.854	1.000	0.718	0.864	0.868	0.935	0.940
Raw coverage	0.081	0.068	0.017	0.089	0.024	0.017	0.069	0.023
Unique coverage	0.054	0.030	0.004	0.058	0.020	0.013	0.022	0.020
Overall consistency	\multicolumn{8}{c}{0.816}
Overall coverage	\multicolumn{8}{c}{0.287}

Notes: $n = 164$. Estimation method is fsQCA. Solid circles (•) refer to the presence of a high operating performance. Circles with a cross (⊗) designate its absence. Large circles represent core condition. The library QCA 3.11 of R 4.0.3 is used.

QCA. Table 4 shows that there are eight core configurations, including configurations of peripheral conditions.

The configurations shown in Table 4 indicate that the presence of a factor marked with ● and the absence of a factor marked with ⊗ represent the condition. For example, according to configuration 4, higher operational performance results from implementing job costing, VLPM-FI, VLPM-NFI, and not implementing LEAN. The resulting condition derived from the absence of assumptions is the simplest QCA solution and is represented by a larger symbol, while the condition derived from a particular assumption is an intermediate solution and is represented by a smaller symbol.

Configuration 1 is the so-called "direct standard costing." Its effectiveness has been confirmed regardless of scale or production system.

Configuration 2 can be the effectiveness of profit management by a process that includes allocation based on job costing. It can be said that the effectiveness of combining standard setting of material and labor costs with VLPM of non-financial information has been validated, especially in large factories. Configuration 3 has also been validated as effective when paired with direct costing and VLPM of both financial and non-financial information. Profit management by process uses both job costing and direct costing. This results in multiple levels of profit representation for each process, including marginal profit before allocation and operating profit. The effectiveness of this approach is not limited by size or production system. The effectiveness of configuration 4 applies to factories that are not implementing lean manufacturing. This configuration consists of job costing and VLPM of both financial and non-financial information. The effectiveness of configuration 5 is limited to small factories where a mix of process costing, PMP, and VLPM of both financial and non-financial information is used. It excludes the allocation of manufacturing overhead using process costing or job costing. Instead, it uses PMP and VLPM with non-financial information. Configurations 6 and 8 show that in large factories implementing lean production PMP and VLPM of non-financial information are used instead of various product cost accounting. Configuration 7 is effectiveness in large factories where lean production practices are absent, which combines job costing, PMP, and VLPM with non-financial information.

5. Discussion

Based on the results shown in Table 4, the following three points can be summarized as effective management accounting system configurations in manufacturing.

The first point is direct standard cost accounting. Although the coverage in QCA is 5.4%, the simple structure does not require mechanisms such as VLPM, making it highly effective. Second, effective management accounting systems often include management accounting systems based on job costing, PMP, or a configuration of both. Furthermore, all configurations have been confirmed to be combined with VLPM of non-financial information. The third point is that it has been suggested that when lean manufacturing is implemented, it may not be compatible with product cost accounting. Configurations 6 and 8 require the implementation of lean production, but the condition for their high effectiveness is that they do not use product cost accounting.

6. Conclusion

In this study, we conducted a QCA based on survey data collected from factories in Gunma Prefecture, Japan. The aim was to answer the research question, "What is the configuration of effective management accounting systems?" It is evident that there is no single effective management accounting system, but rather multiple effective configurations of such systems. In particular, configurations involving direct standard costing, job costing, PMP, and VLPM of non-financial information were identified.

This chapter has three research contributions. The first point is that an effective management accounting system is not a single system but a diverse configuration. The second point is that it suggests that the analysis method QCA is effective. In order to investigate valid configurations, the only option in regression analysis is to increase the number of interaction terms, and using an interaction term of no more than three items can be said to be the limit. The QCA analysis in this study confirmed the effects of five to seven configurations, and the superiority of QCA analysis over regression analysis became clear. The third contribution is that we have confirmed that traditional management accounting systems such as job costing and standard setting of costs of material and labor are still effective today.

Despite these contributions, this study has limitations. These limitations include the fact that it is limited to a sample from Gunma Prefecture, and the fact that performance is measured by a questionnaire, which is not objective. To infer causal relationships with a higher level of evidence, it will be necessary to verify the relationship between these configurations and long-term objective performance.

References

Arai, K. (2020). *The Evolution of Operations Management Accounting.* Chuokeizaisha (in Japanese).

Arai, K., Kato, Y., Sakaguchi, J. and Tanaka, M. (2009). Design principle of cost accounting. *Kanrikaikeigaku*, 18(1), 46–69 (in Japanese).

Arai, K., Kitada, H., and Oura, K. (2013). Using profit information for production management: Evidence from Japanese factories. *Journal of Accounting and Organizational Change*, 9(4), 408–426.

Banker, R. D., Potter, G., and Schroeder, R. G. (1993). Reporting manufacturing performance measures to workers: An empirical study. *Journal of Management Accounting Research*, 5, 33–53.

Bedford, D. S., Malmi, T., and Sandelin, M. (2016). Management control effectiveness and strategy: An empirical analysis of packages and systems. *Accounting, Organizations and Society*, 51, 12–28.

Cardinaels, E. (2008). The interplay between cost accounting knowledge and presentation formats in cost-based decision-making. *Accounting, Organizations and Society*, 33, 582–602.

Cooper, R. (1995). *When Lean Enterprises Collide: Competing Through Confrontation*. Harvard Business Press.

Fiss, P. C. (2011). Building better causal theories: A fuzzy set approach to typologies in organization research. *Academy of Management Journal*, 54(2), 393–420.

Foster, G., and Horngren, C. T. (1988). Cost accounting and cost management in a JIT environment. *Journal of Cost Management*, 2(4), 4–14.

Fullerton, R. R., Kennedy, F. A., and Widener, S. K. (2014). Lean manufacturing and firm performance: The incremental contribution of lean management accounting practices. *Journal of Operations Management*, 32(7–8), 414–428.

Fullerton, R. R. and Wempe, W. F. (2009). Lean manufacturing, non-financial performance measures, and financial performance. *International Journal of Operations and Production Management*, 29(3), 214–240.

Fukushima, K. (2009). Historical development of standard costing in Japanese companies: Literature review of empirical research. *Shogaku-Ronso*, 56(1), 77–97 (in Japanese).

Hayashi, A. (2008). *Why Aren't You Making a Profit Even Though You're Calculating Costs? Introduction to "ABC" to Visualize Cost*. Nippon Jitsugyo Shuppansha (in Japanese).

Iwasawa, K. (2020). Cost information utilized: Evidence from factory survey. *Kaikei Progress*, 21, 32–45 (in Japanese).

Johnson, H. T. (1983). The search for gain in markets and firms: A review of the historical emergence of management accounting systems. *Accounting, Organizations and Society*, 8.

Johnson, H. T. and Kaplan, R. S. (1987). *Relevance Lost: The Rise and Fall of Management Accounting*. Harvard Business School Press.

Kennedy, F. and Brewer, P. (2005). Lean accounting: What's it all about? *Strategic Finance*, November, 27–34.

Maskell, B. H., Baggaley, B., and Grasso, L. (2011). *Practical Lean Accounting* (2nd ed.). Productivity Press.

Ogura, N. (2017). Cost-benefit analysis of cost accounting: Process costing and job costing. *Kaikei Profession*, 12, 39–51 (in Japanese).

Otani, H. (2012). Profit responsibility and use of accounting information at the field level. *Keiei and Keizai*, 91(4), 67–94 (in Japanese).

Porter, D. M. (1980). Waltham system and early American textile cost accounting 1813–1848. *Accounting Historians Journal*, 7(1).

Rihoux, B. and Ragin, C. C. (2008). *Configurational Comparative Methods: Qualitative Comparative Analysis (QCA) and Related Techniques*. SAGE Publications, Inc.

Shimizu, T. (2018). *Learning Cost Accounting through Discussion Points*. Shinseisha (in Japanese).

Swain, M. R. (2021). A brief history of management accounting. *Management Accounting Quarterly*, 22(2), 12–23.

Yoshida, E. and Fukushima, K. (2010) An empirical research of Japanese cost management. *Genkakeisan-Kenkyu*, 34(1), 78–91 (in Japanese).

Yoshikawa, K. (2008). Development of market-oriented cost management: Revisit of standard costing. *Keizai Ronso*, 182(4), 422–442 (in Japanese).

© 2025 World Scientific Publishing Company
https://doi.org/10.1142/9789811295652_0004

Chapter 4

Japanese Management Accounting Mechanisms from the Perspective of the Management Control Package: Linkage of Target Costing, MPC System, and JIT Production System

Keita Iwasawa

Tokyo University of Science, Tokyo, Japan

Abstract

The purpose of this chapter is to clarify the usefulness of Japanese management accounting and its mechanisms based on frameworks whose findings have been accumulated in the field of management control. In particular, this chapter focuses on characteristic management accounting methods widely observed in Japanese firms, such as target costing and MPC (Micro Profit Center). As a result of case studies, the mechanism by which Japanese management accounting methods function effectively under Japanese-style management has been clarified. Furthermore, this study shows the possibility that the roles and functions required of Japanese management accounting methods will change with the recent changes in the management environment and business models, such as the penetration of job-based employment and the development of servitization and mass customization.

1. Introduction: The Present Conditions of the Innovation in Japan

The objective of this study is to elucidate the mechanisms through which Japanese management accounting operates, framed within the context of Management Control Packages. The term Japanese management accounting refers to the distinctive accounting practices found in Japanese firms, though the term has been interpreted in various ways in academic discourse (Yoshida *et al.*, 2012; Iwasawa and Yoshida, 2016; Okano and Suzuki, 2007). One interpretation encompasses accounting techniques conceptualized from initiatives like target costing and Micro Profit Centers (MPC), while another focuses on the practices of management accounting in relation to Japanese organizational contexts.

Previous research has predominantly conducted empirical studies concentrating on specific techniques to clarify their effects and underlying mechanisms. Various approaches have been employed to understand why and how these techniques are effective, focusing on their inherent orientations and mechanisms.

Recently, however, there is a growing body of research focusing not on individual techniques but on combinations of various Japanese management accounting methods. For example, studies have examined the concurrent use of MPC systems (Amoeba Management) and JIT production methods (Lean Manufacturing and Toyota Production System) (Asada and Kazusa, 2020; Kazusa, 2021; Iwasawa, 2019; Yoshikawa and Yoshimoto, 2020), or the coordination between target costing and cost improvement (Hatakeyama *et al.*, 2013).

However, research on combinations of those Japanese management accounting methods is in its nascent stage, and many aspects remain unexplored. Practically, it has long been noted that firms implement multiple Japanese management accounting techniques simultaneously, and these techniques often share commonalities in their effects and orientations. From the perspective of Management Control Packages, these methods can be seen as complementary, generating synergistic effects. However, prior research often focuses on only two such methods, indicating a need for further empirical evidence. Understanding how Japanese management accounting methods with similar orientations exert their effects through complementarity and synergy holds significance.

This study aims to conduct a case study on Company X, which has sequentially implemented Mini Profit Centers, JIT production systems, and target costing as part of its Japanese management accounting techniques, using the framework of Management Control Packages. This approach enables us to reveal how these individually researched methods coordinate to achieve collective efficacy.

The structure of this chapter is as follows: Section 2 presents the research questions (RQ) that this study aims to address. Section 3 explains the field study conducted for this research, followed by Section 4, which presents its results. Specifically, we describe the case of Company X — a publicly listed manufacturing firm on the Tokyo Stock Exchange — which has not only implemented the MPC system but has also introduced JIT production and, more recently, undertaken initiatives in target costing. Lastly, Section 5 discusses the utility of combining Japanese management accounting techniques.

2. Research Question

In elucidating the research objectives, we first organize discussions and remaining issues about the relationship between Micro-Profit Center (MPC), target costing, and Just-in-Time (JIT) production methods in previous research. Based on that, this research presents the RQ in focus.

2.1. *Prior research on the relationship between Japanese managerial accounting methods*

The MPC system, JIT production methods, and target costing have garnered significant academic and practical attention as managerial techniques originating in Japan. The MPC system holds small functional departments responsible for profits and has been discussed in many case studies, such as Kyocera's amoeba management. JIT production methods, evolving from Toyota's efforts, focus on producing only what is needed, when it is needed, and have been widely adopted beyond the automotive industry. Target costing aims to comprehensively manage profits by setting targets for quality, price, reliability, and delivery times in product planning and development.

Several studies have normatively discussed the many commonalities between these diverse Japanese managerial accounting methods, such as their positive impacts on cost, quality, and lead time. These methods empower frontline workers and stimulate communication and interaction. Moreover, these three methods aim to foster market and cost-improvement awareness in functional departments like manufacturing.

This study aims to address two core issues. First, there is a notable gap in empirical evidence concerning the combined implementation of MPC, JIT production techniques, and target costing. Although prior research indicates that these methodologies are being employed in unison, the bulk of existing studies offer normative rather than empirical insights. Management accounting literature has discussed various outcomes, such as synergies, complementary effects, and potential institutional conflicts when deploying multiple techniques concurrently. Second, even if one assumes the benefit of combining these methods, their significance and underlying mechanisms remain under-explained. While the utility of these integrated Japanese managerial accounting practices is acknowledged, detailed discussions on how and why they are effective have been lacking. Beyond the clear-cut cost calculation and management benefits highlighted in earlier studies, there is an opportunity to delve into the influence of these methods on factors like empowerment, interactive control, and market/customer focus. Moreover, the necessity of using these approaches collectively, given their apparent similarities, presents a compelling question.

2.2. *Changes accompanying systems implementation*

This study focuses on changes resulting from the implementation of Japanese management accounting systems to elucidate their impact. Previous research has examined organizational changes following the adoption of specific methodologies (Tani, 2004). These studies have explored the complex relationships between method implementation, its effects, and factors promoting or inhibiting its adoption. By focusing on these changes, this study aims to clarify the differences when implementing the MPC system and JIT production, either individually or in combination. Particularly, given that both MPC and JIT are often adopted in manufacturing settings and share many similarities, analyzing pre- and post-implementation changes is valuable.

Thus, this study explores the changes in MPC practices and their effects when introducing JIT production and target costing, based on a survey of companies that have recently adopted these methods. Through this, we examine the utility and significance of combining these Japanese management accounting methods (Section 5).

2.3. *Research framework: Management control package*

This study adopts the framework proposed by Merchant and Van der Stede (2012). The concept of a Management Control Package, which argues that various management control methods should function as a coordinated package (Malmi and Brown 2008; Yokota 2018), aligns well with the research focus.

Merchant and Van der Stede identify four controls within a Management Control Package: results controls, action controls, personnel controls, and cultural controls. Results controls focus on outcomes and often relate to financial incentives, making them powerful motivators. Action controls restrict employee behavior, personnel controls manage recruitment and placement, and cultural controls focus on shared norms and values. By adopting this framework, the study can better analyze the changes and synergistic effects due to the adoption of Japanese management methods.

In conclusion, this study aims to explore the following research question (RQ):

RQ: How does the adoption of Japanese management accounting methods affect the four controls within the Management Control Package?

3. Research Methodology

This study adopts a field study approach centered on interview-based research. Field studies are useful for clarifying "why" and "how" research questions (Yin, 2018), and are particularly relevant for exploratively examining the unpredictable changes accompanying JIT production adoption.

The research site is the A business division of Company X, a non-ferrous metals manufacturer listed on the Tokyo Stock Exchange's first section. Company X has been implementing the MPC system and recently started adopting JIT production as well. Most of the facilities managed by the A division have been implementing JIT production since October 2016 due to business restructuring. Targeting this division allows for the examination of pre- and post-JIT implementation changes. As of March 2018, the division reported approximately 100 billion yen in consolidated sales and employs nearly 1,000 people.

The interviewee is the head of the planning department of the A division. As a former member of the accounting department, the interviewee is knowledgeable about various aspects of management control within the division. Interviews were conducted on January 10, 2017 (approximately 100 minutes), September 8, 2017 (90 minutes), May 11, 2018 (60 minutes), and November 16, 2022 (60 minutes). Additional research was also performed via email, and attendance at internal meetings on target costing was noted (January 23, 2020, 120 minutes). All interviews were recorded with permission. To enhance objectivity, several other researchers participated, and secondary sources such as trade journals, investor relations information, and internal documents on MPC and target costing were utilized.

4. Field Study

4.1. *Implementation of the MPC system*

4.1.1. *Previous MPC system: Organizational structure and performance evaluation*

Company X has conventionally implemented the MPC system. First, we provide an overview of the conventional MPC system in light of the framework of Merchant and Van der Stede (2012).

A business unit has two major factories in Japan, and a total of about 30 MPCs have been set up within the factories and assigned profit responsibility. Each MPC is set up based on its main processing facilities and is responsible for processing products. Therefore, the brevity of the business as an MPC and the feasibility of carrying out its objectives (Kubota *et al.*,

2016) are high, with MPCs upstream of the manufacturing process manufacturing metal materials and optical fiber materials, etc., and MPCs downstream of the manufacturing process processing final products according to individual product characteristics. Since products require different processing depending on their characteristics, the MPCs that pass through them are also different. Since MPCs are set up based on processing facilities, each MPC varies in size and bundles an average of about three processes, and the processes in each MPC that pass through MPCs differ according to the characteristics of the products.

The profitability unit for calculating MPC profit is based on the section level, but depending on the size of the section, it is expanded to lower levels called "workplaces." The middle managers (assistant manager or above) of the manufacturing division are assigned as the leaders of each MPC and are responsible for the profit of the MPC in charge and have authority over the formulation of production plans, etc., and are in a leadership position within each MPC. In addition, the middle and higher positions receive a portion of their bonuses according to the performance of the MPC in charge.

In terms of results control, MPC leaders are evaluated based on the profits of the MPCs in their charge, and profit indicators calculated by the income statement are a major factor in the evaluation of MPC performance. (1) The income statement is prepared monthly for each MPC, and operating and ordinary incomes are calculated for each MPC. For internal sales, the transfer price is determined through negotiations as described below, and for external sales, the selling price is used as direct sales. (2) Cost of sales includes the cost of materials, labor, and expenses (including depreciation) consumed by each MPC, and SG&A expenses and other interest expenses are allocated to each MPC in accordance with internal rules. There is no particular device to make the profit chart easy to understand, which is often seen in MPC systems such as amoeba management.

In addition to profit targets, each MPC sets its own KPI, which is broken down from the business unit strategy. Specifically, they include cost ratio reduction for specific products, improvement of production line yield and lead time, and quality targets. These KPIs are disseminated within MPC through meetings, etc., and are also linked to the employee goal management system, so that they are broken down into individual goals for MPC members. In this way, the business unit strategy and individual employee goals are linked through the KPIs of each MPC.

Depending on the performance of the MPC in charge of these indicators, bonuses are increased or decreased and promotions are also affected. These MPC profit targets and KPIs are mainly evaluated at monthly meetings for each business unit, where the status of MPC target achievement is shared, and discussions are held for improvement. In addition, quantity indicators are evaluated and confirmed on a weekly and daily basis within each MPC. The status of target achievement is monitored regularly, and when problems are found, thorough discussions are held for improvement in the next period. Next, regarding behavioral control, as previously mentioned, MPC leaders are evaluated based on profit indices at monthly meetings, so they are required to act like managers. The MPC leader is delegated the authority to make production decisions within each MPC and to assign personnel to workers. Therefore, autonomous decision-making is required according to the market environment and the situation of each MPC.

Another distinctive feature is the setting of sales through internal sales based on negotiations among MPCs. Negotiation-based internal sales and purchases are conducted among MPCs, which are in a front-to-back process relationship, regarding the price, quality, and delivery date of intermediate products. During negotiations, the price is determined by estimating the value added in each process backward from the selling price of the product, while referring to the market price of the intermediate product when available. Therefore, the right of avoidance in the strict sense is not recognized, but if negotiations between MPCs continue to break down and it is recognized that outsourcing would be more effective, production may be halted at the discretion of the business unit.

As for personnel control, assistant section chiefs or higher in the manufacturing division are assigned as the leaders of MPCs. Another characteristic of personnel control is the borrowing and lending of personnel among MPCs. MPCs that are busy in operations or experiencing production delays request support, and personnel are dispatched from MPCs with spare capacity. In such cases, the labor costs of the dispatched workers and the associated expenses are recorded in the income statement as the cost of the MPC to which the workers are dispatched. This system of lending and borrowing personnel between MPCs has the effect of enabling flexible personnel assignment based on on-site judgment and avoiding production delays. While different products require different processing, MPCs are set up based on the main processing facilities, resulting in differences in facility operating status at each MPC. Since production delays at upstream MPCs adversely affect the production of downstream MPCs, it is useful to have a mechanism to support MPCs that may become bottlenecks by lending and borrowing personnel among MPCs.

As for cultural control, it is important to foster a sense of profit within MPCs. For this purpose, it is important to conduct internal sales and purchases based on negotiations among MPCs, as described above. The implementation of negotiated internal sales and purchases has the effect of fostering market awareness throughout the entire process and encouraging spontaneous improvements. The company's strength is that it has an integrated in-house process from the production of metal materials such as copper alloys to the processing of final products. In addition, the price of raw materials fluctuates widely. When raw material prices rise, the entire process must strive to reduce costs. For example, when final product prices fall, market information is communicated from back-end MPCs to front-end MPCs through price negotiations, and each MPC is encouraged to make cost-reduction efforts to achieve the target profit. Conversely, when raw material prices rise, cost fluctuations are communicated from front-end to back-end MPCs.

4.1.2. *Challenges faced by Company X's MPC system: Inertness in behavior, culture, and personnel control*

Although Company X had flexible production activities under the MPC system, it had several control problems. First, there was a lack of cultural control in terms of production activities with a market awareness of "manufacturing waste." Since each MPC had the discretion to make production plans, order materials, and determine production quantities, they often ordered more raw materials as a buffer for fear of running out, or stocked up on inventory when there was room. Since there are many processes in manufacturing that require delicate temperature control, etc., it is less time-consuming to stockpile large batches while maintaining stable operation. Also, it is better to keep an inventory in case of an emergency to meet delivery deadlines. Such actions did not always allow production activities to match market demand, and although market information was disseminated through price negotiations among MPCs, it could not be said that market-conscious production activities were being carried out completely. As mentioned in the words of the interviewee, Company X attempted to improve such manufacturing waste by encouraging management of yield rate indicators in addition to MPC profits. In addition, since profit indicators were a major part of the evaluation process, priority tended to be given to these indicators. In addition, since production rods differed greatly depending on the characteristics of the processing facilities, it was difficult to make comparisons among MPCs, and it was also difficult to determine the optimal production rods and inventory volume for each MPC.

The cost ratio was high compared to other companies. So we started (introducing the JIT production system) by asking ourselves, "We have created a lot of cost management indicators and systems, but are they useful?"

In addition, although market awareness was communicated, there was a problem in terms of action control, as the status of achievement varied depending on the difference in the management ability of each MPC. Since the formulation of production plans was left to each MPC, even though market awareness was communicated, efforts to achieve specific goals were dependent on the management capabilities of MPCs. As a result, the level of cost, quality maintenance, and production control varied among MPCs, and even when information was shared, many MPCs were not able to conduct production activities in response to the market environment. MPCs that were insecure about quality and facility maintenance tended to make the previously described no-productions because it was better to keep inventories in case of emergency to meet delivery deadlines, leading to a vicious cycle that further deteriorated the yield rate and cost ratio.

Second, the aforementioned manufacturing waste within MPCs hindered flexible personnel allocation by lending and borrowing personnel among MPCs in personnel control, resulting in "unevenness in operation." The behavior of stockpiling in the midst of a surplus often impedes the lending and borrowing of surplus personnel among MPCs, and prevents the smooth provision of support to MPCs experiencing production delays. As a result, MPCs with an imminent delivery date were often forced to operate unevenly and unevenly, for example, by making temporary operations on holidays and hiring temporary workers. Such deteriorated operating conditions also put pressure on labor costs and expenses.

As described earlier, although Business Unit A conducted flexible manufacturing activities through the MPC system, the MPC system did not fully function to achieve the control effect that was originally expected of the MPC system, and there were some problems that could not be compensated for by the MPC system alone, resulting in unevenness and waste in production. These problems manifested themselves as financial performance issues, such as a high cost ratio when compared to other companies in the same industry, and deterioration in productivity indicators such as yield, lead time, and inventory turnover.

4.2. *Introduction of the JIT production system and changes in control*

In response to the problems described in the previous section, Company X has recently been working to introduce the JIT production system on a company-wide basis, with the introduction and implementation of the JIT production system being led by a cross-departmental promotion office directly under the president, and with guidance from a consultant from Toyota Motor Corporation in the early stages of implementation. As previously mentioned, most of the A business units that are the subject of this study have been implementing the JIT production system since October 2016.

In introducing the JIT production system, Company X adopted the *kanban* system in a way that is compatible with the MPC system. Specifically, the company introduced inter-MPC *kanban* and intra-MPC *kanban* for internal transactions. The former, inter-MPC *kanban*, is operated to receive orders from customers and facilitate production instructions between MPCs, and is exchanged between MPCs in a front-to-back process relationship. The production of the front-end MPC is performed when the production order *kanban* is brought from the back-end MPC to the front-end MPC.

The latter intra-MPC *kanban* is operated between production lines within MPCs to eliminate bottleneck processes within MPCs. Each MPC has an average of about three manufacturing processes, and since the lines that pass through each MPC differ according to the characteristics of the products, management between processes within the MPC is also important.

In addition, in order to realize the JIT production system, efforts are being made in parallel to achieve production leveling, work standardization, and reduction of setup changeover time (Ohno, 1978, pp. 52–92; Monden, 2006, pp. 10–22), all of which are required for *kanban* operation.

As changes in the MPC system due to the introduction of the JIT production system, activation of behavioral control and cultural control were confirmed.

The first change entailed activating market-conscious production activities and fortifying behavioral controls through the use of *kanban*, a mechanism traditionally expected to serve as cultural control. Before the JIT production system's implementation, MPCs had the liberty to determine both material purchasing and production volumes. However, this level of autonomy diminished with the advent of inter-MPC *kanban*. Production would only commence upon receipt of a production order *kanban*, effectively tying each MPC to market demand and eliminating their ability to hold materials or inventory as a buffer. While there was initial strong resistance to this curtailment of authority at the shop-floor level, such objections gradually subsided as the actual flow of manufacturing improved through JIT production system training and consultant guidance.

Additionally, escalating pressure from sales partners and downstream MPCs intensified the focus on market awareness. As previously noted, the introduction of the JIT production system negates the need for buffer inventory, meaning that any delays or quality issues from upstream MPCs directly impact the production of downstream MPCs. Consequently, each MPC has been revising its oversight of upstream MPCs and suppliers while also tightening quality checks during material receipt. This has led to heightened requirements for price, quality, and delivery from sales partners and downstream MPCs, thereby boosting the market awareness of each MPC.

As a second change, noticeable shifts in behavioral control were also observed. Specifically, the enhancement of MPC management capabilities led to an elevated risk of line stoppages. However, this increased transparency made bottlenecks within each MPC more evident to their leadership. Consequently, personnel naturally converged on problematic or bottleneck areas, facilitating improvement-focused communication. These changes collectively uplifted the management capabilities of MPCs. Prior to JIT's introduction, there existed varying degrees of management proficiency among MPCs. The JIT system, through the utilization of in-house *kanban* operations, markedly improved yield and cost-ratio metrics, especially for MPCs that previously struggled with production planning and bottleneck management. This enabled more straightforward achievement of profit objectives, guided by market conditions communicated through the MPC system, and amplified the positive effects of horizontal interactions on production performance.

The third change is the smoothing of personnel allocation by lending and borrowing personnel among MPCs, which was expected as a personnel control measure in MPCs. In the past, flexible personnel allocation was not always implemented, as in the case where a company sometimes had to make up its own MPC's inventory in spite of excess production capacity. Under these circumstances, the JIT production system has reduced the decision-making authority regarding production planning, and manufacturing does not start unless inter-MPC *kanban* is brought in. This clarified personnel surpluses within MPCs and made the borrowing and lending of personnel among MPCs more flexible. Since holding on to excess personnel means incurring labor costs as fixed costs, dispatching them to other MPCs can also improve the performance of their own MPCs. This change can also be seen in the following words of an interviewee.

> "There was still a mindset (within the MPC) that 'we will use it someday anyway, so why don't we just make it and leave it there for the time being? But that kind of thinking was thoroughly rejected by the JIT philosophy, which made it clear that there was a surplus.' Then, since everyone could see that the waiting list was useless, they would say, 'Well, let's send these people over there,' which made it much smoother to manage the workforce."

4.3. *Introduction of target costing and change in control*

Despite its initial success in enhancing control through the MPC system and the JIT production system, Company X faced new challenges due to shifts in the competitive landscape, prompting the adoption of target costing. Previously, as an infrastructure-related business, Company X's sales team would collaborate with the manufacturing department to estimate product costs and decide on accepting orders, all under the oversight of a division manager. However, the rise of competitors from China and other parts of Asia intensified cost-cutting pressures, pushing Company X's manufacturing division to its limits. For example, it became crucial to work with the maintenance department to estimate not just the costs of product sales and setup but also ongoing repair and inspection costs, which would then be proposed to customers. With foreign products often coming in cheaper, Company X had to emphasize lifecycle costs, including low maintenance expenses due to higher product quality, in its product planning and sales negotiations.

Against this background, Company X was considering the establishment of a committee to determine product costs and selling prices based on discussions among multiple functional departments (design and development, manufacturing, sales, maintenance, etc.), and was proceeding with the introduction of such a committee.

Cultural control and behavioral control were activated with the introduction of target costing. Behavioral control is the increase of interactions among functional departments. As expected with the introduction of target costing, the maintenance and servicing departments, which had not interacted with each other on a regular basis, began to participate in the product design and development stage through the establishment of a meeting body. This has enabled the company to reduce costs and increase sales from various perspectives through product development and sales activities that take maintenance costs into account, whereas previously cost reduction using the MPC system and the JIT production system in the manufacturing division was the main means of securing competitiveness.

The first is to further strengthen market awareness and profit consciousness regarding cultural control. The activation of behavioral control has deepened competitive awareness and understanding of the market environment in which they are placed in order to win over competitors more than ever before.

On the other hand, the possibility of a change in the evaluation of the manufacturing division in terms of profit indicators, which is the resultant control of the MPC system, has emerged in the future. As cost control is applied to maintenance and servicing as well, for example, business models and contracts that generate profits in the maintenance and servicing stage, even if profits are not generated in the manufacturing stage, are expected to increase. In such a case, if the selling price is calculated by negotiation among MPCs from the upstream based on the market price as in the past, there is a possibility that no profit will remain in each MPC and a reasonable valuation will not be made. Changes in appropriate valuation methods in accordance with such changes in business models should be observed in the future.

5. Discussion

Our field study in Company X's A business unit showed that the JIT production system addresses gaps in the conventional MPC system, enhancing control and boosting production performance. Such issues in Company X's MPC system have been noted in prior studies and are common in MPC systems. In the following section, we delve into the mechanisms behind these observed changes, drawing on prior research.

Firstly, in enhancing market-conscious production, the two methods complement each other in cultural control focused on market awareness. Under the MPC system, smaller units often maintain inventories as a buffer for sudden orders, making it ill-suited for production and inventory adjustment. Therefore, a mechanism for these adjustments is needed (Ootani, 2018, pp. 102–104). For instance, Kyocera's amoeba management charges inventory interest to the sales department (Inamori, 2006), while Sumitomo Electric Industries explicitly states inventory costs in their line company system (Matsuki, 2003).

This study shows that JIT's *kanban* system aids the MPC in adjusting production and inventory. Specifically, the MPC excels in conveying market price data, while JIT focuses on market demand and production volume. Combining both methods enriches the overall market insight and fosters proactive improvement activities. Moreover, tying production instructions to market demand enhances market-aware production.

The second key finding is that JIT enhances management capabilities within MPCs by facilitating information sharing. A shortcoming of the traditional MPC system is its lack of cost or production control, relying instead on the experience of each MPC leader (Kubota et al., 2004). Prior to JIT's introduction, the study observed varying management skills and production performance within MPCs.

This study empirically shows that JIT serves as an effective tool for MPCs (Monden, 2006). Specifically, JIT helped identify bottlenecks in MPCs, easing their management and fostering internal interactions for improvements. Post-JIT introduction, previously underperforming MPCs exhibited notable gains in performance metrics. JIT's role as a tangible tool for enhancing productivity and reducing costs (Fujimoto, 2001) synergizes with MPCs to activate cost management.

The third point highlights how JIT minimizes suboptimal behavior within MPCs. While MPCs can focus solely on their own objectives, leading to issues like reluctance to share staff, JIT counteracts this. Previous studies (Maruta, 2010; Fujino and Lee, 2016) note that merely relying on management accounting systems is insufficient to facilitate smooth horizontal interactions. In our case study, despite surplus production capacity, a myopic focus on their own goals led MPCs to prioritize their immediate needs, such as stockpiling parts, over inter-departmental cooperation.

JIT compels MPCs to wait for a production-order *kanban* before manufacturing, highlighting excess staffing. Idle staff becomes a cost liability, prompting MPCs to lend personnel to others, reducing overall costs. This promotes a more efficient "lending and borrowing" of staff between MPCs. This finding aligns with Ueso's 2017 observation that both methods aim to create surplus production capacity while avoiding opportunity loss.

However, JIT can address common issues in MPC systems but is not a universal fix. In simpler manufacturing environments, complex systems like JIT may be overkill. Moreover, other solutions exist; for example, internal inventory interest rates or straightforward profit charts could resolve issues without adopting JIT. Still, some firms successfully integrate JIT with other methods, such as Kyocera-style amoeba management, as indicated by Nikkei Strategy (2008).

In addition, the field study in Division A of Company X revealed that target costing enhanced the controls inherent in both the MPC and JIT systems. Furthermore, all three methods shared a market and profit-oriented cultural focus. By incorporating cross-functional roles, target costing extended market and profit orientation to areas not initially covered by MPC and JIT, which were limited to manufacturing and sales.

However, the study notes potential challenges to the MPC system's performance evaluation due to the introduction of target costing and the broadening scope of profit management. Specifically, if the business model evolves to include not just manufacturing but also maintenance and servicing divisions, the existing system of internal sales pricing — based on negotiated or market rates — may no longer accurately capture the manufacturing division's contribution. Future research should explore how to adapt negotiated pricing under these conditions.

6. Conclusion

This study aims to explore how Japanese management accounting practices affect the management control package, focusing on Company X's transition from an MPC system to a JIT production system integrated with target costing. Results indicate that JIT resolves many issues inherent to the traditional MPC system, boosting control efficiency and performance. Additionally, the integration of target costing enhances cross-functional collaboration, further strengthening control mechanisms within the MPC and JIT systems.

This study has three main contributions. First, it empirically validates previous normative claims about the synergistic benefits of combining Japanese-style management accounting methods. We conducted a field study that supports these claims, revealing that the combination enhances market orientation and fosters a dynamic personnel management system, areas previously overlooked.

The role of management accounting within JIT production has long been a subject of discussion (Hansen and Mouritsen, 2007). The seminal work "Relevance Lost" (Johnson and Kaplan, 1987) underscored the diminishing utility of traditional management accounting in modern manufacturing. However, this study reveals that the MPC system remains relevant and effective under JIT production conditions, offering empirical evidence that cost control informed by management accounting is still valuable in contemporary settings.

Second, this study adds to MPC research by detailing Company X's MPC system's functionality and initial challenges. Notably, the study suggests the JIT production system as a solution to these challenges. Furthermore, Company X's unique practice of tying manager compensation to MPC performance merits further exploration.

This study is rich in many implications in that it empirically demonstrated the significance of combining the MPC system and the JIT production system/target costing, two typical Japanese management methods that have developed from different backgrounds but have been claimed to have many affinities with each other. In the future, it would be desirable to elucidate the relationship between the MPC system and other methods at manufacturing sites, as well as the effects of their combined use, based on the findings of this study.

References

Asada, T. and Kazusa, Y. (2020). Overcoming control system stagnation: The evolution of amoeba management at Maruto–Mizutani. *Genkakeisankenkyuu*, 44(1), 88–101 (in Japanese).

Banker, R. D., Bardhan, I. R., and Chen, T. Y. (2008). The role of manufacturing practices in mediating the impact of activity-based costing on plant performance. *Accounting, Organizations and Society*, 33(1), 1–19.

Fujino, M. and Li, Y. (2016). The use of management accounting in horizontal interactions. *Melco Management Accounting Research*, 8(2), 17–33 (in Japanese).

Fujimoto, T. (2001). *Introduction to Production Management I, Production Systems*. Nikkei Publishing Inc.

Hansen and Mouritsen (2007). Management accounting and operations management: Understanding the challenges from integrated manufacturing. *Handbook of Management Accounting Research of Management Accounting Research*, 2, 729–752.

Hatai, T., Suzuki, A., Matsuo, T., and Kato, Y. (2013). Linkage between cost improvement and cost planning in practice: A case study of three manufacturing companies. *Genkakeisankenkyuu*, 37(1), 40–52 (in Japanese).

Inamori, K. (2006). *Amoeba Management: Each and Every Employee Plays a Leading Role.* Nikkei Publishing Inc, Japan (in Japanese).

Iwasawa, K. (2020). The changes of Micro-Profit Center system influenced by the introduction of Just-in-Time production system. *The Journal of Management Accounting, Japan*, 28(1), 37–53 (in Japanese).

Iwasawa, K. and Yoshida, E. (2016). Contribution of Japanese management accounting to global research: A bibliographic study of English journals. *International Journal of Business Management and Research*, 6(5), 33–42.

Johnson, H. T. and Kaplan, R. S. (1987). *Relevance Lost: The Rise and Fall of Management Accounting,* Harvard Business School Press.

Kazusa, Y. (2017). Amoeba management profit chain management and Toyota production system: Typical opportunity loss management in Japanese-style management. In *Amoeba Management Studies: Theory and Evidence*, Chuokeizai-sha, pp. 121–140 (in Japanese).

Kazusa, Y. (2021) Introduction of TPS to overcome "difficulty" of Amoeba Management: Case study of Maruto Mizutani Co. *Management Accounting Review, Japan*, 2(1), 15–32.

Kubota, Y., Shima, Y., and Yoshida, E. (2004). The usefulness of mini profit centers for interdependence management: Through the case of an electronic parts manufacturer, Company A. *Genkakeisankenkyuu*, 28(2), 27–38 (in Japanese).

Kubota, Y., Miya, H., and Tani, T. (2016). Does amoeba management bring results to firms (bottom): Components and summary of amoeba management. *Kigyoukaikei*, 68(1), 124–130 (in Japanese).

Matsuki, T. (2003). Characteristics and effects of mini profit center systems: Through a preliminary investigation of Sumitomo Electric Industries, Ltd. *Aomorikouritsudaigakukeieikeizaigakukenkyuu*, 9(1), 21–49 (in Japanese).

Maruta, K. (2010). A study of responsibility accounting in kyocera amoeba management: From the perspectives of computational structure theory, social psychology, and cultural anthropology. *Melco Journal of Management Accounting*, 3, 27–37.

Merchant, K. A. and Van der Stede, W. A. (2012). *Management Control Systems; Performance Measurement, Evaluation and Incentives*, 3rd edition. FT Prentice Hall.

Monden, Y. (2006). *Toyota Production System: Its Theory and Systematics on Demand Edition*. Diamond Inc.

Ohno, T. (1978). *Toyota Production System: Toward Management of De-Scale*. Diamond Inc., Japan (in Japanese).

Ootani, H. (2018). *Case Study: Amoeba Management and Management Accounting*. Chuokeizai-sha, Inc., Japan (in Japanese).

Okano, H. and Suzuki, T. (2007). A history of Japanese management accounting. *Handbook of Management Accounting Research*, 2, 1119–1137.

Tani, T. (2004). *Successful Management Accounting Systems: Their Introduction and Evolution*. Chuokeizai-sha, Inc. (in Japanese).

Tani, T. (2013). *Essential Management Accounting*, 3rd edition, Chuokeizai-sha, Inc.

Yin, R. K. (2018). *Case Study Research and Applications: Design and Method*, 6th edition. Sage Publications.

Yoshikawa, K. and Yoshimoto, M. (2020). Overcoming the challenges of amoeba management by introducing lean production systems: The case of Hirai Corporation. *Genkakeisankenkyuu*, 44(2), 37–50 (in Japanese).

Yokota, E. (2018). Rethinking the management control framework: A focus on process. *Mitashougakukenkyuu*, 61(1), 163–181 (in Japanese).

© 2025 World Scientific Publishing Company
https://doi.org/10.1142/9789811295652_0005

Chapter 5

Adapting Value-Based Management Practices to a Non-Anglo-Saxon Context: A Case Study of a Project to Implement ROIC Measures in a Japanese Company

Keita Masuya

Keio University, Tokyo, Japan

Abstract

This chapter examines the implementation style of value-based management (VBM) in Japanese companies. Previous studies on VBM have often focused on Anglo-Saxon countries, such as the United Kingdom and the United States, making Japanese companies a unique setting. The research method is a case study of Japanese companies that have newly introduced ROIC for the purpose of corporate value creation. The analysis shows that although the technical and political fit between VBM and the Japanese organizational context is low, the cultural fit between them is high. This difference in fit is the source of the selective VBM style in Japan, which eschews hard controls and emphasizes soft controls. This chapter successfully extends the findings of previous research by elucidating the implementation style of VBM and its causes in a non-Anglo-Saxon setting.

1. Introduction

Creating shareholder value remains a complex challenge. Value-based management (VBM), which aims to increase shareholder value by developing effective management systems and fostering a supportive organizational culture, is a key enabler. The adoption of VBM has expanded beyond its traditional Anglo-Saxon realm to include countries as diverse as Japan and Germany. This expansion raises an important question: How is VBM adapted in different organizational context?

This study focuses on the distinctive implementation and adaptation strategies of VBM in non-Anglo-Saxon environments. It focuses on the integration of return on invested capital (ROIC) measures within a Japanese company and contrasts this approach with Anglo-Saxon practices.

Findings suggest that the Japanese organizational contexts, such as an emphasis on autonomy and employee participation, are culturally consistent with VBM while posing technical and political challenges. This leads to a fusion of control through shared values and the selective application of rigorous management accounting practices.

The research highlights the significant role of organizational context in influencing the selective adoption of VBM dimensions. Existing literature (Burkert and Lueg, 2013; Firk *et al.*, 2019; Nowotny *et al.*, 2022) emphasizes top-down strategies, such as executive support and mechanistic structures, for VBM implementation. In environments that value employee autonomy and participation, a strict top-down approach may be resisted. Therefore, delaying the implementation of advanced VBM, especially in the early stages, may be beneficial. Examining how specific national organizational context influences VBM adaptation provides insights into the diverse practices of VBM globally.

The remainder of the chapter is organized as follows. Section 2 presents the analytical framework. Section 3 describes the case study methodology, the research setting, and the data collection and analysis methods. Section 4 describes the ROIC implementation project, while Section 5 discusses the VBM implementation style and adaptation mechanisms in the chosen context. Section 6 concludes with the contributions and limitations of the study.

2. Analytical Framework

Figure 1 presents the analytical framework of this study. Table 1 shows the dimensions and definitions of key concepts.

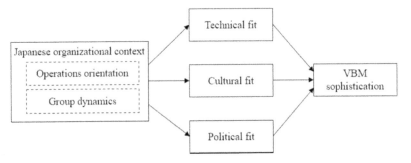

Figure 1. Analytical framework.

Table 1. Dimensions and definition of key concepts.

Key Concepts	Definition
VBM sophistication[1]	
Strategy selection	Choosing the optimal strategy based on the highest potential for value creation in the company's portfolio
Financial value drivers	Supplying information on relevant, fundamental financial value drivers
Non-financial value drivers	Supplying information on relevant, fundamental non-financial value drivers
Empowerment and action plans	Empowering employees and formulating action plans based on key performance measures
Target setting	Setting goals that prioritize long-term value creation, including the realization of synergies
Value-based mindset	Instilling a value-based mindset throughout the workforce
Three types of fit[2]	
Technical fit	The degree of compatibility between the characteristics of the practice and the techniques currently used by the adopters.

(*Continued*)

Table 1. (*Continued*)

Key Concepts	Definition
Cultural fit	The degree of compatibility between the characteristics of the practice and the cultural values, beliefs, and practices of the potential adopters
Political fit	The extent to which the normative aspects, implicit or explicit, of the dissemination activity are aligned with the interests and challenges of potential adopters
Organizational context[3]	
Strategy orientation	
Operations orientation (Japan)	Concentration on production strategies, accumulation of knowledge, and inductive, incremental adaptation to environmental changes
Product orientation (US)	Concentration on product strategy and adaptation to environmental changes through deductive reasoning and flexible resource allocation
Organizing orientation	
Group dynamics (Japan)	Achieving organizational integration through frequent interactions among members and groups based on shared values and information, and respond to environmental variety.
Bureaucratic dynamics (US)	Establishing a formalized organizational hierarchy to address organizational integration and environmental variety through rules and plans

Notes: Each key concepts are based on ...
[1]Burkert and Lueg (2013), [2]Ansari *et al.* (2010), [3]Kagono *et al.* (1985).

2.1. *VBM sophistication*

VBM aligns decision-making at all levels of an organization with the goal of increasing shareholder value (Copeland *et al.*, 1994; Ittner and Larcker, 2001). Fostering a value-creating mindset throughout an organization is essential because commitment to this goal is not always inherent in managers and employees. It involves integrating systems and processes to motivate action (Copeland *et al.*, 1994). VBM achieves normative status when its various elements are fully implemented.

In practice, however, the implementation of normative VBM is not uniform. Studies have found differences in how organizations use VBM measures for goal setting, performance evaluation, etc. (Claes, 2006; Malmi and Ikäheimo, 2003; Ryan and Trahan, 1999). These variations led Malmi and Ikäheimo (2003) to conclude that the normative model of VBM is not universally applicable. In addition, cases have been observed where implemented VBMs have not been integrated or have been abandoned within organizations (Claes, 2006; McLaren *et al.*, 2016). Furthermore, a discrepancy in satisfaction with VBM methods has been noted, highlighting the need for adaptation to specific organizational context (Ryan and Trahan, 1999).

As a result, research has evolved to assess the degree of VBM implementation rather than its mere adoption (Wobst *et al.*, 2023). The concept of "VBM sophistication" was introduced by Burkert and Lueg (2013) to measure the level of implementation, which includes six dimensions (Table 1). Previous research has consistently highlighted factors that contribute to increased VBM sophistication, such as top management support, the emphasis on VBM by CFO, and a centralized organizational structure (Burkert and Lueg, 2013; Firk *et al.*, 2019; Nowotny *et al.*, 2022).

2.2. Japanese organizational context

This study examines the impact of the Japanese organizational context on VBM, drawing on the strategic orientation and organizing orientation outlined by Kagono *et al.* (1985). The framework proves valuable for this study because it empirically and clearly highlights the differences in organizational context between the Anglo-Saxon United States and Japan. These researchers analyzed data from Japanese and US companies and identified different behaviors based on two key dimensions.

US companies typically exhibit a "product orientation and bureaucratic dynamics" approach. This perspective, rooted in the belief that companies belong to shareholders (Kagono *et al.*, 2010), drives resource allocation based on financial logic (Imai and Itami, 1993). To manage diverse businesses, US companies establish finance functions at headquarters and use return on investment (ROI) metrics. Top management often comes from outside the company, leading to sophisticated management accounting focused on capital efficiency (Kagono et al., 1985; Sakurai, 1992).

Conversely, Japanese companies are characterized by an "operations orientation and group dynamics" model. Here, business units and factories have more power than finance and accounting departments (Imai, 1983; Kagono et al., 1985). Planning and control functions are often delegated to these units (Okano, 2012), with top management typically coming from sales and production departments (Tanaka, 2002). Thus, corporate management is seen as an extension of cost and revenue centers (Tanaka, 2002). Japanese management accounting is often criticized for its lack of focus on capital efficiency and investor perspective, as ROI and residual profit are not emphasized as performance measures (Tanaka, 2002; Watanabe, 2001). In Japanese management accounting, there is a strong focus on employee participation and common purpose, which emphasizes understandability over complexity and often excludes detailed accounting information (Okano and Suzuki, 2007; Sakurai, 1992).

Normative VBM is more in line with the Anglo-Saxon "product orientation and bureaucratic dynamics." Product orientation justifies the flexible allocation of resources, and this is reinforced by a bureaucratic dynamics. Normative VBM would provide top management with a means to flexibly allocate resources (Burkert and Lueg, 2013; Firk et al., 2019; Nowotny et al., 2022).

This contrast in organizational context presents a unique research opportunity. What style of VBM is implemented in these different contexts, and why? One approach might be to adapt VBM to the Japanese organizational context, similar to how budgeting, standard costing, and frontline improvement techniques from the United States have been modified for Japanese settings (Hioki, 1998; Okano and Suzuki, 2007; Sunaga and Nonaka, 1995). In the context of VBM, it has been confirmed that Japanese companies that introduced EVA between 1998 and 2000 adapted EVA to existing performance measures and employee understanding (Ogura, 2000).

2.3. *Technical, cultural, and political fit*

Figure 1 illustrates the role of technical, cultural, and political fit as mediating variables, drawing on Ansari *et al.* (2010) to explore the dynamics of VBM fit in different organizational context.

Ansari *et al.* (2010) point out that research on the diffusion of management innovations often focuses only on the adoption decision and overlooks the actual implementation of these innovations. Factors internal to the organization are likely to influence "implementation," including the integration and adaptation or rejection of the new management innovation into the organization.

Ansari *et al.* (2010) postulate that the adoption pattern of a practice depends on its fit with the adopting organization. In this context, "fit" is defined as the extent to which the characteristics of the practice are consistent with the needs, goals, and structure of the organization (Nadler and Tushman, 1980). The concepts of technical, cultural, and political fit are instrumental in generating different mechanisms and patterns of fit within the organization. By introducing a mediating variable, the analysis of the VBM fit mechanism gains depth and precision.

3. Method

This study examines the implementation of VBM in non-Anglo-Saxon context, focusing particularly on the how and why aspects. The chosen method is a case study, which is appropriate for exploring such a dynamic topic. The focus is on Company A, a prominent manufacturing company listed on the Prime Market of the Tokyo Stock Exchange. With a massive scale of three trillion yen in consolidated sales, 100,000 employees, and over 100 plants, Company A operates through four regional SBUs: Japan, Asia, Europe, and the United States.

In FY2021, Company A began implementing ROIC as a new measure of corporate value. This initiative extends to all of its SBUs, with each unit independently designing its management accounting systems.

The focus of this study is the Japanese SBU, referred to as NihonSBU. The NihonSBU is characterized by its focus on operational efficiency and employee participation through Total Quality Management (TQM). These attributes have a significant impact on the use of ROIC and the management of its implementation, providing a lens into the Japanese adaptation of VBM.

Data collection for this case study is multifaceted. It includes four in-depth interviews, each lasting 60–90 minutes, with the head of accounting at the headquarters (secretariat) who is leading the ROIC initiative. The interviews covered the application, implementation, and management of ROIC at the NihonSBU, as well as perceptions of practices at the overseas SBUs. Interviews were recorded with consent and transcribed on the same day. Additional data sources include internal documents such as the ROIC implementation roadmap, e-learning materials, and internal newsletters.

4. Case Study

4.1. *Developing a management accounting system focused on ROIC*

Company A's approach to measuring ROIC is structured around its SBU system, which includes regions such as the United States, Europe, Asia, and Japan. Within these regions, further subdivisions are made, such as dividing Europe into India and the Middle East. In NihonSBU, ROIC is calculated for each of the four business units.

The introduction of ROIC in FY2021 was accompanied by a long-term target through FY2023. This target took into account the total cost of capital ratio, various simulations, and management intentions. ROIC became a component of executive compensation, calculated using adjusted operating income (with a fixed tax rate of 30%) and the book value of working capital and fixed assets. A single cost of capital is applied across the company, and by the end of FY2021, business units began managing ROIC independently, subject to quarterly review by the management committee.

At the business unit level, the initial focus was on autonomy rather than strict accounting control. Although ROIC budget targets were set for each business unit, the goal was the company's consolidated ROIC targets. In the early stages of implementation, actual results were reported to emphasize the importance of ROIC.

Creating a detailed ROIC tree with quarterly measured KPIs is feasible, but introducing new reporting requirements for traditionally unreported KPIs may be perceived as merely bureaucratic and risk ROIC rejection. In particular, indirect departments often struggle with setting quantitative KPIs. As a result, the secretariat has chosen not to mandate detailed or quantified ROIC trees, allowing each department to develop its own approach. There's no single, integrated ROIC tree for the company.

> Creating a detailed ROIC tree can be an exhaustive task that involves setting complex KPIs, collecting them at the corporate office, tracking them, and reporting on them. However, such an approach runs the risk of being rejected by the frontline workers, or of reducing the process to reporting for the sake of reporting. (Head of the secretariat)

The design of the performance evaluation system also remains decentralized. Although ROIC has a significant impact on executive compensation and is part of management incentives, other performance measures are often used, depending on the growth stage and specific challenges. The secretariat does not enforce an integrated approach.

Concerns about enterprise resource planning (ERP) systems within the NihonSBU further complicate matters. While popular ERP systems are in use, a reliance on Excel persists due to ERP limitations in data collection and disaggregation. This leads to problems such as incomplete data, extensive manual work, and errors. Immediate quantification and target setting for KPIs could overwhelm business units with reporting tasks, potentially hindering thorough analysis and improvement of ROIC and KPIs.

Despite the initial obstacles, ROIC adoption gradually improved. Three years after its introduction, the company shifted to a more quantitative evaluation of business units, driving actions such as the sale of underperforming assets based on ROIC analysis. In addition, the company broadened its KPI focus to include assets in addition to profits, reinforcing its commitment to accounting control.

4.2. *Fostering a culture of ROIC awareness*

The secretariat's goal was to ensure that everyone in Company A, from senior management and department heads to technical staff in indirect departments and factories, knew and understood ROIC. Taking advantage of the company-wide adoption of TQM, the secretariat recognized the need to instill an understanding of ROIC at the individual level. In other words, the secretariat believed that if ROIC was not instilled in each and every employee, it would become a skeleton over time. Therefore, the secretariat's focus is on line workers. The secretariat believed that a broad understanding of ROIC among the line workers who support Company A's manufacturing function would help build momentum for ROIC management throughout the company.

Gaining the support of top management was critical to the implementation of these objectives. The importance of this approach is amplified by the fact that its influence extends to line workers at the base of the organizational hierarchy.

Nevertheless, the secretariat was concerned that relying solely on top management support might lead to resistance from line workers. ROIC is not easy to understand for line workers. Therefore, the secretariat wanted to make ROIC itself important, so instead of measuring ROIC or value drivers, it was necessary to penetrate ROIC through translation. The core method was to combine ROIC with TQM. NihonSBU has been practicing TQM for over 50 years with the goal of increasing customer and social value. Concretizing the meaning of ROIC, which was introduced to restore profitability, leads to the point of appropriately creating customer and social value. Based on this recognition of commonality, ROIC and TQM have been combined in such a way as to reduce *muri* (unreasonableness), *muda* (waste), and *mura* (unevenness), and to create customer value while maintaining the perspective of ROIC in terms of invested capital and return. In addition, a new "ROIC Award" was introduced in the TQM Activity Presentation Competition, where case of TQM activities are presented.

Despite these efforts, the secretariat remained cautious about overemphasizing ROIC figures and the ROIC Award. Concerns were raised that an excessive focus on accounting aspects could overshadow important local values such as quality improvement and autonomy. Therefore, it was clarified that the primary goal for line workers was the "TQM Grand Award," not the ROIC Award. The message was clear: maintaining the usual TQM practices with an added ROIC perspective was the desired approach.

> ROIC seems to be a natural extension of TQM principles. However, a strong focus on accounting figures could lead to an overemphasis on financial aspects. While financial awareness is part of the daily routine for front-line employees, it's important not to overemphasize it. Therefore, we consider ROIC to be only one element of the essence of the TQM activity presentation conference. (Head of the secretariat)

The implementation strategy is also reflected in the ambassador system. The ambassadors are appointed to translate the ROIC concept into the target culture and language. They are arranged hierarchically according to the distance between the secretariat and the target. In many cases, the production manager and factory accountant at headquarters are the primary and secondary ambassadors for the line worker, respectively. They were instructed not to emphasize achieving specific accounting targets for ROIC and value drivers. Rather, their role was to philosophically facilitate the integration of ROIC into TQM practices.

This approach of integrating ROIC into the decision-making processes of line workers has begun to bear fruit. Financial awareness has increased, especially with regard to profit and invested capital. In the second year after the introduction of ROIC, there was a noticeable increase in the number of improvement cases related to invested capital in the TQM Activity Presentation Competition. Winners of the ROIC Award were particularly praised for their financial impact. By the third year, most improvement cases included references to ROIC, indicating a successful integration of ROIC concepts into daily operational decisions.

4.3. *Leveraging a ROIC measure in SBUs abroad*

The secretariat observed a significant difference in the application of ROIC between Japan and other regions. In the overseas SBUs covering Europe, the US, and Asia, ROIC is primarily used as a performance measure for top management, often at larger organizational levels than in

Japan. Its incorporation into the incentive plans of SBU top management underscores its criticality and the need to improve ROIC. In these regions, a top-down approach is more common, where ROIC is embedded in KPIs, with clear accountability for each KPI. On the other hand, ROIC itself has not been disseminated throughout the organization. Such an approach suggests a belief that achieving ROIC targets is primarily the responsibility of top management, without the need for widespread awareness of ROIC throughout the organization.

> In Europe and the U.S., ROIC improvement activities are particularly emphasized as a key performance measure for top management. Instead of saying, "This is a collective activity that everyone is doing. So, let's do it," the method of driving ROIC improvement activities is sort of top-down, with the goal of making sure that ROIC is achieved throughout the company,"You have to manage your inventory properly." (Head of the secretariat)

5. Discussion

5.1. *Operations orientation and group dynamics*

The implementation process and management of ROIC by the secretariat clearly shows an "operations orientation and group dynamics" approach. By targeting line workers in manufacturing for ROIC integration, NihonSBU's operations-centric approach is evident. The reasoning behind this was strategic: it was believed that without embedding ROIC at the individual level, it risked becoming a mere formality. Focusing on line workers, pivotal to manufacturing and representing the largest employee segment, was deemed crucial for fostering a company-wide momentum in VBM.

In designing the ROIC-based management control system and establishing the organizational culture, there was a constant concern that the frontline would feel a sense of compulsion. Respecting the frontline culture was a priority. This was evident in the ambassador system, which was critical to managing the implementation process and was tailored to avoid cultural conflicts between the secretariat and the frontline. The initial avoidance of communicating accounting figures and targets and the respect for autonomy also reflect the consideration given to the human impact.

5.2. Technical, cultural, and political fit as mediating variables

The Japanese organizational context, characterized by "operations orientation and group dynamics," is closely related to the full participation of employees and frontline autonomy. They lead to the technical, cultural, and political fit between organizational context and VBM, as shown in Table 2.

The emphasis on frontline autonomy in the Japanese organizational context results in low technical fit. Because ERP systems are not integrated, standardized, and customized, the collection of accounting information often relies on manual, Excel-based processes. As a result, frontline employees often view detailed value driver identification as a "reporting exercise." In response, the secretariat has avoided asking for accounting specifics or detailed ROIC trees. Decentralized business systems hinder the effective use of key performance measures (Cavalluzzo and Ittner, 2004;

Table 2. Influence of the Japanese organizational context on the three fit.

Dimensions of fit	Effects	Summary
Technical	−	• ERP systems are built for each business unit, placing a heavy burden on the collection, aggregation, and reporting of accounting data.
		• Business units are expected to participate in the allocation of invested capital, but a limited information infrastructure makes the budgeting process cumbersome and challenging.
		• The detailed accounting nature of KPIs risks creating a perception of coercion among frontline employees.
Cultural	+	• Values focused on capital efficiency, such as prioritizing manufacturing process efficiency, have become ingrained.
		• A culture of participation by all, as exemplified by TQM, has taken root.
Political	−	• Respecting the autonomy and culture of frontline employees poses a challenge to the diffusion of headquarters-led management innovations.
		• The secretariat uses a variety of influence tactics to spread ROIC to frontline employees.

Lee and Yang, 2011). Hence, automated data collection mechanisms are essential for the ongoing sustainability of VBM (Copeland *et al.*, 1994). The low technical fit challenges the establishment of value drivers, which are crucial for normative VBM (Burkert and Lueg, 2013).

In terms of political fit, the Japanese organizational context makes it difficult for headquarters-driven management innovation. While the rationale for implementing ROIC may be clear at the headquarters level, it's not necessarily aligned with the interests of the frontline. Managers frequently reject the idea that a company should be solely dedicated to its shareholders' interests (Arnold, 2000), especially as their own power within the company increases (Nowotny *et al.*, 2022). The low political fit requires a tailored strategy for implementing ROIC at the frontline, including approaches such as ambassador systems and downplaying accounting numbers. Studies suggest that the success of diffusion is determined by the relationship between senders and receivers, as well as who oversees the diffusion process (Rogers, 1995; Szulanski, 1996).

In contrast, the Japanese organizational context was highly culturally compatible with VBM because it emphasized the importance of full participation. A typical example was the establishment of a value-based mindset by combining TQM and ROIC. The cultural fit between TQM and ROIC was high, as they were characterized by the creation of customer and social value and the participation of all employees. Using the high cultural fit as leverage, the secretariat tried to get them to understand the need for ROIC and how they could contribute to it. Care was taken to maintain this cultural fit by giving the ROIC Award a secondary role and instructing ambassadors not to emphasize accounting targets on the frontline. As Swidler (1986) notes, organizational culture can structure behavior, and high cultural fit helps diffuse management innovations (Ax and Greve, 2017; Detert *et al.*, 2000). Taking advantage of this high cultural fit, the secretariat promoted a values-based mindset.

In this landscape of low technical/political fit and high cultural fit, NihonSBU's VBM practice has taken on a distinctive form. It prioritizes soft controls, such as fostering a value-based mindset and empowerment, over hard controls, such as performance evaluation and compensation linkage. This approach contrasts with overseas SBUs, where different organizational context favors hard controls.

6. Conclusion

How is VBM implemented in non-Anglo-Saxon countries? This study assumed that the Japanese organizational context influences the implementation of VBM through technical, cultural, and political fit. The case study results showed that the Japanese organizational context, characterized by "operations orientation and group dynamics," was associated with high cultural fit and low technical/political fit. These patterns limit the effectiveness of hard controls, such as performance evaluation and value drivers, and increase the importance of soft controls, such as empowerment and value-based mindset.

This study advances current research in three significant ways. First, it sheds light on the nascent area of VBM implementation in a non-Anglo-Saxon context. With the adaptation of management accounting practices in different countries still emerging (Merchant *et al.*, 2011), VBM's adaptation is similarly underexplored (Burkert and Lueg, 2013). By identifying a unique VBM implementation style within a Japanese organizational context and exploring its causes, this study expands understanding beyond conventional approaches. Second, this research addresses a gap by focusing on VBM in organic organizations. While previous studies have highlighted the role of mechanistic structures in enhancing VBM sophistication (Nowotny *et al.*, 2022), the adoption of VBM in organic structures is on the rise. Understanding VBM's adaptation in these settings is crucial. This study contributes by detailing VBM implementation styles and their adaptation mechanisms in organic organizations. Third, this study suggests that it may be critical to refrain from increasing the sophistication of VBM, especially in the early stages of implementation. While the normative view suggests the benefits of advancing VBM (Burkert and Lueg, 2013), striving for a highly sophisticated VBM model from the outset might lead to resistance due to a misfit with the organizational context. Thus, it is suggested that aiming for a more advanced VBM may not be beneficial in the early stages. This highlights the importance of considering both organizational context and timing in understanding the variability of VBM implementation.

However, the study has its limitations and opens avenues for future research. The first limitation lies in its generalizability, as it focuses on a single company with a distinct "operations orientation and group dynamics." To validate or adjust these findings, a broader analysis involving Japanese companies with similar context and Anglo-Saxon companies is needed. The second limitation concerns the time frame of data collection. Collecting data from later stages of VBM implementation is essential to understand how implementation evolves over time. Finally, while the study sheds light on the diversity of VBM practices centered on soft controls, it does not fully explore their effects relative to normative VBM, nor their impact on organizational performance. Examining the interplay between organizational context, VBM sophistication, and organizational performance is an important area for future research.

References

Ansari, S. M., Fiss, P. C., and Zajac, Z. J. (2010). Made to fit: How practices vary as they diffuse. *Academy of Management Review*, 35(1), 67–92.

Arnold, G. (2000). Tracing the development of value-based management. In Arnold, G. and Davies, M. (eds.). *Value-Based Management: Context and Application*. John Wiley & Sons, pp. 7–36.

Ax, C. and Greve, J. (2017). Adoption of management accounting innovations: Organizational culture compatibility and perceived outcomes. *Management Accounting Research*, 34, 59–74.

Burkert, M. and Lueg, R. (2013). Differences in the sophistication of value-based management: The role of top executives. *Management Accounting Research*, 24(1), 3–22.

Cavalluzzo, K. S. and Ittner, C. D. (2004). Implementing performance measurement innovations: Evidence from government. *Accounting, Organizations and Society*, 29(3–4), 243–267.

Claes, P. C. M. (2006). Management control and value-based management: Compatible or not? In M. Epstein, and J. F. Manzoni (eds.). *Studies in Managerial and Financial Accounting*, Vol. 16, Elsevier, pp. 269–301.

Copeland, T., Koller, T., and Murrin, J. (1994). *Valuation: Measuring and Managing the Value of Companies*. John Wiley & Sons.

Detert, J. R., Schroeder, R. G., and Mauriel, J. J. (2000). A framework for linking culture and improvement initiatives in organizations. *Academy of Management Review*, 25(4), 850–863.

Firk, S., Schmidt, T., and Wolff, M. (2019). CFO emphasis on value-based management: Performance implications and the challenge of CFO succession. *Management Accounting Research*, 44, 26–43.

Hioki, K. (1998). On-site principles in the Japanese system. In E. Hamaguchi, (ed.), *What is Japanese Society: A "Complex Systems" Perspective*. Japan Broadcast Publishing, pp. 135–148 (in Japanese).

Imai, K. (1983). *Japan's Industrial Society: Paths of Evolution and Transformation*. Chikuma-Shobo (in Japanese).

Imai, K. and Itami, N. (1993). Interpenetration between the organization and the market. In N. Itami, T. Kagono, and M. Ito, (eds.), *Leading Japanese Corporate System 4: Firms and Markets*. Yuhikaku, pp. 22–48 (in Japanese).

Ittner, C. D. and Larcker, D. F. (2001). Assessing empirical research in managerial accounting: A value-based management perspective. *Journal of Accounting and Economics*, 32(1–3), 349–410.

Kagono, T., Isagawa, N., and Yoshimura, N. (2010). *A New Paradigm of Japanese Corporate Governance*. Yuhikaku (in Japanese).

Kagono, T., Nonaka, I., Sakakibara, K., and Okumura, A. (1985). *Strategic vs. Evolutionary Management: A U.S.-Japan Comparison of Strategy and Organization*. North-Holland, Amsterdam; Sole distributors for the U.S.A. and Canada, Elsevier Science Pub. Co.

Lee, C. L. and Yang, H. J. (2011). Organization structure, competition and performance measurement systems and their joint effects on performance. *Management Accounting Research*, 22(2), 84–104.

Malmi, T. and Ikäheimo, S. (2003). Value based management practices: Some evidence from the field. *Management Accounting Research*, 14, 235–254.

McLaren, J., Appleyard, T., and Mitchell, F. (2016). The rise and fall of management accounting systems: A case study investigation of EVA™. *The British Accounting Review*, 48(3), 341–358.

Merchant, K. A., Van der Stede, W. A., Lin, T. W., and Yu, Z. (2011). Performance measurement and incentive compensation: An empirical analysis and comparison of Chinese and Western firms' practices. *European Accounting Review*, 20(4), 639–667.

Nadler, D. and Tushman, M. (1980). A model for diagnosing organizational behavior. *Organizational Dynamics*, 9(2), 35–51.

Nowotny, S., Hirsch, B., and Nitzl, C. (2022). The influence of organizational structure on value-based management sophistication. *Management Accounting Research*, 100797.

Ogura, N. (2000). Economic value added as management accounting in Japanese companies. *Kaikei*, 157(5), 662–678 (in Japanese).

Okano, H. (2012). Institutionalization process of Japanese management accounting. In T. Hiromoto, Y. Kato, and H. Okano, (eds.). *Management Accounting Systems of Japanese Companies*, Tokyo, Chuokeizai-Sha, pp. 49–92 (in Japanese).

Okano, H. and Suzuki, T. (2007). *A History of Japanese Management Accounting*. In C. Chapman, A. Hopwood, and M. Shields, (eds.). *Handbook of Management Accounting Research*, Vol. 2. Elsevier, pp. 1119–1137.

Rogers, E. M. (1995). *Diffusion of Innovations*, 5th edition. Free Press.

Ryan, H. E. and Trahan, E. A. (1999). The utilization of value-based management: An empirical analysis. *Financial Practice and Education*, 9(1), 46–58.

Sakurai, M. (1992). Basic characteristics of modern U.S. management accounting. *Kaikei*, 141(5), 530–545 (in Japanese).

Sunaga, I. and Nonaka, I. (1995). Introduction and transformation of American business management techniques in Japan. In H. Yamazaki and T. Kikkawa (eds.), *A History of Japanese Management (Vol. 4): Continuity and Discontinuity in "Japanese-style" Management*. Tokyo, Iwanami Shoten, Publishers (in Japanese).

Swidler, A. (1986). Culture and action: Symbols and strategies. *American Sociological Review*, 51(2), 273–286.

Szulanski, G. (1996). Exploring internal stickiness: Impediments to the transfer of best practice within the firm. *Strategic Management Journal*, 17, 27–43.

Tanaka, T. (2002). Strategy implementation and performance evaluation: In relation to strategic management systems. *Kaikei*, 161(4), 477–491 (in Japanese).

Watanabe, Y. (2001). Capital management and cost of capital to support management strategies: As management diversifies. *Kigyo Kaikei*, 53(5), 672–677 (in Japanese).

Wobst, J., Tanikulova, P., and Lueg, R. (2023). Value-based management: A review of its conceptualizations and a research agenda toward sustainable governance. *Journal of Accounting Literature*, https://doi.org/10.1108/JAL-11-2022-0123.

Chapter 6

The Effect of Management Accounting Capabilities on the Use of Management Accounting Systems

Kazunori Fukushima

Chuo University, Tokyo, Japan

Abstract

The purpose of this study is to explore how the use of management accounting differs according to the organizational ability to use management accounting for management purposes (management accounting capabilities). In this study, we focus on two management accounting capabilities: experiential learning capability and absorptive capacity. The results of the analysis confirmed that high experiential learning capability promotes the active use of advanced management accounting methods and management control. On the other hand, it was only confirmed that high absorptive capacity promotes the use of advanced management accounting methods, suggesting that there is a possibility that the use of management accounting is affected differently depending on management accounting capabilities. In addition, it was inferred that having both experiential learning capabilities and absorptive capacity is important for the use of advanced management accounting methods.

1. Introduction

Recent studies have focused on the relationship between management accounting and organizational capabilities with the goal of clarifying the impact of management accounting on performance. When a direct relationship between management accounting and performance is assumed, the results are mixed. We explore this relationship by assuming it is affected by certain organizational capabilities such as organizational learning and creativity (Henri, 2006). There are (at least) three ways in which management accounting and organizational capabilities could be related. The first is via a mediation model, which assumes that using management accounting improves performance by affecting organizational capabilities. The second relies on a moderation model, which assumes that organizational capabilities affect the relationship between the use of management accounting and performance. The third approach assumes a relationship in which organizational capabilities influence performance by determining the use of management accounting.

This study focuses on the third approach. The mediation model approach has been the subject of much discussion (Franco-Santos et al., 2012), but a clear relationship has not yet been found. The moderation model shows that organizational capabilities enhance the effectiveness of management accounting, but many aspects of how this occurs remain unclear, such as the correlation between the type of organizational capabilities and the type of management accounting (Fukushima, 2015, 2016). Studies using the third approach find that higher organizational absorptive capacity facilitates the use of sophisticated management accounting systems (MAS) (Libby and Waterhouse, 1996; William and Seaman, 2001) and interorganizational cost management (Fayrad et al., 2012); however, further analysis of the impact of organizational capabilities other than absorptive capacity on the use of management accounting is needed to understand this relationship.

The purpose of this study is to determine how the use of management accounting varies with organizational capabilities. Using data collected through a questionnaire survey, we examine how the characteristics and use of performance measurement systems differ with management accounting capabilities (Fukushima, 2015, 2016), i.e., the ability to meet an organization's objectives. The remainder of the study is organized as follows: Section 2 presents our research framework based on a review of previous studies, Section 3 describes our data collection, measurements, and variables, Section 4 presents our analytical results, which are discussed in Section 5, and Section 6 concludes.

2. Literature Review and Research Framework

2.1. *Literature review*

Previous studies discuss two types of management accounting capabilities: organizational capabilities related to the use of a specific MAS (Yook, 2003; Yoshida, 2001, 2002) and organizational capabilities related to the use of management accounting in general (Elbashir *et al.*, 2011; Fayrad *et al.*, 2012; Fukushima, 2015, 2016; Libby and Waterhouse, 1996; Williams and Seaman, 2001). In the first type of study, one of the management accounting capabilities analyzed is target cost management, focusing on the organization's ability to accumulate and utilize knowledge related to target cost management effectively and efficiently. Yoshida (2001, 2002) shows that strong target cost management capabilities are effective in preventing burnout among the engineers in charge of design, which is one of the reverse functions of target cost management, and that it improves the results of target cost management (Yook, 2003).

An organizational capability that has been the focus of the latter type of study is absorptive capacity (Elbashir *et al.*, 2011; Fayrad *et al.*, 2012; Fukushima, 2015, 2016; Libby and Waterhouse, 1996; Williams and Seaman, 2001). A high absorptive capacity of organizations has been shown to facilitate the use of advanced MAS (Libby and Waterhouse, 1996; William and Seaman, 2001). Fayrad *et al.* (2012) also find that the use of intra-organizational cost management, and information-sharing with external organizations such as suppliers, increases an organization's absorptive capacity, including the frequency, depth, and ease of communication and the ability to search for and evaluate knowledge, and even the use of inter-organizational cost management. Furthermore, Elbashir *et al.* (2011) find that higher absorptive capacity of top management promotes more effective use of business intelligence (BI), and that higher absorptive capacity in a business unit not only directly promotes the use of BI but it also helps to refine IT systems and thus has an indirect impact by facilitating the use of BI.

Other general management accounting capabilities also suggest that organizational capabilities influence the ability to implement experiential learning (Kaplan and Norton, 1996; Tani *et al.*, 1994). Kaplan and Norton (1996) argue that introducing a Balanced Scorecard does not mean that it will function effectively immediately, but that smoother operations become possible through a trial-and-error process and by gradual upgrading. Tani *et al.* (1994) show that when a target cost management system is first introduced it may not be effective. Furthermore, although the initial introduction of target cost management is oriented toward manufacturing that achieves both cost and quality, as time passes it also tends to be used for product development that better meets customer needs and to facilitate more timely introduction of new products.

These studies suggest that for management accounting to function effectively, knowledge that enables adaptive use for management purposes is essential (Mata *et al.*, 1995). They also point out that learning through experience is important for organizations to acquire, accumulate, and utilize knowledge (Kolb, 1984; Yeung *et al.*, 1999). We can infer that organizations acquire the use of management accounting through experiential learning, in which knowledge is accumulated by reflecting on the use of management accounting (Huber, 1991; Kolb, 1984).

2.2. Research framework

This study examines the impact of two organizational capabilities, absorptive capacity and experiential learning capability, on the use of management accounting. Some studies suggest that absorptive capacity and experiential learning capability may have different effects on the use of management accounting. For example, Fukushima (2016) suggests that higher organizational absorptive capacity promotes the adoption of more sophisticated MAS, whereas higher experiential learning capability of organizations promotes a more diverse use of management accounting. Other studies note that absorptive capacity may be affected by experiential learning, pointing out that an organization's previous experience influences the knowledge and information it is willing to obtain (Cohen and Levinthal, 1990; Zahra and George, 2002).

Based on the above, the discussion in this study assumes a relationship between a combination of absorptive capacity and experiential learning capabilities, and the different uses of management accounting.

3. Methods

3.1. *Data collection*

In this study, we attempt to clarify the kinds of differences that exist in the use of MAS according to management accounting capabilities. Data for the analysis were collected through a questionnaire survey distributed through the mail. The survey, which was conducted in 2013, targeted 847 manufacturing firms listed on the First Section of the Tokyo Stock Exchange (those whose industry codes according to the Securities Code Council are between 3050 and 3800). Questionnaires were sent to managers within those firms who were expected to be familiar with the actual performance management practices of major business units. To provide an incentive for responding to the questionnaire, those who participated were eligible to receive a report describing the results. Reminder letters were also sent to improve the collection rate. The final number of responding firms, including those received after the collection deadline, was 76 (collection rate: 9.0%). The analysis uses a final sample of 73 firms, after excluding data with missing items for the questions used in the analysis.

To examine non-response bias, two analyses were conducted on the data of the 73 firms that responded. First, a goodness-of-fit test was conducted on the industry distribution of the firms in the final sample, which confirmed that the industry distribution of the sample firms was consistent with the industry distribution of the firms in the manufacturing industry as listed on the first section of the Tokyo Stock Exchange ($\chi^2 = 13.461$, df = 15, $p = 0.567$). Second, tests to identify a difference in firm size (based on consolidated sales and number of employees) between the firms in the sample and those that did not respond to the questionnaire revealed no significant difference. These results indicate there is no significant non-response bias in the data used in the analysis.

3.2. Definition of variables

First, we investigate the organizational capabilities that are thought to influence the use of MAS: absorptive capacity and experiential learning capability. We measure absorptive capacity using seven of the survey questions about how knowledge of performance measurement and evaluation is acquired, referring to discussions in the literature on organizational absorptive capacity (Jansen et al., 2006; Szulanski, 1996). Experiential learning capability is measured using six of the survey questions about how the process of performance measurement and evaluation is reviewed based on studies of experiential learning at the individual level (Kolb, 1984) and at the organizational level (Huber, 1991; Matsuo, 2011). We performed an exploratory factor analysis of these 13 questions and extracted two factors with an eigenvalue of 1 or higher (see Table 1). We identify the first factor (F1) as being related to "absorptive capacity" ($\alpha = 0.901$) because it indicates that the survey respondents actively obtain knowledge from outside their organizations and consider and utilize improvement plans based on that knowledge. The second factor (F2) is associated with "experiential learning capability" ($\alpha = 0.824$) because it indicates that the firms reflect on their business activities based on performance evaluations and use those results in subsequent performance measurement and evaluations. In operationalizing the variables, we score the mean value of the responses to questions that show high factor loadings (0.4 or higher) for each factor.

Next, we investigate the characteristics of MAS and the ways in which MAS are used. First, we analyze the characteristics of contemporary performance measurement systems (CPMS) to examine how a sophisticated MAS is used in this arena. CPMS, also called comprehensive performance measurement systems or strategic performance measurement systems, assume that the relationship between strategy and performance indicators common to both types of performance measurement systems is a function of the relationship between strategy and performance indicators. We measure the characteristics common to both systems, such as the assumed relationship between strategy and performance indicators, the combination

Table 1. Results of factor analysis on management accounting capabilities.

	Mean	S.D.	F1	F2
Improvement based on acquired knowledge will be reflected in performance measurement and evaluation	4.23	1.124	**0.875**	−0.022
Considering performance measurement and evaluation improvement plans based on acquired knowledge	4.22	0.961	**0.855**	−0.010
Attending study groups with people outside the company to gain knowledge	4.00	1.225	**0.843**	−0.038
Based on the feedback obtained, the firm is considering ways to improve performance measurement and evaluation	4.52	1.132	**0.765**	0.134
Seeking input from outside experts	3.53	1.625	**0.718**	−0.139
Improvement based on the feedback obtained will be reflected in performance measurement and evaluation	4.36	1.218	**0.714**	0.238
Attending business school or other schools to gain knowledge	3.42	1.246	**0.605**	−0.049
Review of business activities during the fiscal year	5.85	1.028	−0.254	**0.827**
Verify and review the relationship between business strategy and performance targets	5.41	0.969	−0.090	**0.827**
Verification and review of business strategies	5.55	1.028	0.048	**0.757**
Manager's explanation of the situation based on the performance of the department under his/her jurisdiction	5.42	1.079	0.144	**0.583**
Reflection on next year's goals	5.95	0.880	0.087	**0.512**
Verification and review of performance measurement and evaluation methods	4.71	1.079	0.183	**0.426**

Note: Principal factor method, factor patterns after promax rotation. Theoretical range of each scale is 1 to 7. Bolded values are at 0.4 or higher.

of financial and non-financial indicators, and the link between performance and compensation, using 15 questions based on Franco-Santos *et al.* (2012) and Speckbacher *et al.* (2013).

As shown in Table 2 (Panel A), three factors with an eigenvalue of 1 or higher were extracted from an exploratory factor analysis. The first

Table 2. Results of factor analysis on CPMS characteristics and use.

	Mean	S.D.	F1	F2	F3
Panel A: Characteristics of CPMS					
Linkage between upper managers' performance and promotion	4.32	1.257	**0.849**	0.098	−0.278
Linking middle managers' performance to financial rewards	4.32	1.342	**0.789**	−0.122	0.283
Linkage between middle managers' performance and promotion	3.99	1.149	**0.760**	0.182	−0.165
Linking upper managers' performance to financial rewards	4.75	1.470	**0.723**	−0.138	0.242
Evaluation of non-financial performance that is difficult to measure	4.01	1.253	0.039	**0.860**	−0.122
Setting financial performance targets that are difficult to measure	4.03	1.166	0.102	**0.859**	−0.207
Evaluation of measurable non-financial performance	4.90	1.082	−0.093	**0.688**	0.363
Setting measurable non-financial performance targets	5.04	1.020	−0.035	**0.675**	0.370
Setting performance targets in consideration of business strategy	5.71	1.136	−0.039	−0.077	**0.703**
Develop action plans to achieve performance goals	5.53	1.029	0.199	0.050	**0.629**
Consideration of the relationship between financial and non-financial performance	4.67	1.214	−0.138	0.068	**0.447**
Panel B: Use of CPMS					
Understanding the results of business activities	5.96	0.934	**0.765**	0.003	
Tracking progress toward achieving goals	5.79	1.013	**0.756**	0.016	
Comparison of established targets/forecasts with actual results	6.30	0.617	**0.708**	−0.140	

(*Continued*)

Table 2. (*Continued*)

	Mean	S.D.	F1	F2	F3
Evaluation of achievement of key performance indicators (KPIs)	5.27	1.170	**0.652**	−0.057	
Ongoing review and discussion of Action Plan	4.97	1.093	**0.625**	0.154	
Foster a common understanding within the business units regarding the current status of the business	5.37	0.825	**0.518**	0.361	
Improved cohesion within business units	4.55	1.354	−0.166	**1.024**	
Facilitate discussions with supervisors and subordinates	4.42	1.040	0.104	**0.579**	

Note: Principal factor method, factor patterns after promax rotation. Theoretical range of each scale is 1 to 7. Bolded values are at 0.4 or higher.

factor (F1) is named "performance-reward link" ($\alpha = 0.851$) because it indicates characteristics related to the link between the compensation of top-level (business unit head class) and mid-level (section manager class) managers and their performance. The second factor (F2) is named "non-financial performance" ($\alpha = 0.856$) as it indicates the characteristics of goal-setting and evaluations related to both measurable or difficult-to-measure non-financial performance, such as market share and corporate/product reputation. The third factor (F3) is named "strategic performance management" ($\alpha = 0.673$) as it relates to characteristics that consider the relationship with strategy and the relationship between financial and non-financial goals. In operationalizing the variables, we score the mean value of the items with high factor loadings (0.4 or higher) for each factor.

We then investigate the use of MAS with respect to management control using CPMS. Specifically, based on the framework in Simons (1995, 2000), we measure the interactive and diagnostic use of performance measurement systems with eight questions, referring to Henri (2006). As shown in Table 2 (Panel B), two factors with an eigenvalue of 1 or more are extracted from the exploratory factor analysis. The first factor (F1) is named "diagnostic control" ($\alpha = 0.842$) because it shows the characteristics of control regarding the achievement of prior goals, such as the status of key performance indicators and comparisons of target and forecast values with actual values. The second factor (F2) is named "interactive control" ($\alpha = 0.712$), as it relates to characteristics of active interaction, such as thorough discussions between upper and lower managers and the intent to improve cohesion. In operationalizing the variables, we score the mean of the items with high factor loadings (0.4 or higher) for each factor. For the tension generated by the combination of diagnostic and interactive controls (dynamic tension), we score the product of each variable for the diagnostic and interactive controls.

4. Results

In this study, we attempt to clarify the kinds of differences that exist in the use of MAS according to management accounting capabilities. Therefore, we classify organizations according to their absorptive capacity and experiential learning capability, and examine what differences exist in the use of MAS among these groups of organizations. First, based on the medium values of each organization's experiential learning capability (5.67) and absorptive capacity (4.29), we divided the organizations into high and low capability groups and combined them into four organizational groups. In the four groups of organizations, those with high experiential learning capability and high absorptive capacity are classified as "high management accounting capabilities firms" (Group A, $n = 26$), those with a high experiential learning capability only are classified as "experiential learning capability specialized firms" (Group B, $n = 14$), those with high absorptive capacity only are classified as "absorptive capacity specialized firms" (Group C, $n = 11$), and those with low experiential learning capability and low absorptive capacity are classified as "low management accounting capabilities firms" (Group D, $n = 22$).

We conduct a one-way ANOVA on the management accounting capabilities and size of the four groups and find significant differences in both experiential learning capability (F = 42.814, $p < 0.01$) and absorptive capacity (F = 36.151, $p < 0.01$). Conversely, we find no significant differences for either consolidated sales (F = 1.077) or total number of employees (F = 1.186) for size. These results indicate that the groupings are based on management accounting capabilities.

Table 3. Differences in management accounting between groups.

	one-way ANOVA					Tukey multiple comparison					
						(A)			(B)		(C)
	(A)	(B)	(C)	(D)	F-value	(B)	(C)	(D)	(C)	(D)	(D)
Performance-reward link	4.74	4.23	4.11	4.06	1.947						
Non-financial performance	4.79	4.70	4.23	4.16	2.390*		*				
Strategic performance management	5.77	5.69	5.30	4.52	14.443***			***		***	**
Interactive control	5.31	5.39	4.64	4.43	5.528***			***		**	
Diagnostic control	5.88	5.85	5.06	4.89	17.558***	***	***	***		***	
Dynamic tension	31.40	31.55	23.81	21.99	11.116***	**	***	**		***	

Notes: (A) high management accounting capabilities firms, (B) experiential learning capability specialized firms, (C) absorptive capacity specialized firms, (D) low management accounting capabilities firms. *** $p < 0.01$, ** $p < 0.05$, * $p < 0.10$.

We then examine the differences in the use of MAS among the four organizational groups in terms of the characteristics and use of CPMS using a one-way ANOVA. For items for which significant differences are found, we also conduct a Tukey multiple comparison test (Table 3).

The results show there are no significant differences among the four groups of organizations in the performance-reward link with respect to the characteristics of CPMS. Conversely, for non-financial performance we confirm that firms with high management accounting capabilities use these systems more than firms with low management accounting capabilities ($p < 0.10$). Regarding strategic performance management, we find that firms with low management accounting capabilities use it less than the other three groups ($p < 0.01$ and $p < 0.05$ only for firms with high levels of absorptive capacity).

Regarding the use of CPMS, we confirm that firms with high management accounting capabilities ($p < 0.01$) and firms with strong experiential learning capabilities ($p < 0.05$) were more likely than firms with low management accounting capabilities to use interactive controls. With respect to diagnostic controls, we find that firms with strong management accounting capabilities and experiential learning capabilities use them more frequently than firms with high absorptive capacity and firms with low management accounting capabilities ($p < 0.01$). In addition, firms with strong management accounting capabilities and firms that are strong in experiential learning were more likely to exhibit dynamic tension than firms exhibiting strong absorptive capacity ($p < 0.05$) and those with low management accounting capabilities ($p < 0.01$).

Based on these results, we present key characteristics regarding the use of MAS within each group of organizations classified by their management accounting capabilities. The firms with low management accounting capabilities (Group D) do not have a sophisticated performance measurement system and their utilization of such systems is not high compared to the other three groups. In contrast, the firms with strong management accounting capabilities (Group A) are have the most sophisticated and most utilized performance measurement systems. Firms with strong experiential learning capabilities (Group B) actively use performance measurement systems. Firms with strong absorptive capacity (Group C) have introduced sophisticated performance measurement systems.

5. Discussion

Based on the above analysis, we offer some observations regarding the influence of management accounting capabilities on the use of MAS. First, we infer that experiential learning capabilities encourage the active use of MAS and the adoption of sophisticated MAS. The analysis confirms that firms with strong management accounting capabilities use performance measurement systems more actively than firms with a strong absorptive capacity. In addition, firms with a strong experiential learning capability are more active in their use of performance measurement systems and adopt more sophisticated performance measurement systems than firms with low management accounting capabilities. For a management accounting system to function effectively, knowledge is essential to enable its adaptive use for management purposes (Mata *et al.*, 1995). We also note that the ability to learn through experience is important for organizations in order to acquire, accumulate, and utilize knowledge

(Kolb, 1984; Yeung *et al.*, 1999). Furthermore, previous studies suggest that learning through experience when using MAS enables more effective use of MAS (Kaplan and Norton, 1996; Tani *et al.*, 1994). The results of this study are consistent with these findings. In other words, we show that experiential learning capabilities play a role in facilitating the use of sophisticated MAS and the active use of MAS.

Second, our results suggest that absorptive capacity encourages the use of sophisticated MAS. We find that firms with strong absorptive capacity adopt more sophisticated performance measurement systems than firms with low management accounting capabilities. Previous studies show that high absorptive capacity promotes adoption and use of sophisticated MAS (Elbashir *et al.*, 2011; Fayrad *et al.*, 2012; Libby and Waterhouse, 1996; Williams and Seaman, 2001). Our results are consistent with those findings, as high absorptive capacity promotes the use of sophisticated MAS such as strategic performance measurement and evaluation, but see no relationship between the use of sophisticated MAS and the active use of performance measurement systems such as interactive controls, diagnostic controls, and dynamic tension. In other words, the effect of absorptive capacity on the use of MAS may be limited to promoting the use of advanced MAS.

Third, we infer that having both experiential learning capability and absorptive capacity is important in using sophisticated MAS. Our results also confirm that firms with strong management accounting capabilities employ not only strategic performance management but also non-financial performance indicators more extensively than firms with weak management accounting capabilities. Zahra and George (2002) point out that an organization's prior experience influences the type of knowledge and information it seeks to obtain. A recognition of the limitations of the management accounting system in use through experiential learning leads firms to acquire, assimilate, and exploit other advanced MAS that have the potential to resolve those limitations (Lane *et al.*, 2006), which may facilitate their use.

6. Conclusion

In summary, this study explores differences in the use of MAS as a function of two management accounting capabilities, namely experiential learning capability and absorptive capacity.

Our results show the importance of including a firm's experiential learning capability in the discussion. Previous studies have mainly focused on the impact of absorptive capacity on the use of MAS. This study confirms that experiential learning capabilities also affect the use of MAS. Research has shown that learning through experience in using MAS may lead to more effective use of MAS (Kaplan and Norton, 1996; Tani et al., 1994). We find it is important to consider experiential learning capability as an influential factor in adopting MAS.

Our results also enrich the understanding of the influence of absorptive capacity on the use of MAS. Previous studies suggest that high absorptive capacity promotes the adoption and use of sophisticated MAS (Elbashir et al., 2011; Fayrad et al., 2012; Libby and Waterhouse, 1996; Williams and Seaman, 2001). Consistent with prior studies, our results do not show that absorptive capacity affects the use of MAS. This indicates that the impact of absorptive capacity may be limited to the adoption of MAS.

This study has several limitations. First, we were unable to clarify the influence of the relationship between a firm's experiential learning capability and absorptive capacity regarding the adoption and use of MAS, which we inferred from previous studies. Although we found differences in the adoption and use of MAS between firms with high management accounting capabilities and firms with strong absorptive capacity and low management accounting capabilities, no significant differences were found between firms with high experiential learning capabilities and firms that are strong in terms of absorptive capacity. Future studies should examine the use of MAS other than with respect to the adoption and use of performance measurement systems.

Next, we examined the effects of the adoption and use of MAS for each group of organizations classified according to their management accounting capabilities. While we examined the effect of management accounting capabilities on the use of MAS, management accounting capabilities also have an effect on the relationship between the use of MAS and organizational performance (Fukushima, 2015, 2016). The use of influential MAS may differ depending on management accounting capabilities; therefore, future research should clarify whether the combination of management accounting system use and management accounting capabilities has a positive impact on performance.

Finally, it is important to refine the questions used to assess management accounting capabilities and expand the sample size in order to generalize the results of the analysis. In this study, we used questions originally developed with reference to previous studies; these questions need to be refined. For example, a more precise scale could be developed by referring to the discussion on organizational learning ability in Jerez-Gómez *et al.* (2005). In addition, since the sample size for this study is fairly small, there were limitations on the statistical analyses employed and in the generalization of the results. Therefore, further analysis with a larger sample size and more refined questionnaire items is required.

References

Cohen, W. M. and Levinthal, D. A. (1990). Absorptive capacity: A new perspective on learning and innovation. *Administrative Science Quarterly*, 35(1), 128–152.

Elbashir, M. Z., Collier, P. A., and Sutton, S. G. (2011). The role of organizational absorptive capacity in strategic use of business intelligence to support integrated management control systems. *The Accounting Review*, 86(1), 155–184.

Fayrad, D., Lee, L. S., Leitch, R. A., and Kettinger, W. J. (2012). Effect of internal cost management information systems integration, and absorptive capacity on inter-organizational cost management in supply chains. *Accounting, Organizations and Society*, 37(3), 168–187.

Franco-Santos, M., Lucianetti, L., and Bourne, M. (2012). Contemporary performance measurement systems: A review of their consequences and a framework for research. *Management Accounting Research*, 23(2), 79–119.

Fukushima, K. (2015). An exploratory study of management accounting capabilities: Effects of relationship between performance measurement systems and absorptive capacity on organizational performance. *The Journal of Cost Accounting Research*, 39(1), 65–75.

Fukushima, K. (2016). The moderating effects of management accounting capabilities on relationship between management accounting system and organizational performance. *Accounting Progress*, 17, 42–54.

Henri, J.-F. (2006). Management control systems and strategy: A resource-based perspective. *Accounting, Organizations and Society*, 31(6), 529–558.

Huber, G. P. (1991). Organization learning: The contributing processes and the literatures. *Organization Science*, 2(11), 88–115.

Jansen, J. J. P., Van den Bosch, F. A. J., and Volberda, H. W. (2005). Managing potential and realized absorptive capacity: How do organizational antecedents matter? *Academy of Management Journal*, 48(6), 999–1015.

Jerez-Gómez, P., Céspedes-Lorente, J., and Valle-Cabrera, R. (2005). Organizational learning capability: A proposal of measurement. *Journal of Business Research*, 58(6), 715–725.

Kaplan, R. S. and Norton, D. P. (1996). *The Balanced Scorecard: Translating Strategy into Action*. Harvard Business School Press.

Kolb, D. A. (1984), *Experimental Learning: Experience as the Source of Learning and Development*. Prentice-Hall.

Lane, P., Klka, B. R., and Pathak, S. (2006). The reification of absorptive capacity: A critical review and rejuvenation of the construct. *Academy of Management Journal*, 31(4), 833–863.

Libby, T. and Waterhouse, J. H. (1996). Predicting change in management accounting systems. *Journal of Management Accounting Research*, 8, 137–150.

Mata, F. J., Fuerst, W. L., and Barney, J. B. (1995). Information technology and sustained competitive advantage: A resource-based analysis. *MIS Quarterly*, 19(4), 487–505.

Matsuo, M. (2011). *Learning from Experience: An Introduction*. DIAMOND, Inc. (in Japanese).

Simons, R. (1995). *Levers of Control: How to Managers Use Interactive Control Systems to Drive Strategic Renewal*. Harvard Business School Press.

Simons, R. (2000). *Performance Measurement and Control Systems for Implementing Strategies*. Prentice-Hall.

Speckbacher, G., Bischof, J., and Pfeiffer, T. (2003). A descriptive analysis on the implementation of balanced scorecards in German-speaking countries. *Management Accounting Research*, 14(4), 361–388.

Szulanski, G. (1996). Exploring internal stickiness: Impediments to the transfer of best practice within the firm. *Strategic Management Journal*, 17, 27–43.

Tani, T., Okano, H., Shimizu, N., Iwabuchi, Y., Fukuda, J., and Cooray, S. (1994). Target cost management in Japanese companies: Current state of the art. *Management Accounting Research*, 1, 67–81.

Williams, J. J. and Seaman, A. E. (2001). Predicting change in management accounting systems: National culture and industry effects. *Accounting, Organizations and Society*, 26(4/5), 443–460.

Yeung, A. K., Ulrich, D. O., Nason, S. W., and von Glinow, M. A. (1999). *Organizational Learning Capability: Generating and Generalizing Ideas with Impact.* Oxford University Press.

Yook, K.-H. (2003). The effect of group maturity and organizational capabilities on performance of target cost management. *The Journal of Management Accounting, Japan*, 11(1), 3–14 (in Japanese).

Yoshida, E. (2001). Empirical study about the relationship between organizational capabilities for target cost management and performance: Comparison among three divisions at a Japanese Electric Company. *The Journal of Cost Accounting Research*, 25(2), 1–9.

Yoshida, E. (2002). Relationship between performance and organizational capabilities in target cost management: Mail survey to design engineers. *The Journal of Management Accounting, Japan*, 10(1), 39–52.

Zahra, S. A. and George, G. (2002). Absorptive capacity: A review, reconceptualization, and extension. *Academy of Management Journal*, 27(2), 185–203.

© 2025 World Scientific Publishing Company
https://doi.org/10.1142/9789811295652_0007

Chapter 7

Influence of DX Promotion on Knowledge Sharing via Management Control Systems

Haruo Otani

Chuo University, Tokyo, Japan

Abstract

This study explores how the promotion of digital transformation (DX) affects knowledge sharing through Management Control Systems (MCS). After reviewing previous studies on DX, MCS, and knowledge sharing, the case of Kyocera's DX promotion is described. In conclusion, DX promotion can enhance knowledge externalization and combination through MCS and increase knowledge sharing. Additionally, if DX promotion entails the issue of knowledge internalization, it is important for actors with combinative capabilities to discover opportunities for knowledge internalization.

1. Introduction

This study aimed to determine how the promotion of digital transformation (DX) affects knowledge sharing through Management Control Systems (MCS). This study addresses the intersection of three areas: DX, MCS, and knowledge sharing, with a particular focus on developing the discussion to contribute to management accounting research. This study explores how DX-driven organizations employ knowledge sharing via

MCS based on findings from research on (1) MCS and knowledge sharing, (2) MCS and DX, and (3) DX, MCS, and knowledge sharing.

The use of digital technology is attracting attention in corporate management, but synonymous terms can cause confusions. Examples include, "digitization," which refers to the technological process of converting analog information to a digital form, "DX," which denotes the use of digital technology to bring about major organizational transformation and significant changes in strategy and management behavior, and "digitalization," which implies both digitization and DX (Knudsen, 2020). Furthermore, the definitions of these terms differ among authors. The Ministry of Economy, Trade, and Industry (METI, 2022) states that DX enables the transformation of products, services, and business models based on the needs of customers and society, and changes operations, organization structures, processes, and corporate culture and climate to establish a competitive advantage by utilizing data and digital technology when organizations must adapt to drastic changes in the business environment.

Fähndrich (2022) defines digitalization as a fundamental change in business activities and models based on knowledge gained from digital technology. In summary, digitalization is a concept intended for organizational transformation using digital technology. This chapter consistently uses "DX" as a broad concept that encompasses digitization, DX, and digitalization following Horii (2022) to avoid confusion of terms.

We also clarify the meaning of MCS in this study. Management control is "the process by which managers influence other members of the organization to implement an organization's strategies" (Anthony, 1965, p. 17). Managers require useful information for decision-making and support systems to achieve organizational goals. Accordingly, presuming that digital technology could support decision-making, this study defines MCS as "an information system that influences managers' decision-making." Data information, and knowledge are considered to be similar concepts in information systems. Bhimani and Willcocks (2014) regard data, information, and knowledge as records, messages, and models (meaning how things work), respectively. An information system can be described as a sequence of processes, including the processing of data as information after it is stored in the system and subsequently provided to actors as knowledge.

Enterprise Resource Planning (ERP) has been discussed as an example of MCS concerning digital technology in the management accounting field since the 1990s, and a certain amount of research has already accumulated. However, there are a few skeptical views of the usefulness of ERP. For instance, Chapman (2005) points out that ERP, as an information system, may impede rather than extend the traditional perspective of management control which suggests its influence on managers' decision-making. Quattrone (2016) also doubts whether today's innovation and diffusion of digital technology, despite mass-producing knowledge associated with the purpose of decision-making, actually provide useful information. A few academic studies have attempted to explore decision-making with digital technologies (Möller *et al.*, 2020), and a certain amount of practical research exists on these challenges. It is assumed that innovation in digital technology and its diffusion in practice will further increase in the future. Thus, it is important from both academic and practical perspectives to examine the impact of digital technology on decision-making via MCS.

The remainder of this chapter is organized as follows. The next section reviews the literature on DX, MCS, and knowledge sharing. Section 3 explains the analytical perspective of knowledge sharing via MCS in organizations that actively use DX. Section 4 describes the Kyocera Corporation's efforts as a case study of the affirmative use of DX. Section 5 discusses the case study from an analytical perspective, and the final section summarizes the study's conclusions and limitations.

2. Literature Review

This section briefly reviews the literature in the following order: studies on (1) MCS and knowledge sharing, (2) MCS and DX, and (3) DX, MCS, and knowledge sharing, to identify topics in knowledge sharing using digital technology.

2.1. *Research on MCS and knowledge sharing*

Knowledge sharing and transfer are the key concepts in knowledge management research. The theoretical background of knowledge can be found in resource-based theory, which suggests that knowledge creation and sharing (transfer) leads to a firm's competitive advantage (Argote and Ingram, 2000). Knowledge to support high technological capabilities within an organization is expected to bring about new knowledge combinations or innovation when it is not utilized only in specific departments, but also transferred and shared across departments to save the cost of acquiring it from (Fukuda, 1999).

Management accounting research is concerned with how to design and use MCS to promote knowledge sharing within organizations. For example, Hartmann and Vaassen (2003) argued that management control can expedite knowledge creation and knowledge integration, which correspond to knowledge sharing and utilization based on Merchant's MCS (action, results, personnel, and culture). Ditillo (2012) discussed the importance of knowledge integration as a means of knowledge creation, sharing, and utilization. Ditillo (2012) also mentioned that management control is an important method of knowledge circulation.

However, knowledge sharing can lead to the leakage of knowledge and loss of competitive advantage in one's own division, which may discourage knowledge transfer to other divisions. It has been suggested that such impediments to knowledge transfer can be overcome by combining incentives and collaborative actions (Morris and Empson, 1998). In particular, group-level incentives can promote knowledge sharing (transfer) (Haesebrouk et al., 2018). Thus, the more organizations emphasize knowledge sharing, the more they prefer group-level outcome measures (Hwang et al., 2009). It seems that the ideal design and use of MCS have been explored in terms of internal knowledge sharing to enhance the competitive advantage across the entire company.

2.2. *Research on MCS and DX*

Recently, there has been interest in DX in Japanese accounting practice and research. METI (2022) has prepared guidelines for the promotion of corporate DX and published them as the "Digital Governance Code 2.0" (formulated in 2020 and revised in 2022). The October 2021 issue of *Accounting* (a representative journal of Japanese accounting practices) prepared a special issue on accounting and Artificial Intelligence (AI), while the November 2022 issue produced academic and practical research on accounting and DX. Accounting and DX were also adopted as the unified themes of the 71st Kansai Section of the Japan Accounting Association, and academic research has been published in *Accounting* (one of the academic journals regarding Japanese accounting). However, few studies have been conducted on DX in management accounting in Japan (Horii, 2022).

Comparing several literature reviews in foreign journals can help identify the stream of research. Granlund (2011) reviewed the relationship between management accounting and accounting information systems (mainly ERP) from an original perspective, while Rom and Rohde (2007) conducted a systematic review of the relationship between management accounting and integrated information systems. Both studies indicates that most scholars have explored the relationship between management accounting and ERP.

In contrast, Knudsen (2020) conducted a systematic review of the relationship between accounting (financial and management accounting) and digitalization in the literature since 2007 adding the financial accounting field to the analytical framework of Rom and Rohde (2007), which focused only on management accounting. Fähndrich (2022) also carried out a systematic review of literature published since 2000 that was associated with the relationship between management control and digitalization including the fields of management accounting and management. Knudsen (2020) and Fähndrich (2022) confirmed two trends through literature reviews. The first wave represented a group of studies related to ERP in the 1990s and the 2000s, whereas the second wave displayed a group of studies related to AI, Business Intelligence (BI), big data, cloud computing, blockchain, and social network services (SNS) from 2011 to 2022. Notably, the second wave considered ERP to be a "legacy system (technological debt)" (METI, 2022) and sought to find ways to overcome its limitations through new digital technologies. Although ERP is suitable for increasing efficiency because the entire system integrates standardized data, it is not adaptable to dynamic changes in the current environment. Therefore, people are increasingly interested in the agility of AI and other digital technologies.

2.3. *Research on DX, MCS, and knowledge sharing*

There are two phases in the process of explaining research on DX; MCS, and knowledge sharing. The first describes the relationship between shared knowledge and DX, and the second examines knowledge sharing via MCS in DX-promoting organizations. Organizations may adopt personalization and codification strategies for knowledge sharing (Hansen *et al.*, 1999; Newell *et al.*, 2003). The personalization strategy expresses the sharing and creation of knowledge (mainly tacit knowledge) through face-to-face interactions, whereas the codification strategy displays the transfer (sharing) of written documents (explicit knowledge) between individuals or groups utilizing information technology (digital technology) (Hansen *et al.*, 1999). The context of DX promotion emphasizes the development of knowledge through MCS to implement the codification strategies.

However, knowledge codification is not always appropriate for knowledge sharing (Morris and Empson, 1998). Knowledge is identified as explicit and can be coded, and tacit, pre-coded, or decodable. However, not all knowledge can be coded as explicit knowledge even if digital technology is introduced. This is because it is technically impossible to fully capture tacit knowledge as computer data (Bhimani and Willcocks, 2014). Thus, while knowledge is both complex and codifiable (Kogut and Zander, 1992), codifiability and complexity may create a paradox in its replication (Kogut and Zander, 1992). The implication that the codification of knowledge corresponds to simplification may harm the complexity inherent in knowledge. The question remains as to whether simplified knowledge can be useful for decision-making, even though knowledge can be coded through DX promotion.

The production and exploitation of knowledge using digital technologies may increase the risk of decision-making because information is disconnected from the original context (e.g., Newell *et al.*, 2003; Knudsen, 2020) owing to the inherent characteristics of path dependence in knowledge. Codification requires knowledge to be removed from the embedded context and then re-embedded in a different context. Furthermore, it has been pointed out that user-generated information, such as word-of-mouth sites, is exogenous in nature and too ambiguous to be shared as knowledge within an organization for decision-making (Knudsen 2020). Thus, careful attention should be given to the use of knowledge shared by digital technologies in MCS to avoid misleading decision-making.

In summary, knowledge sharing using digital technology involves three issues: (1) codification, (2) simplification, and (3) decontextualization.

First, the target of knowledge sharing through digital technology is codable (explicit) knowledge because there are technical limitations in sharing tacit knowledge. Second, the complexity of knowledge is compromised (misled), whereas knowledge codification is simplified. Third, the coded knowledge may differ from (distort) the meaning in the original context since knowledge possesses the nature of path dependence. Therefore, the problem seems to lie in the fact that knowledge codification, simplification, and decontextualization reduce the usefulness of decision-making via knowledge sharing in MCS utilizing digital technology.

The next section deals with these issues in terms of the knowledge conversion mode between tacit and explicit knowledge (Nonaka and Takeuchi, 1995). In addition, the impact of DX promotion on knowledge sharing via MCS is thoroughly discussed, which is the objective of this study.

3. Analytical Perspective of Knowledge Sharing via MCS in DX-Driven Organizations

Nonaka and Takeuchi (1995), who proposed the theory of knowledge creation, stated that knowledge conversion between explicit and tacit knowledge enables actors to create new knowledge in an organization. There are four modes of knowledge conversion; (1) socialization: from tacit to tacit knowledge; (2) externalization, from tacit to explicit knowledge; (3) combination, from explicit to explicit knowledge; and (4) internalization, from explicit to tacit knowledge. Socialization refers to the sharing of experience among actors without any coding; externalization shows that the use of language codifies actual phenomena; combination reflects that the incorporation of explicit knowledge among actors can create new knowledge; and internalization indicates that documents (e.g., manuals) enable actors to experience vicariously following actual contexts.

These four types of knowledge conversion have different expressions based on the strategic pattern of knowledge sharing; that is, individualization and codification (Hansen et al., 1999). Collaboration is applied to individualization strategies because of the conversion from tacit to tacit knowledge. Externalization and combination contain a codification strategy owing to the conversion of tacit or explicit knowledge into new explicit knowledge. In contrast, internalization converts coded explicit knowledge into tacit knowledge, and can be called a "de-codification strategy." In fact, there are two digital terms: "encode," which translates data into a code, and "decode," which restores the original data. However, this study regards a de-codification strategy as the different meanings of embedding knowledge into a new context rather than restoring it to the original data. As mentioned previously, the main modes of knowledge conversion related to digital technology are externalization, combination, and internalization.

In addition, actors' capabilities can be important factors in knowledge sharing. Kogut and Zander (1992) point out that the combinative capabilities of knowledge incorporate existing knowledge (tacit or explicit) to create new applications (equivalent to innovations). Networks with such combinative capabilities treat a central organization, group, or individual as knowledge brokers in the process of knowledge co-creation (Abbate and Coppolino, 2011). It is presumed that actors with combinative capabilities utilizing digital technologies are knowledge brokers who promote knowledge sharing via MCS in the context of DX-driven organizations.

Moreover, actors involved in knowledge sharing must be able to understand and exploit the knowledge gained. Cohen and Levinthal (1990) conceptualize the absorptive capacity of knowledge and define it as "an ability to recognize the value of new information, assimilate it, and apply it to commercial ends" (Cohen and Levinthal, 1990, p. 128). Prior knowledge may reinforce actors' absorptive capacity. However, exposure to absorptive capacity also depends on the organizational culture or climate. For example, Elbashir *et al.* (2011) found that cultural controls with respect to knowledge creation may encourage an organization to promote assimilation and enhance the absorptive capacity of management and business unit managers when BI and MCS are assimilated in organizations that introduce BI. In other words, an organizational culture that inspires the adoption of new digital technologies affects the absorptive capacity of actors, leading to knowledge sharing and creation that promote DX.

The following section explores knowledge sharing via MCS in DX-driven cases, including the three modes of knowledge conversion, combinative capability, knowledge broker, and absorptive capacity from an analytical perspective.

4. Kyocera's DX Promotion Case Study

This study treats the Kyocera Corporation (hereafter referred to as Kyocera) as a DX-driven organization. Qualitative data were collected using the company's published secondary data, which consisted of an Integrated Report (FY2020–FY2022 associated with DX promotion), newspapers and magazines articles, websites, and other archives. Although the data are secondary, several sources, such as the Integrated Report are employed after verifying the consistency of descriptions and authenticity of the information.

DX was first promoted in Kyocera after its current president took office in 2017 and launched "the Project of Doubling Productivity" (Nihon Keizai Shimbun, 2020). This project aims to realize a smart factory by introducing AI-based defect prognosis, failure prognosis, and automatic monitoring, as well as robot-based automatic production and autonomy to manufacturing settings, resulting in doubling (improvement) hourly profitability. The company has emphasized DX promotion in response to the current labor shortage and reshoring of production due to COVID-19 since 2020. Kyocera's FY2020 Integrated Report explicitly states that it will promote digitalization (DX); April 2020, it established a Digital Business Promotion Division to accelerate company-wide DX promotion. As a result, Kyocera acquired the "Certified Business Operator of DX" status from METI in 2022. Kyocera's DX promotion enables it to implement company-wide development along with organizational transformation. Therefore, Kyocera's case matches our interest in knowledge sharing through MCS. However, Kyocera's promotion of DX is still in its infancy and provides only limited information based on the content of ongoing initiatives.

Kyocera's DX promotion has three characteristics. The first is the strong leadership of top management. As mentioned above, Kyocera began to shift toward the active use of DX around 2017, when its current president was inaugurated. Kyocera announced a policy of aggressive investment in DX, with plans to invest approximately 10 billion yen annually in digitizing operations in the manufacturing, sales, and back-office divisions by 2020. Additionally, the technical terms corporate transformation (CX) business transformation (BX) were used one after another to visualize the causal chain of organizational transformation for the sake of DX expansion (See the left side of Figure 1).

The second is the initiation of organizational transformations. The Ministry of Economy, Trade, and Industry (2022, p. 7) lists the items for organizational design and human resource development for which DX-driven organizations should aim. Some excerpts of the items include ensuring the autonomy of organizational members, developing a personnel system based on human resource development, and improving their digital literacy. As depicted in Figure 1 and Table 1, Kyocera has already addressed organizational design and human resource development, taking the above into consideration. Kyocera now struggles to consolidate data because each business division has built its own database and the company employs amoeba management with a focus on divisional profitability systems (Nihon Keizai Shimbun, 2020). Hence, the Digital Business Promotion Division launched a common platform for data collection using the internet of things (IoT) and data analysis to gather internal and external human resources. DX promoters from each division work concurrently with the Digital Business Promotion Division, and bring their experience back to their own divisions to engage in data coding on a common platform. Specifically, they actively convert the tacit knowledge embedded in the operations of each amoeba into explicit knowledge, storing not only existing explicit knowledge but also explicit knowledge coded from

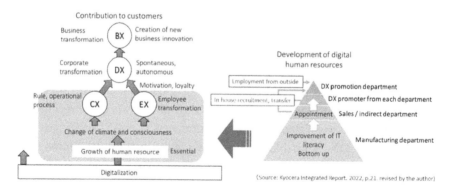

Figure 1. The development of DX and Digital Human Resource in Kyocera.

Table 1. Management issues and DX project in Kyocera.

Issue	Management policies	DX project
Management foundation from individual to overall optimization	**Transition to a segmented system** • Quick decision making Via empowerment • Improvement of human resource mobility between departments	**Information sharing Via DX** • DX department is composed of members who concurrently work in their settings • Information fluidity through data sharing infrastructure
Transformation of organizational culture towards a culture of freedom and open mindedness/activation of young employees	**Change in personnel system/ work environment** • Carrier double-tracking and 360-degree evaluation • Hoteling workstation	**Use of IT Data** • Breaking down hierarchical relationship based on reverse mentoring by young generation • Converting tacit explicit knowledge from digitization

Source: Kyocera Corporation, Integrated Report 2021, p. 25.

tacit knowledge on the platform to encourage knowledge sharing among departments. In addition, improving employees' IT literacy and fostering a mindset in which employees are proactively involved in DX facilitate increases in levels of digital human resources.

The third is the spread of the DX via MCS, with the doubling of productivity plans as one of the outcome indicators and the doubling of hourly profitability indicating control over goals and results. Additionally, Kyocera has developed digital human resources across divisions as personnel control and increased their mobility, thereby raising the next generation from a company-wide perspective. Additionally, it has improved IT literacy (including knowledge coding). Moreover, it seems that the company fosters an organizational culture or climate that embraces DX as a cultural control and promotes decision-making using digital technology, that is, it aims for data-oriented management.

5. Discussion

The characteristics of knowledge sharing in Kyocera's DX promotion were discussed from the perspective of the modes of knowledge conversion: externalization, combination, and internalization. Externalization and combinations are noticeable in the construction of common company-wide platforms. Specifically, they suggest a platform for data collection via the IoT and data analysis. Data collection and analysis, which were previously developed independently by each business unit, are now consolidated on a common platform, dramatically increasing data accessibility. Additionally, converting the tacit knowledge embedded in the operations of each amoeba into explicit knowledge (externalization) encourages knowledge sharing through socialization with digital technology. The emphasis on externalization stimulates the improvement of the efficiency of knowledge sharing and contributes to the development of young generations.

In addition, the company concentrates on leading an organizational culture that encourages externalization and a combination of knowledge. Kyocera emphasizes employee autonomy through empowerment, while holding DX promotion divisions and their own divisions concurrently increases the mobility of human resources. The company incorporates a legitimate evaluation into its personnel system, thereby encouraging organizational members to actively implement the DX project. Kyocera challenges organizational transformation based on the dimensions of both DX and organizational culture. Consequently, it can be said that Kyocera's DX promotion encompasses the standardization of databases, the development and evaluation of digital human resources across divisions, and the encouragement of the organizational culture accompanied by digitalization to develop a codification strategy that emphasizes the externalization and combination of knowledge.

However, there is no specific description in the Integrated Report or other documents regarding the internalization of knowledge. Explicit knowledge shared on a common data platform requires each amoeba to first decode it in order to understand and utilize it. Therefore, this study deals with the combinative capabilities of actors, their roles as knowledge brokers, and their absorptive capacity.

As mentioned in Section 3, actors with combinative capabilities are expected to promote knowledge sharing as knowledge brokers. In Kyocera, DX promoters in manufacturing, sales, and indirect departments who concurrently work with the DX Promotion Department (the Digital Business Promotion Division) are expected to play the role of knowledge brokers. DX promoters are likely to be familiar with not only the knowledge of digital technology but also the local knowledge used in their operations. Hence, they can combine the knowledge stored in a common platform with the local one in order to create opportunities for internalization of knowledge.

DX proponents have also found that an improvement in absorptive capacity (i.e., the ability to assimilate and adapt acquired knowledge to a particular context) may lead to decoding strategies for knowledge internalization. Knowledge coded on a common platform must be reinterpreted according to the context of the site on which it is adapted. It is important for DX promoters to demonstrate their absorptive capacity to translate explicit knowledge into tacit knowledge and embed it in the context of their settings.

This suggests that actors' combinative capabilities, the role of knowledge brokers, and their absorptive capacities may compensate for issues with respect to knowledge internalization via digital technology in DX-driven organizations.

6. Conclusions and Limitations

This study reviews previous studies on DX, MCS, and knowledge sharing and describes and discusses the case of Kyocera's DX promotion to explore its impact on knowledge sharing via MCS. Two conclusions can be drawn from the discussion.

First, DX promotion can enhance knowledge externalization and combination through MCS and increase knowledge sharing through a common data platform, cross-functional development, mobility of human resources, and an organizational culture that embraces digitalization. The first finding supports the results of Elbashir *et al.* (2011), who noted the importance of organizational culture in the adoption of digital technologies while also pointing to the importance of an organic connection between the DX project, human resource development, and organizational culture.

Second, if DX promotion entails the issue of knowledge internalization, it is important for actors with combinative capabilities to discover opportunities for knowledge internalization as knowledge brokers and to translate the knowledge encoded by means of their absorptive capacities according to the context to which it is to be adapted. Although prior research has highlighted the advantages and disadvantages of knowledge coding (Morris and Empson, 1998) and its technical limitations (Bhimani and Willcocks, 2014), few studies have examined how to firmly embed coded knowledge into new settings. Compared with previous studies, our findings imply that an actor's capability and role can overcome the issues of internalization.

However, some issues remain to be addressed in future studies. First, it takes a certain amount of time for DX promotion to penetrate the entire company and to develop the ideal digital human resource because Kyocera's DX project is a work in progress. Therefore, the findings from the Kyocera case study indicates limited interpretation from the perspective of a company currently implementing DX promotion in an ongoing manner. Additionally, this study did not address the measurement and evaluation of the outcomes of DX promotion. This issue, including Kyocera's hourly profitability, needs to be studied further. Finally, there is little discussion of MCS based on specific management accounting practices. Further studies should be conducted to explore inherent knowledge sharing via MCS.

Acknowledgments

Special thanks to Kazuki Hamada (Okayama Shoka University), Yoshitaka Myochin (Kaishi Professional University), Syufuku Hiraoka (Soka University), Hiroshi Obata (Meiji Gakuin University), Makoto Tomo (Seijo University), and Tsutomu Yoshioka (Toyo University) for their valuable comments in the workshop of the Japan Society of Organization and Accounting held at Rikkyo University on March 11, 2023. Sincere gratitude to Makoto Nonaka (Toyo University), co-researcher at the DX Promotion Organization, provided informative advice. The author takes full responsibility for the integrity of this chapter. This research was supported by a JSPS Grant-in-Aid for Scientific Research (JP22K01794).

References

Abbate, T. and Coppolino, R. (2011). Knowledge creation through knowledge brokers: Some anecdotal evidence. *Journal of Management Control*, 22, 359–371.

Anthony, R. N. (1965). *Planning and Control Systems: A Framework for Analysis*. Boston, MA: Harvard Business School Press.

Argote, L. and Ingram, P. (2000). Knowledge transfer: A basis for competitive advantage in firms. *Organizational Behavior and Human Decision Processes*, 82(1), 150–169.

Bhimani, A. and Willcocks, L. (2014). Digitisation, "Big Data" and the transformation of accounting information. *Accounting and Business Research*, 44(4), 469–490.

Chapman, C. S. (2005). Not because they are new: Developing the contribution of enterprise resource planning systems to management control research. *Accounting, Organizations and Society*, 30, 685–689.

Cohen, W. M. and Levinthal, D. A. (1990). Absorptive capacity: A new perspective on learning and innovation. *Administrative Science Quarterly*, 35(1), 128–152.

Ditillo, A. (2012). Designing management control systems to foster knowledge transfer in knowledge-intensive firms: A network-based approach. *European Accounting Review*, 21(3), 425–450.

Elbashir, M. Z., Collier, P. A., and Sutton, S. G. (2011). The role of organizational absorptive capacity in the strategic use of business intelligence to support integrated management control systems. *The Accounting Review*, 86(1), 155–184.

Fähndrich, J. (2022). A literature review on the impact of digitalisation on management control. *Journal of Management Control*, 34, 9–65.

Fukuda, J. (1999). The role of management accounting system in knowledge management: Limited to the phase of knowledge transfer. *Keiei Shirin (The Hosei Journal of Business)*, 36(3), 57–70 (in Japanese).

Granlund, M. (2011). Extending AIS research to management accounting and control issues: A research note. *International Journal of Accounting Information Systems*, 12, 3–19.

Haesebrouk, K. and Cools, M. (2018). Status differences and knowledge transfer: The effect of incentives. *The Accounting Review*, 93(1), 213–234.

Hansen, M. T., Nohria, N., and Tierney, T. (1999). What's your strategy for managing knowledge? *Harvard Business Review*, March–April, 1–10.

Hartmann, F. G. H. and Vaassen, E. H. J. (2003). The changing role of management accounting and control systems: Accounting for knowledge across control domains. In A. Bhimani (ed.). *Management Accounting in the Digital Economy*. Oxford University Press, pp. 112–132.

Horii, S. (2022). Possibility of development of management accounting via DX. *Aikei*, 201(6), 80–91 (in Japanese).

Hwang, Y., Erkens. D. H., and Evans III, J. H. (2009). Knowledge sharing and incentive design in production environments: Theory and evidence. *The Accounting Review*, 84(4), 1145–1170.

Knudsen, D. R. (2020). Elusive boundaries, power relations, and knowledge production: A systematic review of the literature on digitalization in accounting. *International Journal of Accounting Information Systems*, 36, 1–22.

Kogut, B. and Zander, U. (1992). Knowledge of the firm, combinative capabilities, and the replication of technology. *Organization Science*, 3(3), 383–397.

Kyocera Corporation (2023). https://www.kyocera.co.jp/sustainability/digital/index.html. (Last visited March 9, 2023).

Kyocera Corporation 2020, 2021, 2022 Integrated Report (in Japanese).

METI Ministry of Economy, Trade and Industry. 2022. "Digital Governance Code 2.0" (Revised September 13, 2022) (in Japanese).

Möller K., Schäffer, U., and Verbeeten, F. (2020). Digitalization in management accounting and control: An editorial. *Journal of Management Control*, 31, 1–8.

Morris, T. and Empson, L. (1998). Organisation and expertise: An exploration of knowledge bases and the management of accounting and consulting firms. *Accounting, Organizations and Society*, 23(5/6), 609–624.

Newell, S., Huang, J. C., Galliers, R. D., and Pan, S. L. (2003). Implementing enterprise resource planning and knowledge management systems in tandem: Fostering efficiency and innovation complementarity. *Information and Organization*, 13, 25–52.

Nihon Keizai Shimbun (2020). *Kyocera, 3000 "Amoeba" Collaboration*. May 28, 2020 (in Japanese).

Nikkei Business (2022). Charisma's teachings, deepening [Kyocera President]. *Hideo Tanimoto*, 2164, 44–48 (in Japanese).

Nonaka, I. and Takeuchi, H. (1995). *The Knowledge-Creating Company: How Japanese Companies Create the Dynamics of Innovation*. Oxford University Press.

Quattrone, P. (2016). Management accounting goes digital: Will the move make it wiser? *Management Accounting Research*, 31, 118–122.

Rom, A. and Rohde, C. (2007). Management accounting and integrated information systems: A literature review. *International Journal of Accounting Information Systems*, 8, 40–68.

© 2025 World Scientific Publishing Company
https://doi.org/10.1142/9789811295652_0008

Chapter 8

The Role of Informal Controls When Concurrently Used with Tight Formal MCS

Koki Mori

Chiba University of Commerce, Chiba, Japan

Abstract

This chapter sheds light on investigating the function of informal controls when concurrently used with tight formal management control systems. Based on the case study of 3M Company that uses archival data, I captured the mechanism that informal controls balance MCS and create dynamic tension while formal control is used tightly. Furthermore, this study emphasizes the importance of viewing management controls comprehensively and the role of informal controls.

1. Introduction

In management accounting studies, researchers have expanded the field of management accounting and are seen to encourage vigorous discussions (Scapens, 2014). While some literature narrowly define management accounting as formal "systems" (McWatters and Zimmerman, 2016), others that are considering such expansion conceptualize it as a wider variety of the field (Hopper *et al.*, 2009; Macintosh and Quattrone, 2010). Furthermore, the importance of understanding management accounting practices comprehensively through multiple systems and mechanisms is being acknowledged (Malmi and Brown, 2008; Mundy, 2010; Otley, 2016). In particular, research that focuses on tensions arising from seemingly contradictory systems and concepts has been developed (Bedford, 2015; Bedford *et al.*, 2019; Henri 2006; Tillema and van der Steen, 2015; van der Kolk *et al.*, 2020). According to these arguments, to understand the substance of management accounting in organizations especially the dynamism of management controls, consideration of comprehensive dimensions, such as narrow management accounting and broad control mechanisms, and formal and informal exploration, is required.

In recent years, management accounting papers on informal controls have been published (Kaufman and Covaleski, 2019; Newman, 2014; Pitkänen and Lukka, 2011; Stouthuysen *et al.*, 2017). They revealed the separate and complementary effects of formal and informal controls.

Based on the findings of these studies, in this chapter, the author focuses on investigating the function of informal controls when concurrently used with tight formal management control systems. This study examines 3M Company as a case that sets and achieves tight performance targets in parallel with using informal controls for organizational growth. 3M Company has used informal controls such as "15% rule" traditionally to achieve tight target and grown continuously in the long term. Meanwhile, in the 2000s, James McNerney, the then CEO, imported GE's vaunted Six Sigma program. It is argued that later this change turned out to be a tension that interrupted informal controls within the company that had accomplished economic benefits and development of innovative products simultaneously (Hindo, 2007). The management of the 3M Company has been picked as a subject of notable books such as *In Search of Excellence* (Peters and Waterman Jr., 1982) and *Built to Last* (Collins and Porras, 1994), etc. I comprehend the management of 3M company in terms of generating dynamic tensions through tight controls by formal systems and informal controls and changing the balance between them. This perspective enables us to analyze management controls comprehensively and understand significant implications of the dynamism of management accounting that only focusing on formal systems cannot.

The remainder of this chapter is organized as follows. Section 2 provides a review of the relevant prior literature to discuss the scope of management accounting concept and research, and then select the research topic. Section 3 presents the case analysis methods. Section 4 describes the case of 3M company and considers tensions that could be generated by formal and informal controls. Section 5 offers the findings and limitations of this study as conclusions.

2. Literature Review and Theoretical Development

2.1. *Informal controls in management accounting studies*

This section is described based on Mori (2020) written in the Japanese language.

The conventional definition of management accounting appears in the report of 1958 Committee on Management Accounting of the American Accounting Association as follows.

> Management accounting is the application of appropriate techniques and concepts in processing the historical and projected economic data of an entity to assist management in establishing a plan for reasonable economic objectives and in the making of rational decisions with a view toward achieving these objectives. (Brummet *et al.*, 1959, p. 210)

Thereafter, some textbooks such as McWatters and Zimmerman (2016) define management accounting as the formal systems. Its premise is that management accounting practice means the use of management accounting systems. Accordingly, they propose the narrow definition of management accounting as the concept within this scope.

Meanwhile, other textbooks and literature broaden the field of management accounting and conceptualize it in that manner, e.g., Hopper *et al.* (2009) use the word "Management Accounting Systems" while arguing that social processes, including informal information and controls, depend on researchers' orientation. Macintosh and Quattrone (2010) conceptualize management accounting systems narrowly while proposing that it is necessary to see them in relation to the entire array of control mechanisms used by organizations. They offer a wider concept of management accounting in contrast to a narrower definition by Horngren and Sundem (1990) and point out the differences between them.

Furthermore, Scapens (2014) describes in his final editorial of *Management Accounting Research* that the journal deliberately avoided defining "management accounting" and relegated the development of this discussion to researchers. He argues that the scope of management accounting is defined by the papers that are in the journal. This attitude of the journal means they accept new ideas, topics, theories, methods, etc., however, in so doing, authors should justify the need to extend the scope of management accounting. In other words, Scapens intentionally did not define management accounting over his tenure as the editor of *Management Accounting Research* to stimulate free and fluid discussion of research development. Nevertheless, when a researcher attempts to broaden the research field and concept of management accounting, mutual agreement in a community of experts through the peer review system in response to arguments of the paper by the author is essential. To conclude this paragraph, Scapens (2014) emphasizes the importance of researchers' consideration for allowing deterrence against a disorderly conceptual expansion.

In addition to these arguments, studies that examine informal controls as a main research topic are being published. It means informal controls could be an analysis subject to reveal the mechanism of management accounting practice in organizations. Malmi and Brown (2008) propose the package framework of management controls and indicate that managers are available to formally and informally direct employee behavior. Therefore, to consider management controls comprehensively through multiple systems and mechanisms (Malmi and Brown, 2008; Mundy, 2010; Otley, 2016), management accounting researchers needs to take account of informal controls.

2.2. *Research question*

Prior to discussing the research question, I clarify the distinction between formal and informal controls. Formal controls are utilized by formal rules, procedures through contracts and structured involving many organizational members, whereas informal controls rely on organizational norms and cultures, provided through unplanned and instant person-to-person dialogue (Das and Teng, 2001; London and Smither, 2002; Plesner Rossing, 2013; Wohlgemuth *et al.*, 2019). Sometimes, informal controls are regarded as synonymous with social controls (Eisenhardt, 1985) or clan control (Eisenhardt, 1985) in research (Das and Teng, 2001; Wohlgemuth *et al.*, 2019).

Informal controls having such features are considered not included in narrowly defined management accounting on the premise of using formal systems; nevertheless, it is approaching as a main research subject of management accounting studies in recent years. For instance, Pitkänen and Lukka (2011) indicate that the coexistence of regular formal feedback through performance measurement systems and cultural and trust-based informal feedback enables making quick problem-solving decisions and additional discussion. In addition, Stouthuysen *et al.* (2017) find when firms that form alliance use informal controls, the positive relationship between outcome and behavior controls is enhanced. They adopt informal controls as the main variable of research question in management accounting study.

Furthermore, other studies emphasize the importance of informal controls due to its supplemental dimension for conventional management accounting concepts. Some research that focuses on levers of control (Simons, 1995), especially interactive control systems and reference informal controls. Collier (2005) argues that the framework proposed by Simons (1995) pays too little attention to the function of informal controls. Rossing (2013) suggests that, in addition to interactive control systems, informal interaction has a stimulatory effect on it. Moreover, Ferreira and Otley (2009) emphasize the importance of informal controls through the use of performance measurement systems and offer to reveal the effect of informal controls when performance evaluations are subjective as the future research theme.

While these studies shed light on the relationship between various management control types and informal controls, one of the remaining topics that has not been completely investigated yet is tight management control. The tightness of management control means it has a difficult goal and requires organizational members to meet this target (Van der Stede, 2001). It is suggested that tight control and other types of control are mutually complemented (Mundy, 2010), however, this mechanism has not been adequately examined yet. Lau (1999) indicates managers under tight control tend to create slack (excess resources in organizations), which implies organizations somehow use management controls to maintain balance.

With these studies in mind, this study examines the function of informal controls when concurrently used with tight formal management control systems.

3. Research Method

Considering the simultaneous use of tight formal management control systems and informal controls, a case analysis of 3M Company is adopted. Using archival data for research enables longitudinal analysis of organizational activities on a long-term basis, compared with surveys or interviews at a certain time. There are only a few management accounting studies using archival documents of firms. However, Spraakman (2006) analyzes Hadson's Bay Company and Quinn (2014) analyzes the Guinness Brewery, and each uses archival records. The subject of both studies is management accounting change (Burns and Scapens, 2000) and it requires longitudinal analysis of management control systems and related actions in an organization. Archival research is capable of not only following an organizational process or aspect over time but examining the effects of events as well (Quinn, 2014).

This study focuses on the function of informal controls when it is concurrently used with tight formal management control systems and attempts to investigate their relationship in a longitudinal manner. Using tight control among organizations perhaps causes side effects such as creating slack temporarily. To address this issue, losing control tightness might be considered but it lacks sustainability of management control mechanism. Despite that, if research could investigate organizations using both formal tight control and informal control and this combined use is performing well, it is expected that findings about the effect of informal controls and mechanisms of management control could be generalized.

3M Company is a firm that meets these conditions and has achieved continuous organizational growth as described in the following section.

Thus, this study examines the archival records of 3M Company to analyze a long-term mechanism of management controls.

4. Case Analysis

4.1. *Traditional management of 3M Company*

In 1902, 3M Company was founded in Two Harbors, Minnesota, then named Minnesota Mining and Manufacturing Company. They were grown through manufacturing abrasive as their main product at an early stage. In 1923, the restorer of the company William McKnight set rigorous targets as annual sales growth at 10% and profitability at 15% and showed a policy that a product or business is shed when it no longer meets these goals (3M Company, 2002). Meanwhile, they also implemented a strategy that focuses on the process of variation and selection to find a germ of new business from numerous ideas, compared to "branching and pruning" (Collins and Porras, 1994). Hence, 3M Company aimed for organizational growth and allowed employees to spend time for developing new products simultaneously from the first.

In 1948, McKnight introduced divisional lines into the company due to firm growth, and then set a policy that allowed employees to use 15% of their work time freely to pursue independent product development or resolve an issue. In this era, 3M Companies faced rapid expansion of its own organization, i.e., listed on the New York Stock Exchange (in 1946), opened 3 new plants (in 1947), and reached $100 million in sales (in 1948). Therefore, McKnight promoted decentralization and held divisions responsible for making profits. This kind of change that decentralization is implemented in accordance with organizational growth coincides with the framework of the organizational life cycle (Miller and Friesen, 1984).

In the meantime, organizational members were able to coordinate with their colleagues at their own discretion while using resources of the organization within 15% culture. It means that the mechanism of informal controls was arranged at 3M. Then, 3M created few innovative products, e.g., Scotch cellophane tape and Post-it note. The meaning of 15% culture is the fact that management deliver employees a fixed freedom for development rather than the number "15." In this regard, Dr. William E. Coyne,

Senior Vice-President Research and Development at 3M spoke the following in 1996 (Kippenberger, 1997, p. 31).

> Some of our technical people use much more than 15% of their time on projects of their choosing. Some use less than that; some use none at all.

Dr. Coyne suggested the view that the number of "15%" is meaningless. It means that 15% culture is set as an official rule at 3M Company, whereas an organizational member is implicitly allowed to work independently on his own product idea using organizational resources. This time-honored practice is called "bootlegging." In summary, 15% culture and bootlegging are informal controls through spontaneous actions by employees that would be developed on an unplanned basis.

However, here we must be aware that 3M Company achieved to combine creating innovative products with economic outcome through using formal control systems in addition to informal controls. One of these systems is tight performance target called "stretch goals," and the other one is formal systems to support product development.

Stretch goal, presented by then Chairman Ray Herzog in 1977, is the target that "25% of our sales in any one year should come from products that are less than five years on the marketplace" (Coyne, 1996). In 1992, the target was raised to "30% of all sales from products introduced in the past four years," in both percentage and term (Kippenberger, 1997). Garud et al. (2011, p. 750) show that the division's general manager strongly considered this stretch target.

> In view of the rapid changes in the electronic display market, if we were to just meet 3M's internal new-product-to-sales ratio objective, we would not be able to stay in the business very long. That is because the industry and the markets and the technologies are changing a lot faster than a goal of 30% new products over four years could support. So we had to learn how to grow this business based on new technologies, new products, and based on a new-product-to-sales ratio substantially higher than the aggregate corporate objective for all divisions in 3M.

Regarding this kind of mechanism for achieving tight target, Garud et al. (2011) argue, as the activities for product development shape, the efficient use of organizational resources is available to employees with support from formal systems. They investigate the process of two product development projects that were implemented in the 1980s–1990s. One of these projects, the development of Brightness Enhancement Film, began from bootlegging during the Christmas season. As the development proceeded, this project obtained funds from inside the company called Genesis Grants, which organizational members who were working on explorative activities could apply for. Then, the division put together people from not only new hires but also other divisions, in addition to bootlegging equipment and facilities from other divisions, and successfully developed innovative products that met the stretch goal at last. In the meantime, over 150 people from across 3M Company worked on the projects at no cost to the division. Another observed project by Garud *et al.* (2011) is the development of the Trizact abrasive. This project utilized 15% culture at their initial stage of technical development, later was helped through Genesis Grants and interacted with diverse experts from different parts of the company, as well as Brightness Enhancement Film case. Furthermore, the project secured funding under the newly established Pacing Plus program to hasten development and market introduction. These programs enable quick product development.

Garud *et al.* (2011) indicate concurrent formal and informal controls result in the effective use of organizational resources, e.g., people, goods, and money, to achieve tight performance targets. Informal controls lead to productive outcomes in association with formal controls, under the tension between generating innovation and the achievement of tight financial performance targets. The use of formal systems and informal controls hereby creates dynamic tensions by being complementary to each other when formal controls are tight.

4.2. *Organizational change through the introduction of Six Sigma*

Even though the 3M Company had accomplished organizational expansion and innovation together, they faced the decrease of sales growth rate in the 1990s. To break the *status quo*, James McNerney was hired by 3M Company as the CEO, from GE. He immediately introduced Six Sigma to improve efficiency. Six Sigma is management techniques that includes tools such as DMAIC (Define, Measure, Analyze, Improve, Control) and DFSS (Design For Six Sigma) to improve process efficiency, aims quality of products within 3.4 defects per million. In this section, I analyze 3M Company while under the implementation of Six Sigma, referring to Hindo (2007) and Canato *et al.* (2013).

In 3M Company, the tension arose between introduction of Six Sigma and their traditional product development policies. Previously, organizational members had enough time for research and development, and the company supported a project from these works that was granted potential through funds (Garud *et al.*, 2011). However, DMAIC of Six Sigma is the framework to resolve the problem systematically, and DFSS is the technique to optimize new product development by incorporating metrics reflecting customers' critical needs from an early stage of the process. It means introduction of Six Sigma intended to produce results in a short-term in terms of both development and manufacturing process. Moreover, McNerny trained all employees to have knowledge of Six Sigma, and some of them were selected and became "Black Belt."

In spite of that, top management were supposed to realize the tension between innovation and efficiency through Six Sigma and to deal with it. For instance, the description in the 2002 annual report that was published immediately after introducing Six Sigma states the following.

> At the same time, we realize that efficiency alone cannot generate growth, so we're driving organic growth as hard as we're driving operational excellence.

> Against these goals, we've established metrics and set some tough objectives for ourselves. The integration of Six Sigma tools into the new product development process will ensure that the voice of the customer is at the heart of our process. (3M Company, 2003, pp. 2–3)

Nevertheless, eventually tension arose in 3M Company. On the one hand, some employees felt that Six Sigma interferes with their free practice through 15% culture and bootlegging and prevents creation of innovation.

> We all came to the conclusion that there was no way in the world that anything like a Post-it note would ever emerge from this new system. (Hindo, 2007, p. 14)

Six Sigma killed entrepreneurship, which was one of the fundamental traits of 3M. The rush to rationality killed what made our company great that is innovation at all levels, the capacity to find new ways. (Canato *et al.*, 2013, p. 1739)

On the other hand, other employees recognized the effect of Six Sigma which specified objectives and monitoring mechanisms that 3M had been lacking before. Furthermore, several years after the introduction, some organizational members argued Six Sigma would be effective if appropriate department implemented it.

3M has never been used to measure or monitor; there was no follow up. One of the positive and innovative things was the increased emphasis on monitoring, in every activity. (Canato *et al.*, 2013, p. 1736)

Six Sigma taught us how to ask ourselves clearly what we want to be included within the boundaries of a project. Now when we discuss a project we ask ourselves explicitly what the goal is.

What remained is the idea of control plans, of setting up a structured process to monitor the results of our policies and see if they keep working. (Canato *et al.*, 2013, p. 1742)

McNerney promoted it to improve efficiency through restructuring and suppressing capital investment in parallel with implementing Six Sigma. Thereafter, 3M Company achieved 1.3-fold in sales and 2.2-fold in profit from 2001 to 2005 during McNerney's service as CEO.

In contrast, George Buckley, McNerney's successor, not only inhibited implementing Six Sigma at research division but also invested in them, to arrange an environment for innovation. In his era, sales and profit consequently rose 1.2-fold over the 5 years, up to 2010. Moreover, New Product Vitality Index (NPVI), one of their important KPIs, was improved to 31% in 2010, compared with numbers in the low 20s just a few years ago (3M Company, 2011). Buckley hereby achieved continuous organizational growth through loosening management by Six Sigma and its tight control.

However, as Canato *et al.* (2013) suggest in their study, the efficiency of Six Sigma has not been denied at all in 3M Company. As indeed the use of Six Sigma has been specified at their annual report up to 2021 business year (3M Company, 2022). Therefore, it is considered that Six Sigma was utilized in accordance with various purposes at some sections, after company-level intensive implementation had terminated.

4.3. *Findings from 3M Company case*

3M Company case suggests the mechanism of creating dynamic tension through parallel use of formal and informal controls and the importance of maintaining their balance.

Traditional management of 3M Company set tight financial performance targets such as NPVI and tried to achieve it. Basically, the general formal control, division managers are accountable for their performance, is used. In addition to that, informal controls, e.g., 15% culture and bootlegging, are implemented. The company uses formal systems such as Genesis Grants to turn promising ideas generated from these informal controls into business and thus lead to achieving the goal. It should be noted that 3M company intended to formulate these comprehensive controls and created dynamic tension.

In contrast, the tension between innovation and efficiency, that arose from introducing Six Sigma, was problematic for the company as it may decrease the positive traditional dynamic tension. Six Sigma is the management technique to achieve targets through improving process efficiency, and it turns into tighter use of formal controls in 3M Company. Hindo (2007) and Canato *et al.* (2013) suggest the company began to lose the balance between formal and informal controls that had been maintained before.

To create dynamic tension through management controls, balancing controls based on contradicting concepts is important (Mundy, 2010), e.g., levers of control (Bedford, 2015; Henri, 2006) proposed by Simons (1995), performance measurement systems that simultaneously encourage incremental and radical innovation (Bedford *et al.*, 2019), and elements of controls (van der Kolk *et al.*, 2020) proposed by Merchant and Van der Stede (2007). Based on the 3M Company case, it is suggested that there is difficulty maintaining balance between the combined use of formal controls for achieving tight targets and informal controls that secure degrees of freedom within working time for employees. Introduction of Six Sigma was changed with the need to deal with business problems, slowing down organizational growth, that then 3M Company faced. In fact, prior to this change, they intended to develop, commercialize, and monetize products quicker than before through Pacing Plus program. Use of Six Sigma is considered as an extension of this aim. But overall, management reforms by McNerny affected the balance that had delivered dynamic tension and 3M Company maintained before.

It was fortunate for 3M Company that McNerney moved out to Boeing in 2005, and subsequently to this event, his successor Buckley paid attention to managing traditional balance and Six Sigma was adopted according to circumstances. These changes caused "swinging back" to the balanced use of formal controls for achieving tight target and flexible informal controls, which resulted in the improvement of NPVI.

Through the 3M Company case, the mechanism that informal controls balance and create dynamic tension while formal control is used tightly, is found. However, the difficulty of maintaining this balance during management reforms in accordance with environmental change is also revealed.

5. Conclusions

I examined the 3M Company case by analyzing archival data. Conclusively, this study contributes to the literature in three ways.

First, this study finds an effect of informal controls in field of management control. It reveals the mechanism that formulating and using balanced comprehensive management controls including informal controls enable to create dynamic tension. In addition to findings from research regarding tight management accounting systems, this study argues that it is important to perceive management controls comprehensively and consider the role of informal controls.

Second, this study points out, during organizational change, the difficulty and significance of maintaining a balance of management controls to create dynamic tension. In 3M Company, introduction of Six Sigma had a certain level of validity due to facing stagnation of financial performance by traditional management controls. Even though introducing a management tool that has efficiency in some respects, this study sheds light on the mechanism that such change may induce to loss of balance of management controls. Prior literature revealed the importance and aspects of management controls that create dynamic tension, and this study adds a new perspective, that is the continuous balancing over time with management change.

These findings have implications for practice as well. Leaving place for informal controls while using formal controls tightly and maintaining its balance deliberately are significantly important to a manager, especially for modern management that requires the coexistence of conflicting concepts, such as ambidexterity.

Third, this study uses archival data and examines chronological organizational change to explore a research question regarding mechanism of management controls. Analysis of archival data enables to examine dynamics of case company's management controls in the long term and finding knowledge through not only temporary relations between variables but its change as well. In addition to the literature regarding management accounting change including Quinn (2014) showed the validity of analyzing archival data. This kind of methodology could be adopted for other management accounting studies, e.g., based on organizational life-cycle (Miller and Friesen, 1984). If the framework of Miller and Friesen (1984) is applied in the case of this study, it is possible to interpret that 3M Company has enabled to remain at the revival stage (i.e., later growing phase) thanks to creating dynamic tension through management controls. This is the new perspective in the stream of management accounting studies citing organizational life cycle (e.g., Auzair and Langfield-Smith, 2005; Kallunki and Silvola, 2008; Moores and Yuen, 2001; Su et al. 2015). It indicates the room for future research by adopting archival data to analyze.

However, this study has some potential limitations. First, the analysis is based on single organization and thus findings should be deliberately interpreted for generalization. Second, despite this study focuses the case that has a large stock of archival data, it is not possible to be absolutely certain of capturing all elements of management controls over time (Quinn, 2014). Therefore, regarding management controls in the case company, the space of different interpretations remains.

Third, this study describes just one of the patterns that create dynamic tension through management controls as well as prior studies. This study has set the effectiveness of informal controls as a research topic and accomplished its aim. However, except for the typology that this study is based on, other "balance" of management controls, e.g., control levers (Bedford, 2015; Henri, 2006), contents of performance measurement systems (Bedford *et al.*, 2019), elements of control (van der Kolk *et al.*, 2020), etc., could gain outcome as dynamic tensions. In other words, if a company lost the balance between formal and informal controls, they possibly omit it and intend to balance from different perspective (*vice-versa*).

Future research could hereby address these limitations to reveal mechanisms of generating dynamic tension more comprehensively. It means there is room for developing discussion to create dynamic tension, perhaps balancing management controls at "somewhere" based on organizational condition or environment, rather than at specific elements. Using archival data would be one of the promising passes to develop literature in this stream because qualitative research and comparative study focusing multiple organizations are required.

References

3M Company. (2002). *A Century of Innovation. The 3M Story*. St. Paul: 3M.

3M Company. (2003). *2002 Annual Report*.

3M Company. (2011). *2010 Annual Report*.

3M Company. (2022). *2021 Annual Report*.

Auzair, S.M. and Langfield-Smith, K. (2005). The effect of service process type, business strategy and life cycle stage on bureaucratic MCS in service organizations. *Management Accounting Research*, 16(4), 399–421.

Bedford, D. S. (2015). Management control systems across different modes of innovation: Implications for firm performance. *Management Accounting Research*, 28, 12–30.

Bedford, D. S., Bisbe, J., and Sweeney, B. (2019). Performance measurement systems as generators of cognitive conflict in ambidextrous firms. *Accounting, Organizations and Society*, 72, 21–37.

Brummet, R. J., Crossman, P. T., Pressler, S. A., Weltmer, W. K., and Welsch, G. A. (1959). Report of Committee on Management Accounting. *The Accounting Review*, 34(2), 207–214.

Burns, J. and Scapens, R. (2000). Conceptualising management accounting change: An institutional framework. *Management Accounting Research*, 11(1), 3–25.

Canato, A., Ravasi, D., and Phillips, N. (2013). Coerced practice implementation in cases of low cultural fit: Cultural change and practice adaptation during the implementation of Six Sigma at 3M. *Academy of Management Journal*, 56(6), 1724–1753.

Collier, P. M. (2005). Entrepreneurial control and the construction of a relevant accounting. *Management Accounting Research*, 16(3), 321–339.

Collins, J. and Porras, J. I. (1994). *Built to Last: Successful Habits of Visionary Companies*. Harper Business.

Coyne, W. E. (1996). *Building a Tradition of Innovation*. United Kingdom Department of Trade & Industry Innovation Lecture. London.

Das, T. K. and Teng, B.-S. (2001). Trust, control, and risk in strategic alliances: An integrated framework. *Organization Studies*, 22, 251–283.

Eisenhardt, K. M. (1985). Control: Organizational and economic approaches. *Management Science*, 31, 134–149.

Ferreira, A. and Otley, D. (2009). The design and use of performance management systems: An extended framework for analysis. *Management Accounting Research*, 20(4), 263–282.

Garud, R., Gehman, J., and Kumaraswamy, A. (2011). Complexity arrangements for sustained innovation: Lessons from 3M Corporation. *Organization Studies*, 32(6), 737–767.

Henri, J.-F. (2006). Management control systems and strategy: A resource-based perspective. *Accounting, Organizations and Society*, 31(6), 529–558.

Hindo, B. (2007). At 3M, a struggle between efficiency and creativity. *Business Week*, 11(11), 8–14.

Hopper, T., Tsamenyi, M., Uddin, S., and Wickramasinghe, D. (2009). Management accounting in less developed countries: What we know and needs knowing. *Accounting Auditing & Accountability Journal*, 22(3), 469–514.

Horngren, C. T. and Sundem, G. L. (1990). *Introduction to Management Accounting*, 8th edition. Prentice-Hall.

Kallunki, J. P. and Silvola, H. (2008). The effect of organizational life cycle stage on the use of activity-based costing. *Management Accounting Research*, 19(1), 62–79.

Kaufman, M. and Covaleski, M. A. (2019). Budget formality and informality as a tool for organizing and governance amidst divergent institutional logics. *Accounting, Organizations and Society*, 75, 40–58.

Kippenberger, T. (1997). A tradition of innovation at 3M. *The Antidote*, 2(2), 31–33.

Lau, C. M. (1999). The effect of emphasis on tight budget targets and cost control on production and marketing managers' propensity to create slack. *The British Accounting Review*, 31, 415–437.

London, M. and Smither, J. W. (2002). Feedback orientation, feedback culture, and the longitudinal performance management process. *Human Resource Management Review*, 12, 81–100.

Macintosh, N. B. and Quattrone, P. (2010). *Management Accounting and Control Systems: An Organizational and Sociological Approach*, 2nd edition, Wiley.

Malmi, T. and Brown, D. A. (2008). Management control systems as a package — Opportunities, challenges and research directions. *Management Accounting Research*, 19(4), 287–300.

Merchant, K. A. and Van der Stede, W. A. (2007). *Management Control Systems*, 2nd edition, Pearson Education Limited.

Miller, D. and Friesen, P. H. (1984). A longitudinal study of the corporate life cycle. *Management Science*, 30(10), 1161–1183.

Mundy, J. (2010). Creating dynamic tensions through a balanced use of management control systems. *Accounting, Organizations and Society*, 35(5), 499–523.

McWatters C. S. and Zimmerman, J. L. (2016). *Management Accounting in a Dynamic Environment*, Routledge.

Moores, K. and Yuen, S. (2001). Management accounting systems and organizational configuration: A life-cycle perspective. *Accounting, Organizations and Society*, 26(4/5), 351–389.

Mori, K. (2020). The modern concept of management accounting: A focus on informal controls. *The Journal of Chiba University of Commerce*, 58(2), 241–253 (in Japanese).

Newman, A. H. (2014). An investigation of how the informal communication of firm preferences influences managerial honesty. *Accounting, Organizations and Society*, 39(3), 195–207.

Otley, D. (2016). The contingency theory of management accounting and control: 1980–2014. *Management Accounting Research*, 31, 45–62.

Ouchi, W. G. (1979). A conceptual framework for the design of organizational control mechanisms. *Management Science*, 25, 833–848.

Pitkänen, H. and Lukka, K. (2011). Three dimensions of formal and informal feedback in management accounting. *Management Accounting Research*, 22(2), 125–137.

Peters, T. J. and Waterman, Jr., R. H. (1982). *In Search of Excellence: Lessons from America's Best-Run Companies*. Harper Business.

Plesner Rossing, C. (2013). Tax strategy control: The case of transfer pricing tax risk management. *Management Accounting Research*, 24(2), 175–194.

Quinn, M. (2014). Stability and change in management accounting over time — A century or so of evidence from Guinness. *Management Accounting Research*, 25(1), 76–92.

Simons, R. (1995). *Levers of Control: How Managers Use Innovative Control Systems to Drive Strategic Renewal*. Harvard University Press, Boston.

Scapens, R. W. (2014). My final editorial. *Management Accounting Research*, 25, 245–250.

Spraakman, G. (2006). The impact of institutions on management accounting changes at the Hudson's Bay Company. *Journal of Accounting and Organizational Change*, 2(2), 101–122.

Stouthuysen, K., Slabbinck, H., and Roodhooft, F. (2017). Formal controls and alliance performance: The effects of alliance motivation and informal controls. *Management Accounting Research*, 37, 49–63.

Su, S., Baird, K., and Schoch, H. (2015). The moderating effect of organisational life cycle stages on the association between the interactive and diagnostic approaches to using controls with organisational performance. *Management Accounting Research*, 26, 40–53.

Tillema, S. and van der Steen, M. (2015). Co-existing concepts of management control. *Management Accounting Research*, 27, 67–83.

van der Kolk, B., van Veen-Dirks, P. M. G., and ter Bogt, H. J. (2020). How combinations of control elements create tensions and how these can be managed: An embedded case study. *Management Accounting Research*, 48, 100677.

Van der Stede, M. A. (2001). Measuring "tight budgetary control". *Management Accounting Research*, 12, 119–137.

Wohlgemuth, V., Wenzel, M., Berger, M., and Eisend, M. (2019). Dynamic capabilities and employee participation: The role of trust and informal control. *European Management Journal*, 37, 760–771.

© 2025 World Scientific Publishing Company
https://doi.org/10.1142/9789811295652_0009

Chapter 9

Management Control Systems of Japanese Overseas Subsidiaries

Makoto Tomo

Seijo University, Tokyo, Japan

Abstract

This chapter examines the management control system of overseas subsidiaries from the perspective of human resource management and management accounting through case studies of four companies. When the management of overseas subsidiaries is delegated to local personnel (CEO), a management style suited to local customs would be applied. Even if the human resource evaluation is adapted to local customs, applying the same system as the Japanese headquarters would be effective for business performance evaluation. The proportion of overseas subsidiaries acquired through in-out M&A is increasing in Japan. Therefore, it may be effective not only to transfer the Japanese management control system overseas but also to integrate it with the management control system owned by the acquired company or local personnel.

1. Introduction

The proportion of foreign employees with distinct values increases as the number of foreign subsidiaries in a group increases. Cultural frictions could be induced by differences in laws, systems, and cultures in the backgrounds of foreign employees. Human resource management (HRM) is also impacted by local price levels and labor markets. Local management accounting is influenced by Japan. This is because performance is evaluated on a consolidated basis. This study examines the relationship between HRM and management accounting in overseas subsidiaries based on the case studies of four companies.

This study examines the management control system of overseas subsidiaries from the perspective of HRM and management accounting based on case studies. A management style suited to local customs is applied when the management of overseas subsidiaries is delegated to local personnel (CEO). Even if the human resource evaluation is adapted to local customs, applying the same system as the Japanese headquarters would be effective for business performance evaluation. The proportion of overseas subsidiaries acquired through in-out mergers and acquisitions (M&A) is increasing in Japan. Therefore, it may be effective not only to transfer the Japanese management control system overseas but also to integrate it with the management control system owned by the acquired company or local personnel.

2. Changes in Global Group Management and Management Systems of Overseas Subsidiaries

2.1. *Changes in global group management in HRM and management accounting*

According to the Survey of Overseas Business Activities (METI, 2023a), the overseas production ratio in FY2021 was 41% (based on companies operating overseas). According to the FY2009 Basic Survey of Overseas Business Activities (METI, 2019a), 69% of the respondents cited "strong or expected demand in local product markets" and 16% cited "availability of high-quality, inexpensive labor" as influencing factors for their overseas investment decisions. Thus, when making foreign investments, they emphasize the local consumer market than the production side of the investment. Furthermore, an increasing number of companies are using M&A to expand overseas, with In-Out M&A (mergers and acquisitions of overseas companies by Japanese companies) exceeding most M&A in value terms between 2010 and 2019 (RECOFDATA, 2023). The personnel system in Japan is shifting from a seniority-based pay system to a job-based pay system common to other countries. According to a survey by Mercer Japan (2018), more than 80% of foreign-affiliated companies in Japan had job-based pay systems in place at all management and non-management levels (career-track and general office worker). A survey of Japanese companies revealed that 53% of the surveyed companies had already introduced a job-based pay system at the management level. Performance management indicators are impacted depending on whether the personnel evaluation system is seniority- or job-based. Tomo (2019) mentioned that a shift to a job-based pay system would require performance measures based on the controllability principle.

The "Report on Survey of Overseas M&A by Japanese Companies" (METI, 2019b) mentions that "the key to attracting talented people from the global market is to shift from a fixed compensation system to a variable compensation system, which is based on the achieved performance." As discussed earlier, global corporate management is changing in terms of HRM and management accounting as companies globalize.

2.2. Management structure in overseas subsidiaries

I have been conducting interview research with Japanese overseas subsidiaries in Europe, North America, Latin America, and Southeast Asia and their Japanese headquarters for more than 10 years since 2010. The management structure of overseas subsidiaries can be divided into three typical patterns based on this research: (1) adapted to the Japanese system, (2) adapted to the local system and delegated authority, and (3) a fusion of the Japanese and local systems.

(1) A "management style that is adapted to the Japanese system" is often seen in Southeast Asia, which is geographically closer. These overseas subsidiaries often have systems (budget systems, personnel evaluation systems, and production management systems) similar to those of the subsidiaries in Japan. Southeast Asia has geographical proximity to Japan (e.g., the Haneda–Bangkok flight time is approximately 5–7 hours) and has a minor time-zone difference of approximately 1–2 hours. Therefore, if a problem occurs in the region, it can be handled by a business trip from Japan. Local subsidiaries that handle world-class products or products of

extremely high quality tend to adopt this style. Although this management style facilitates a similar level of management as in Japan, local subsidiaries may experience challenges related to HRM, such as poor employee retention rates, if they manage HRM as in Japan.

(2) "Adapting to the local system and delegating authority" is the opposite of (1) and is more common among companies that are geographically distant from Japan, have a long history of overseas expansion, or have a high degree of product localization. For example, Mexico is a long distance from Japan (the Narita–Mexico City direct flight is approximately 12–14 hours long), and the time-zone difference is approximately 14–15 hours, which implies that days and nights are almost opposite.

Although the development of information and communication technology (ICT) has made real-time video-conferencing and teleconferencing possible in recent years, time-zone differences make it difficult to manage or control issues from Japan in a timely manner. Although this style is useful for recruiting human resources — it enables HRM to be tailored to the local labor market — the exercise of control out of Japan is difficult.

(3) "Management that integrates Japanese and local systems" implies management based on the Japanese system, while incorporating a partially localized structure, or delegating authority locally, while partially incorporating Japanese-style management.

If the CEO of an overseas subsidiary is entrusted to local personnel, management can be tailored to the local market. However, Hofstede *et al.* (2013, p. 295) have indicated that even when companies internationalize, their planning, control, and accounting systems remain significantly influenced by their home country's culture. Therefore, even if the CEO of an overseas subsidiary is a local, as long as it is a Japanese overseas subsidiary, it will be influenced to some extent by the management style of the Japanese headquarters.

3. HRM and Management Accounting in Overseas Subsidiaries

This section presents four case studies regarding the relationship between HRM and management accounting in an overseas subsidiary. The first is a case study of an integration process (PMI) following an In-Out M&A in which a Japanese company acquires an overseas company. The next three are case studies of overseas subsidiaries in Mexico. I chose Mexico because it is a Spanish-speaking country with a distinct culture and is geographically distant compared to Southeast Asia. The first case study is based on data from 2019, when I conducted the interviews. Similarly, the second and third are based on data as of 2020, and the fourth is based on data as of 2016.

3.1. *Case study of advertising company A: Integration process (PMI) after in-out M&A*

Company D, an advertising company, acquired Company A, an overseas peer company, in 2013. The acquisition price was approximately 400 billion yen. Goodwill was recorded against the acquisition premium, and total assets increased by 1 trillion yen from before the acquisition, approximately doubling. After the acquisition, the top management of Company A retained the previous president. In 2015, Company D changed its consolidated accounting standards from the Japanese generally accepted accounting principles (GAAP) to the International Financial Reporting Standards (IFRS), and its fiscal year ended from March to December, in line with Company A. The company also changed its business segments to domestic (Company D) and overseas (Company A), and the overseas subsidiaries owned by Company D were incorporated into Company A. Additionally, the overseas subsidiaries owned by Company D began using Company A's performance evaluation system and HRM mechanism. At the beginning of the change, there was slight resistance.

The budget and key performance indicators (KPIs) used by Company A are identical to those used by Company D. The KPIs are gross profit, underlying operating profit, and operating margin (underlying operating profit divided by gross profit). The underlying operating profit is "KPIs to measure recurring business performance, which is calculated as operating profit added with amortization of M&A related intangible assets, acquisition costs, share-based compensation expenses related to acquired companies, and one-off items such as impairment loss and gain/loss on sales of non-current assets." The medium- and long-term KPIs used are gross profit growth, excluding the impact of foreign exchange and acquisitions, and operating margin. The adoption of these indicators based on the manageability principle may have been influenced by Company A, which is actively engaged in acquisitions.

Company A's budget system is integrated with that of Company D. Company A draws up its budget using a bottom-up approach in accordance with the group-wide medium-term management plan. Company A has been delegated performance evaluation by Company D. Unlike Company D, Company A's employee incentive bonuses are reduced to zero if KPIs are not achieved. Company A uses the IFRS for performance evaluation, which differs from Company D, which uses non-consolidated accounting based on the Japanese GAAP.

HRM is not integrated into Companies A and D. Company A has introduced a global grading system as a compensation system for its executives, CEOs of subsidiaries, division heads, and other senior executives (approximately 1% of the total workforce). This system is not implemented in Japan. Additionally, Company A has instituted a "Deferred Cash Plan" as a long-term incentive plan. Under this plan, employees are entitled to receive a fixed amount after three years of service from the date of grant. This plan replaces the performance share plan that Company A had before the M&A. Company D's long-term incentive plan is a performance-based equity compensation plan for executives that is different from Company A's plan.

Company A uses a "Group Code of Conduct" (same as Company D) to promote the cultural integration of employees from culturally and geographically diverse backgrounds. Additionally, Company A regularly conducts employee opinion surveys to identify problems and measure employee satisfaction.

As discussed earlier, Company A had an integrated management accounting system with Company D, including a code of conduct, budget system, and KPIs. Among them, Company A had customized KPIs that reflected its business structure and enabled it to measure performance continuously. Additionally, the operation of the KPIs and HRM was delegated to Company A.

3.2. *Case study of precision equipment manufacturer Company K*

Company K is a sales subsidiary of a precision equipment manufacturer in Mexico. Out of its approximately 80 employees, three — including the president — are sent by a parent company, three are locally hired Japanese, and the rest are sourced through a recruitment agency. The main targets of the Group Master Plan for Company K are sales and profit margins. Other KPIs, such as inventory turnover and receivables turnover, are set for each country. The reporting line for monthly performance reports is the North American headquarters. Additionally, the North American headquarters evaluates the local subsidiary presidents and managers. The format of the monthly performance report is identical worldwide and can be viewed at the headquarters in Japan.

Company K has adopted Ameba Management as its management accounting method and aims for open-book management in which management results are disclosed to all employees. The company provides monthly performance reports to all employees, sharing medium- and long-term goals, monthly targets, and their results. Additionally, it discloses daily sales results to its employees. This does not reach the level of Japan, where profit per hour is disclosed on a weekly basis. However, Company K believes that the disclosure of daily sales results to employees motivates them to achieve KPIs. Employee compensation is based on the base salary rather than performance-based incentives. This system, designed to maintain the basic livelihood of employees, is unique in Mexico.

Moreover, Company K has implemented a philosophy-based management system, which is like "two sides of the same coin" as the Ameba Management system. Every morning, employees read and comment on the philosophy, which is translated into Spanish. Through this process, Mexican employees understand the altruistic spirit of "what is the right thing to do in business." Although Mexico and Japan have distinct cultures and languages, the management philosophy has permeated the Mexican employees, serving as a guideline during moments of confusion or uncertainty.

As discussed above, Company K implemented the Group's common management accounting system, the Ameba Management and Philosophy Management, in Mexico as well as in Japan. Regarding the compensation system, the company adopted a system similar to the fixed salary system in Japan. Thus, Company K can be considered a case of transferring Japanese-style management overseas.

3.3. *Case study of electrical equipment manufacturer Company B*

Company B is a foreign subsidiary of an electrical equipment manufacturer located in Mexico. It has approximately 20 employees, one of whom is seconded from a parent company in Japan. The president is Mexican.

When the company first entered the Mexican market, it dealt with household appliances; however, today its core business is infrastructure projects with repair services. Although there is a regional headquarters in the US, the Mexican operation is essentially a subsidiary of the Japanese operating company. Company B is a commissioner that represents the sales activities of its parent company in Japan and earns a certain percentage of the commission when a deal is closed.

Company B's budget is determined on the basis of its medium-term management plan. The Management by Objectives system (MBO), as at the headquarters, has been adopted. The evaluation of the CEO's performance is conducted by the parent company in Japan based on the MBO. The criteria for KPIs are decided by the headquarters after a mutual agreement with Company B. Regarding bonuses, the headquarters evaluates them after self-evaluation of KPIs. The evaluation is not only based on financial results but also considers qualitative factors such as efforts to obtain orders and local response in executing the contract to avoid penalties. This is partly because the infrastructure business is easily affected by external factors and has few controllable aspects. For example, public tenders tend to decrease dramatically during presidential election years every six years.

The compensation of the Mexican CEO is determined based on the previous compensation and the labor market rate (senior management). Compensation levels are high in the infrastructure business because personal connections are significant and the people who have them are valuable.

In contrast to the seniority system common in Japan, compensation for sales and administrative personnel is job-related, based on duties and position, with annual salary increments based on inflation plus α. Incentives are provided for other employees. While incentives exist for employees in charge of equipment installation and training, compensation for other employees is "base salary + bonus." For sales staff, bonuses are paid as if 100% of sales targets were achieved operationally, regardless of financial results such as sales target achievement, making it effectively a fixed salary. This is based on the same concept as CEO compensation. Administrative staff, however, receive variable bonuses based on the percentage of targets achieved.

As discussed previously, Company B has implemented a management accounting system similar to that in Japan — the MBO. However, it has adapted its compensation system according to the reality of the infrastructure business in Mexico.

3.4. *Case study of automobile parts Manufacturer C*

Company C is a Mexican manufacturing subsidiary of an automotive supplier with approximately 2,000 employees, including management staff and workers. The CEO has been a Mexican national since the company was established in the 1980s. Although the right to select the CEO is retained by the headquarters in Japan, general management and HRM are fully delegated to Company C. HRM differs significantly from that in Japan as follows.

Company C divides its human resources into three major categories: (1) executives, (2) middle managers, and (3) workers. There is no internal rule for training and promoting middle-level employees to general managers, based on the premise that only executives can be assigned to general manager positions. In Mexico, it is common for middle-level employees who have studied at prestigious universities in the country or abroad to become general managers after gaining experience in several companies. Company C usually hires general managers by headhunting from the executive market. The hiring of the general manager at Company C is largely due to the CEO's extensive network of contacts in Mexican industry associations and headhunting firms.

In Company C, the compensation level for general managers is set higher than that for equivalent positions in Japan. For example, the salary level for the CEO and factory managers is two to three times higher than the Japanese standard.

In Mexico, there is a system provided for in the Labor Code: the "PTU" (Participación de los trabajadores en las utilidades de las empresas). Under this system, 10% of the taxable income is distributed to the employee. To reduce the cost burden of the PTU, Company C used a "dispatch agency scheme." Specifically, the company splits its compensation plan using two staffing agencies, one for the top tier and the other for the rest. Although the labor law revision in FY2012 made this more difficult, companies that used this scheme before the law revision were given a reprieve.

At Company C, management accounting is based on the Japanese system, and investment and financing decisions require the approval of the headquarters. For example, budget preparation begins in July. A budget planning meeting is held in the fall, and the draft budget is submitted to the headquarters in December. The budget is approved in March, after the adjustment process. During the term, budget performance is forecast on a semi-annual basis. However, the budget at the beginning of the term remains unchanged and the company is required to achieve it.

Company C's reporting line is directly to the headquarters in Japan, not through the US headquarters. Company C is required by the headquarters to achieve the financial indicators such as sales and profit on the income statement, and the days of inventory and receivables on the balance sheet. In particular, the headquarters strongly demands that the company reduce inventory. The supply contract is FOB (Free on Board) and importing goods by sea freight from China takes approximately a month, including customs clearance, which increases the inventory in transit. Therefore, Company C uses a trading company to reduce its inventory in transit.

As discussed previously, management accounting and financial management aspects are tightly controlled by the headquarters. However, Company C has fully delegated authority over HRM, including compensation levels.

4. Conclusion and Future Research

4.1. *Conclusion*

Figure 1 summarizes the cases of the four companies. In terms of management accounting, all four companies implemented systems similar to those in Japan. In terms of HRM, they employed personnel and applied compensation systems that were adapted to local customs. The CEO was a local person (except for Company K). The longer the CEO was a local person, the higher was the degree of HRM delegation.

Company A, while using a common budget system and KPIs with Japan, was delegated its operations, and adopted a localized HRM system. Company K, under a Japanese CEO, managed human resources in a Japanese way without using an incentive system, using Ameba Management and Philosophy Management. Although Company B had implemented the MBO, it used a qualitative evaluation that was more in line with the local labor market environment than a quantitative evaluation. In Company C, the management accounting system was strongly controlled from Japan, while the HRM system was fully delegated. As aforementioned, these cases suggest that management accounting systems can be standardized globally while adapting to local cultures to revitalize HRM in overseas subsidiaries.

The case of Company A is unique in that it not only transferred Japanese management methods overseas but also reflected, albeit partially, the management methods of the acquired Company A to the group as a whole. First, KPIs for measuring constant profit were established, considering Company A's business structure, and applied to the entire group.

Second, Company D's overseas subsidiaries were reorganized under Company A, and Company A's global management methods were applied to them. Third, Company A instituted a "Deferred Cash Plan" as a long-term incentive plan to manage human resources in a long-term manner, which influenced the introduction of a performance-based equity compensation plan for executives in Company D. This may have influenced the introduction of a performance-based equity compensation plan for executives in Company D.

As the weight of overseas subsidiaries increases through In-Out M&A, etc., the use of the knowledge of the acquired company and local management personnel will be effective for HRM and management accounting in overseas subsidiaries, as shown in the cases of Companies A and C (see Table 1).

Table 1. Summary of the cases.

Case	CEO Nationality	Management accounting	HRM
Co. A	local	Budget system and KPIs: the same as in Japan. The operation methods: different from those in Japan. Co. D's overseas subsidiaries: placed under Company A and Company A's management system is applied.	CEO's personnel right: held by the headquarters. Personnel evaluation and incentive plans: local.
Co. K	local	Ameba Management and Philosophy Management: partial implementation similar to the headquarters in Japan. Management Accounting Indicators: globally standardized format. Reporting line: North America, also can be viewed at the headquarters in Japan.	Philosophy management system: similar to the headquarters in Japan. Compensation system: similar to the fixed salary system in Japan without an incentive system.
Co. B	local (Predecessor was Japanese)	Criteria for KPIs: decided by headquarters after mutual agreement between Company B and the headquarters. KPIs evaluations: performed in accordance with the local market.	MBO: used, but qualitative rather than financial evaluation (also for salespeople). CEO compensation: reflects Mexican labor market rates.
Co. C	local	Budget system: conforms to Japan. Evaluation of financial KPIs: the headquarters involved. Investing or raising funding: no authority (requires HQ approval).	HRM: fully delegated to the local management. CEO's personnel right: held by the headquarters. Local CEO compensation: at the local market level. "Dispatch Agency Scheme": used to reduce the PTU cost burden.

4.2. Future research

Harris *et al.* (2019) indicated the following detrimental effects of "linking strategy to metrics": "Tying compensation to a metric-based target tends to increase surrogation (to confuse what's being measured with the metric being used), an unfortunate side effect of pay for performance." Similarly, Muller (2018) suggested that "Problems arise when such measures become criteria used to reward and punish — when metrics become the basis of pay-for-performance or ratings."

In Europe and the US, performance indicators are generally linked to compensation. Conversely, Yokota (2010) highlighted the weak link between performance indicators and compensation in Japan. Even in the cases in this study (except for Company A), the linkage between performance indicators and compensation is weak, and it can be said that Japanese-style management is also applied to overseas subsidiaries.

In all of these cases, each company reported the performance indicators of its overseas subsidiaries and the results of its analysis at monthly financial reporting meetings. In each company, if budgets were not met, the causes and solutions were discussed among the managers of the local subsidiaries, the regional headquarters, and the headquarters in Japan. Company A, which is considered to have the highest degree of delegation of authority, also did this by having executives from the Japanese headquarters join Company A's board of directors.

Knowledge is shared globally at the stage of reviewing the progress of performance indicators. The achievement of performance indicators in overseas subsidiaries is the result of collaboration with managers in the overseas subsidiaries, the regional headquarters, and the headquarters in Japan. Therefore, it is assumed that performance indicators are not fully linked to the compensation of specific individuals in overseas subsidiaries.

This study is inconclusive in terms of how performance measures should be used in HRM when the acquired company has a distinct culture, such as in incentive-based companies.

As in the case of Company A, a company that acquires an overseas subsidiary through an In-Out M&A rather than a new establishment is likely to be exposed to significant cultural friction. The involvement of management accounting in the PMI of HRM in such companies is a topic for future research.

References

Harris, M. and Tayler, B. (2019). *Don't Let Metrics Undermine Your Business*. Harvard Business Review, 97(5), 62–69.

Hofstede, G. H., Hofstede, G. J., and Minkov, M. (2010). *Cultures and Organizations: Software of the Mind*, 3rd edition, McGraw-Hill.

METI (Ministry of Economy, Trade and Industry). (2019). *Cross-border M&A and Japanese Companies*. https://www.meti.go.jp/policy/external_economy/toshi/kaigaima/image/CrossborderMAandJapaneseCompanies.pdf.

METI (2023). *Summary of the Basic Survey on Overseas Business Activities* (52nd edition). https://www.e-stat.go.jp/stat-search/file-download?statInfId=000040059978&fileKind=2 (in Japanese).

Mercer Japan. (2018). *Survey Report on the Status of Introduction of Fair Evaluation Methods Based on the Clarification of Job*. https://warp.da.ndl.go.jp/info:ndljp/pid/11241027/www.meti.go.jp/policy/jinzai_seisaku/houkokusyo.pdf (in Japanese).

Muller, J. Z. (2018). *The Tyranny of Metrics*. Princeton University Press.

Tomo, M. (2019). Cross-cultural management and management accounting issues: Case studies of pure holding companies and Japanese overseas subsidiaries. *The Journal of Management Accounting, Japan*, 27(2), 13–26 (in Japanese).

Recofdata. (2023). *Mergers & Acquisitions Research Report*, 344 (in Japanese).

Yokota, E. (2010). *Performance Management Accounting and Organizational Behavior*, Vol. 10, Section 3. Chuo-keizai-sha (in Japanese).

Chapter 10

The Influences of Comprehensive Performance Management Systems on Subsidiaries: Comparative Analysis of Foreign Subsidiaries and Domestic Subsidiaries

Yudai Onitsuka

Chiba University, Chiba, Japan

Abstract

This chapter examines a research question: Does the effective usage of a comprehensive performance management system by headquarters differ depending on the type of relationship between headquarters and subsidiaries? The analyses in this chapter reveal that the effective use of comprehensive performance management systems differs depending on the relationship between headquarters and subsidiaries, especially in a hierarchical relationship. In particular, the comparison of the influences on foreign and domestic subsidiaries indicates that the diagnostic use of comprehensive performance management systems by headquarters is more effective for Multinational Companies (MNCs). However, the effects of the interactive use of comprehensive performance management systems are more negative for foreign subsidiaries than for domestic ones.

In addition, the results suggest that the degree of organizational decentralization, which is a characteristic of organizational hierarchical relationships, influences the effective use of a comprehensive performance management system. The results of the analyses in this chapter indicate that organizational decentralization is not only affected by the company's size but also by the distance between headquarters and subsidiaries, which influences the effectiveness of the use of a comprehensive performance management system.

1. Introduction

This chapter discusses performance management systems (PMS) as one of the central mechanisms of management control systems (MCS).

While MCS are necessary and important to successfully implement strategies in any type of decentralized organization (Anthony and Govindarajan, 2007), effective mechanisms and processes depend on the type of decentralized organization (Chenhall, 2003, 2007). The patterns in who has the role and degree of authority in an organization, that is, the role and degree of delegation of authority of each person and department in the organization, are diverse. Based on the contingency theory, the design features and usages of PMS should be compatible with each of these organizational types.

In this regard, previous studies have examined the relationships between organizational structural characteristics (e.g., degree of decentralization, top management-manager interdependence, and match between authority and responsibility) and design features and usages of PMS (e.g., Abernethy *et al.*, 2004, 2010; Dossi and Patelli, 2008; Lee and Yang, 2011; van Veen-Dirks, 2010). However, most of these studies have focused on internal strategic business units (SBUs), and research on headquarters–subsidiary relationships is lacking; moreover, the knowledge of effective design features and usage of PMS in headquarters–subsidiary relationships is limited.

In Japan, research on headquarters–subsidiary relationships has attracted much attention due to the 1997 legal amendment permitting pure holding company systems. In particular, some have argued for the importance of subsidiary management through PMS and have claimed the need to clarify this mechanism (Asada, 2010; Matsuo, 2005). However, the problem is that the research is limited to case studies (e.g., Sonoda, 2017) and fact-finding surveys (e.g., Kimura, 2005).

Therefore, this chapter focuses on both domestic and foreign subsidiaries to clarify the research question: Does the effective usage of a comprehensive PMS by headquarters differ depending on the type of relationship between headquarters and subsidiaries?

2. Hypotheses

Described by Yori *et al.* (2012) as "an old and new problem" (p. 17), the traditionally discussed problem of partial optimization becomes more pronounced in the headquarters–subsidiary relationship; this is because the subsidiary is also legally an independent entity, whereas managers in internal SBUs are considered "pseudo presidents." The creation of "walls" between headquarters and subsidiaries, and among subsidiaries, exacerbates the problems of information asymmetry and monitoring costs (Busco *et al.*, 2008). In particular, the "wall" is higher in the global headquarters–foreign subsidiary relationship than in the domestically developed headquarters–domestic subsidiary relationship; this makes it difficult to control foreign subsidiaries (Bartlett and Ghoshal, 1989). Yori *et al.* (2012) highlight the importance of balancing the centripetal force of the headquarters with the centrifugal force of the subsidiaries and the need for "control systems and mechanisms to encourage autonomous behavior" (p. 18) of the subsidiaries for this purpose. To avoid the problem of partial optimization and integrate the subsidiary's behavior into the overall optimization, it is important to open a "window" in the "wall" between the headquarters and subsidiaries and among subsidiaries, that is, how to share information across the entire corporate group (Busco *et al.*, 2008; Yokota, 2017; Yori *et al.*, 2012). The headquarters need to understand the situation of the subsidiaries and more clearly indicate "what needs to be done" (Kaplan and Norton, 2001; Matsuo, 2005). Therefore, a comprehensive PMS is an effective system for this purpose. Conflicts between headquarters and subsidiaries are reconciled using the PMS to communicate the overall company strategy to subsidiaries and share the information necessary to achieve the company's strategy (Kubota *et al.*, 2014). Communicating "what needs to be done" also reduces the geographic and organizational "wall" between headquarters and subsidiaries and facilitates holistic optimal decision-making by the subsidiaries (Busco *et al.*, 2008).

On the other hand, Nishii (2018) examined the relationship between the cultural distance between headquarters and subsidiaries and the PMS based on a questionnaire survey of Japanese global firms. He classified his sample into six groups according to the cultural distance between headquarters and subsidiaries and whether the president of the foreign subsidiary was local or dispatched from Japan. Using this classification, he examined the impact of cultural distance on the enhancement of control through a PMS using means of multiple-indicator-multiple-cause (MIMIC) modeling. In the group of subsidiaries with a Japanese president of the foreign subsidiary, the coefficients of cultural distance on the enhancement of control through the PMS were all statistically significantly negative. However, in the group in which a local person was appointed president of the subsidiary, the relevant coefficients were mostly statistically significantly positive. Nishii (2018) explains this result in terms of headquarters gathering information on the situation, activities, and results of foreign subsidiaries through human networks. Specifically, when the president of a foreign subsidiary is dispatched from the headquarters, it is easier to collect information through human networks; thus, less emphasis is placed on controlling the subsidiary through the PMS. On the other hand, when a local is hired as the president of a foreign subsidiary, the headquarters have an incentive to emphasize control through the PMS to gather information about the subsidiaries. Although Nishii (2018) does not examine the impact of a PMS on some outcome variables, it suggests that the distance between headquarters and subsidiaries is a factor that creates differences in PMS control.

As mentioned previously, any distance between headquarters and subsidiaries increases the information asymmetry between them. Particularly problematic between headquarters and subsidiaries with large information asymmetries are monitoring cost and intensity, and the subsidiary's commitment to the overall company strategy (Busco *et al.*, 2008; Quattrone and Hopper, 2005). When information asymmetries are large, headquarters may have an incentive to strengthen monitoring to obtain information on the decision-making behavior of subsidiaries' top management and on the activities. However, enhanced monitoring not only increases monitoring costs but may also induce a decline in managers' motivation and commitment (e.g., Merchant, 1990).

Regarding this trade-off relationship, Mahlendorf *et al.* (2012) examine the impact of a comprehensive PMS on the decision-making behavior of foreign subsidiaries' top management based on embedding theory. The analysis results show that the impact of a comprehensive PMS on the decision-making of foreign subsidiaries' top management is stronger when the degree of embeddedness of foreign subsidiaries is high. In other words, when information asymmetry between headquarters and subsidiaries is high, headquarters will focus more on monitoring through the PMS. This result indicates that headquarters try to access diverse information about foreign subsidiaries by setting exhaustive performance indicators, and their intention is more targeted to reflect the foreign subsidiaries' situation.

Regarding the usage of PMS, it has been argued that in decentralized organizations, an elaborate PMS (e.g., a comprehensive PMS) can be effective when used loosely (Koufteros *et al.*, 2014; Smith and Bititci, 2017). Koufteros *et al.* (2014) found that, in decentralized organizations, the diagnostic use of a PMS enhances organizational decision-making capacity. Based on a survey of both foreign and domestic subsidiaries, Asada *et al.* (2020) examined the effects of budget and performance measures on the decision-making of subsidiaries' top management. They found no difference in the regression coefficients for the interaction term between non-financial indicators and the intensity of monitoring by headquarters but confirmed that the interaction term significantly lowers subsidiary performance only in the analysis of foreign subsidiaries. In contrast, the interaction term between non-financial indicators and the degree of involvement of the headquarters in the subsidiary's activities significantly increases the performance of the latter only in the analysis of domestic subsidiaries.

The results of the series of studies presented earlier suggest a combination of PMS design features and usage that are effective in controlling subsidiaries. Thus, this chapter develops two hypotheses. In controlling subsidiaries, it is effective to focus on the design of the PMS to enhance monitoring, but its usage must be loose. When headquarters use the PMS tightly, the subsidiary's top management may perceive it as excessive interference, which leads to a decrease in motivation and commitment. It is also inferred that these effects are stronger (weaker) for foreign subsidiaries (domestic subsidiaries) where information asymmetry is relatively large (smaller). Therefore, the following hypotheses are developed:

H1: The impact of the PMS on the decision-making of subsidiaries' top management is higher when the headquarters uses a comprehensive PMS diagnostically, and it is higher on the decision-making of foreign subsidiaries' top management than on domestic subsidiaries' top management.

H2: The impact of the PMS on the decision-making of subsidiaries' top management is lower when the headquarters uses a comprehensive PMS interactively, and it is lower on the decision-making of foreign subsidiaries' top management than on domestic subsidiaries' top management.

3. Method

3.1. *Data*

This chapter tests the hypotheses using a survey of Japanese and foreign subsidiaries.

3.1.1. *Survey of foreign subsidiaries*

The survey covered Japanese subsidiaries that were wholly owned by their foreign headquarters. A gap may exist between the head office and the subsidiaries in terms of the influence of the control system and the degree of delegation of decision-making authority by the head office; therefore, data had to be collected directly from the subsidiaries to reflect their actual status rather than from the headquarters. Due to the complex structure of MNEs, it is not realistic to conduct a survey of the entire MNE group, which would limit the observability of the impact and effects of the MCS (Mahlendorf *et al.*, 2012; Nohria and Ghoshal, 1997).

The subsidiaries to which the questionnaire was sent were selected from the "List of Foreign Subsidiaries" (in Japanese) published by Toyo Keizai Inc. in July 2016. Questionnaires were sent simultaneously to the 1,758 selected subsidiaries on September 15, 2016, and responses were requested by September 30, 2016. The final number of responses was 250 firms (14.2% response rate), of which 234 (13.3% response rate) were used for the analysis, excluding the sample with significant missing data.

For the sample used in the analysis, the regional breakdown of the responding firms' parent companies was as follows: 83 (35.5%) from North America, 112 (47.9%) from Europe, and 39 (16.7%) from Asia and other regions. To confirm the non-response bias, a goodness-of-fit test (χ^2 test) on the industry distribution of responding firms revealed no statistically significant difference between the sending and responding firms ($p > 0.05$). In other words, the industry distribution of the sample used in this analysis was consistent with that of the questionnaire firms.

3.1.2. *Survey of domestic (Japanese) subsidiaries*

The survey covered subsidiaries that were wholly owned by their Japanese headquarters, and the reason for targeting subsidiaries is the same as that for foreign subsidiaries mentioned above. The companies to which we sent the questionnaire were selected from among the 2,105 largest wholly owned subsidiaries recorded in the "Affiliated Companies Database 2020" (in Japanese), a database provided by Toyo Keizai Inc. Responses were requested by November 9. The final number of responses was 220 (response rate: 10.5%), of which 214 (response rate: 10.2%) were used for the analysis, excluding samples with significant missing data.

The sample used for analysis was checked for non-response bias. Specifically, we conducted goodness-of-fit tests on the distribution of firm size and industry among the 2,105 firms that sent the mailed questionnaire survey and the 214 firms (response rate of 10.2%) used in the analysis. The results showed no statistically significant differences in the number of employees or sales between the sample and the 2,105 firms that sent the questionnaires ($p > 0.05$). However, we found potential incompatibility between the sample and the 2,105 firms that sent the questionnaires ($p < 0.05$) in terms of industry distribution.

3.2. *Measures*

The variable for the characteristics of a comprehensive PMS (comprehensiveness [COMP]) comprised eight items, excluding one item that showed a ceiling effect, out of the nine items in the sample of foreign subsidiaries. As we found no serious problems in the descriptive statistics, all nine items were used in the domestic subsidiary sample.

Next, the diagnostic use (DUSE) and interactive use (IUSE) variables of the PMS by headquarters comprised six items for diagnostic use (DUSE) and five items for interactive use (IUSE), respectively.

Respondents were asked to respond to 14 items about the influence of PMS by headquarters on foreign subsidiaries' decision-making, which is the dependent variable, with reference to previous studies (e.g., Dossi and Patelli, 2008; Onitsuka, 2019). Based on the results of the factor analysis, we identified three dependent variables: influence on internal management decisions (INF-C), influence on sales decisions (INF-S), and influence on manufacturing and service planning (INF-D).

Each variable was combined by summing the items comprising each variable and dividing them by the number of items. To avoid multicollinearity, each variable was centered based on its mean value.

Appendix A presents the descriptive statistics for each item. Appendix B shows the variables used for hypothesis testing.

4. Results of Analyses

To test the hypotheses in this chapter, we established two models for all the dependent variables. We entered the main independent variables (COMP, DUSE, and IUSE) and control variables (AUTH-C, S, D, INDUST_dummy, and SIZE) in the first model. In the second model, we used the interaction variables (COMP*DUSE and COMP*IUSE) between the comprehensiveness of the PMS and its diagnostic and interactive use, respectively. Table 1 presents the results of the analysis and also includes the results of the tests on the difference between the regression coefficients for foreign and domestic subsidiaries.

The results in Table 1 show that the dependent variables (INF-C, INF-S) and the interaction variable (COMP*DUSE) have a statistically

Table 1. Results of hierarchical regression analysis and tests of differences in regression coefficients.

	Dependent variable: INF-C			
	Foreign subsidiaries		**Domestic Subsidiaries**	
	Model1	Model2	Model1	Model2
Independent variables				
COMP	**0.266****	**0.259****	**0.260****	**0.278****
DUSE	−0.052	−0.035	0.029	0.023
IUSE	**0.207***	**0.231***	0.130	0.134
AUTH-C	0.194	0.209	−0.078	−0.087
AUTH-S	−0.080	−0.110	0.115	0.106
AUTH-D	0.020	0.031	−0.063	−0.052
INDUST_dummy	−0.017	−0.027	−0.191**	−0.193**
SIZE	−0.058	−0.046	0.066	0.060
COMP*DUSE		**0.354*****		0.107
Test statistic for difference in coefficients		**5.339*****		
COMP*IUSE		**−0.297****		−0.031
Test statistic for difference in coefficients		**4.190*****		
R^2	0.204	0.242	0.165	0.172
Adj. R^2	0.177	0.209	0.131	0.130
F-Value	7.500***	7.413***	4.873***	4.058***
	Dependent variable: INF-S			
Independent variables				
COMP	**0.152**†	**0.160**†	**0.229***	**0.271****
DUSE	0.032	0.057	−0.011	−0.022
IUSE	0.149	**0.162**†	0.157	0.160
AUTH-C	0.097	0.113	0.110	0.096
AUTH-S	0.008	−0.006†	0.042	0.023
AUTH-D	0.151*	0.155	−0.048	−0.028
INDUST_dummy	−0.037	−0.053	−0.155*	−0.161*

(*Continued*)

Table 1. (*Continued*)

	Foreign subsidiaries		Domestic Subsidiaries	
	Model1	Model2	Model1	Model2
SIZE	−0.115†	−0.110†	−0.026	−0.034
COMP*DUSE		**0.213***		**0.107†**
Test statistic for difference in coefficients		**3.245****		
COMP*IUSE		**−0.121†**		−0.002
Test statistic for difference in coefficients		0.945		
R^2	0.155	0.170	0.148	0.171
Adj. R^2	0.126	0.135	0.113	0.129
F-Value	5.376***	4.763***	4.272***	4.034***

Dependent variable: INF-D

Independent variables				
COMP	0.088	0.103	**0.202***	**0.240***
DUSE	0.090	0.104	0.057	0.045
IUSE	0.029	0.023	**0.203***	**0.210***
AUTH-C	0.092	0.097	0.134	0.116
AUTH-S	−0.108	−0.097	−0.043	−0.061
AUTH-D	0.426***	0.420***	−0.024	−0.002
INDUST_dummy	0.068	0.059	−0.159*	−0.162*
SIZE	0.008	0.003	0.086	0.075
COMP*DUSE		−0.069		**0.208***
Test statistic for difference in coefficients		**2.153***		
COMP*IUSE		0.122		−0.049
Test statistic for difference in coefficients		**1.679†**		

Table 1. (*Continued*)

	Foreign subsidiaries		Domestic Subsidiaries	
	Model1	Model2	Model1	Model2
R^2	0.135	0.169	0.168	0.173
Adj. R^2	0.106	0.133	0.134	0.130
F-Value	4.579***	4.724***	4.980***	4.067***

Notes: ***$p < 0.001$, **$p < 0.01$, *$p < 0.05$, †$p < 0.1$ All tests are two-tailed. INF-C = the influence of parent-PMS on subsidiaries' internal control decision making; INF-D = the influence of parent-PMS on subsidiaries' decision making about developing products and/or services INF-S = the influence of parent-PMS on subsidiaries' decision making about selling processes COMP = Comprehensive PMS; DUSE = Diagnostic use of PMS; IUSE = Interactive use of PMS; AUTH-C = decision-making authority about subsidiaries' internal control; AUTH-S = decision-making authority about selling processes; AUTH-D = decision-making authority about developing products and/or services; INDUST_dummy = Industry of a subsidiary (1 = manufacturing; 0 = not); SIZE = Number of employees to represent the size of the subsidiary.

significant positive relationship in the analysis for foreign subsidiaries, whereas the dependent variables (INF-C and INF-S) and the interaction variable (COMP*IUSE) have a statistically significant relationship with any of the interaction variables. Even in the analysis of domestic subsidiaries, the dependent variables (INF-S and INF-D) and COMP*DUSE have a statistically significant positive relationship.

The test results for the difference in regression coefficients indicate that the coefficient of COMP*DUSE is higher for the analysis targeting foreign subsidiaries than for that targeting domestic subsidiaries when INF-C and INF-S are the dependent variables. Conversely, the difference in the coefficient of COMP*IUSE is statistically significantly lower for foreign subsidiaries when INF-C is used. Therefore, based on the results of the analysis with INF-C and INF-S as dependent variables alone, Hypotheses 1 and 2 are partially supported. However, in the analysis with INF-D as the dependent variable, the results contradict the hypothesis.

5. Discussion

The analysis in Table 1 shows that the effective use of a comprehensive PMS differs depending on the hierarchical relationship between headquarters and subsidiaries.

First, the results of the analysis with INF-C and INF-S as dependent variables indicate that the diagnostic use of a comprehensive PMS by headquarters enables the subsidiary's decision-making behavior to align with the corporate strategy. Conversely, the interactive use of the PMS by headquarters hinders the effectiveness of the comprehensive PMS. These effects are more significant for foreign subsidiaries than for domestic subsidiaries. This result is consistent with Asada *et al.* (2020), who analyzed domestic and foreign subsidiaries. Asada *et al.* (2020) compared domestic and foreign subsidiaries with the same headquarters. Their analysis indicates that excessive involvement by the headquarters in the subsidiary when focusing on non-financial indicators reduces the effectiveness of budgetary control over the foreign subsidiary. Although this study does not assume the same headquarters, its results are consistent with those of previous studies. When the headquarters uses a PMS with elaborate features, such as a comprehensive PMS for its foreign subsidiaries, it should be somewhat loose about how it uses the PMS. Otherwise, the positive effects of a comprehensive PMS will not be realized, but rather, the PMS will negatively affect the subsidiary.

Nevertheless, based on the results of the analysis with INF-D as the dependent variable, the degree of delegation of decision-making authority may be related to the effectiveness of the PMS. This is because AUTH-D, which indicates the degree of delegation of decision-making authority related to INF-D, is 3.543 for foreign subsidiaries, which is below the theoretical mean (= 4), whereas it is 5.174 for domestic subsidiaries, which is significantly higher, and the difference is statistically significant ($t = 13.970$, $p < 0.001$). This chapter assumed that the organizational distance between headquarters and subsidiaries was greater for foreign subsidiaries than for domestic subsidiaries. However, from the perspective of decision-making authority regarding manufacturing and service development, the opposite is true. Thus, although the hypothesis was not supported, the study's assertion that the headquarters–subsidiary hierarchical relationship affects the effectiveness of a comprehensive PMS should not be overlooked.

6. Conclusion

This chapter examined the following research question: Does the effective usage of a comprehensive performance management system by headquarters differ depending on the relationship between headquarters and subsidiaries? The analysis reveals that the effective use of a comprehensive PMS for subsidiary decision-making behavior differs depending on the relationship between headquarters and subsidiaries. Specifically, the diagnostic use of a comprehensive PMS is effective, and the interactive use of a comprehensive PMS is negative, which is more significant in multinational firms. In addition, as a characteristic of the organizational structure that indicates the difference in the relationship between headquarters and subsidiaries, the degree of organizational decentralization by the degree of delegation of decision-making authority influences the effective use of a comprehensive PMS. As assumed in this study, organizational decentralization is not affected by firm size but rather by organizational hierarchical relationships, which in turn determine the effectiveness of using a comprehensive PMS. This is consistent with assertions made in previous studies (Chenhall, 2003; Lee and Yang, 2011).

This study has several implications. First, in the context of promoting decision-making behavior consistent with corporate strategy, the effective use of a comprehensive PMS has diagnostic use both for foreign and domestic subsidiaries, but the headquarters' influence of a comprehensive PMS is stronger for foreign subsidiaries. Second, the diagnostic use of a comprehensive PMS is particularly effective for more autonomous subsidiaries that are structurally decentralized. Third, the negative effects of the interactive use of a comprehensive PMS are more likely to occur in foreign subsidiaries.

This study presents evidence that expands the findings of previous studies. However, this study also faces challenges that must be resolved. The most important issue is that previous studies have reported results that differ from those presented in this section. For example, Guenther and Heinicke (2019), who analyzed medium-sized firms, showed positive effects of the interactive use of an elaborate PMS (comprehensive PMS), contrary to the results of the analysis in this chapter. Information exchange through human networks may be particularly effective when the distance between headquarters and subsidiaries is small. In particular, the interactive use of the PMS is more likely when the distance between top management and the SBU (or its managers) is closer. This finding is supported by studies that examined the size of the organization. The closer the distance between top management and the SBU, the more useful people-oriented controls are (e.g., Bruns and Waterhouse, 1975; Heinicke et al., 2016). However, Simons (2000) states that a prerequisite for the interactive use of the PMS is that this method of operation must penetrate — and information gathered from — every part of the organization; that is, the effective usage of PMS differs between subsidiaries and PMS for internal SBUs. Therefore, it is also necessary to examine the differences in the effective usage of PMS by comparing subsidiaries and internal SBUs.

Appendix A

All items were measured on a 7-point Likert scale.

Descriptive statistics on comprehensive PMS

To what extent do you agree with the following statements about the parent-PMS' characteristics?	Foreign subsidiaries Mean	SD	Domestic subsidiaries Mean	SD
The parent-PMS links together the activities of your Japanese company to the achievement of organizational goals and objectives.	5.551	1.396	5.042	1.419
The parent-PMS provides consistent and mutually reinforcing links between the current operating performance of your Japanese company and the organization's long-term strategies.	5.372	1.503	4.906	1.463
The parent-PMS provides a diverse set of measures related to the key performance areas of your Japanese company.	5.355	1.677	4.836	1.600
The parent-PMS provides a range of measures that cover the critical areas of your Japanese company's operations.	5.013	1.710	4.650	1.496
The parent-PMS provides various information about important aspects of your Japanese company's operations.	5.009	1.570	4.645	1.490

(Continued)

Descriptive statistics on comprehensive PMS

To what extent do you agree with the following statements about the parent-PMS' characteristics?	Foreign subsidiaries Mean	SD	Domestic subsidiaries Mean	SD
The parent-PMS provides information on different dimensions of your Japanese company's performance.	5.004	1.595	4.547	1.484
The parent-PMS is produced in a fully documented form, which provides a record for evaluating performance.	4.949	1.764	4.364	1.589
The parent-PMS provides a broad range of performance information about various areas of your Japanese company.	4.833	1.645	3.967	1.611
The parent-PMS shows how the activities of your Japanese company affect the activities of other business units/subsidiaries within the organization.	4.526	1.731	3.911	1.606

Descriptive statistics on PMS use

To what extent do you agree to the following statements about how to use of the parent-PMS?	Foreign subsidiaries Mean	SD	Domestic subsidiaries Mean	SD
Diagnostic Use				
The parent-company uses the PMS to compare performance and results of your Japanese company's operations to expectations.	5.761	1.353	4.804	1.407
The parent-company uses the PMS to track progress of your Japanese company's activities toward goals.	5.303	1.638	5.210	1.469
The parent-company uses the PMS to monitor performance and results of your Japanese company's operations.	5.278	1.674	4.906	1.350
The parent-company relies heavily on staff specialists in preparing and interpreting information from the parent-PMS.	3.970	1.600	4.051	1.926
The parent-company pays attention on the activities of your Japanese company only when the parent-company knows exception to a plan happened through the parent-PMS.	3.270	1.720	3.738	1.927

(Continued)

(Continued)

Descriptive statistics on PMS use

To what extent do you agree to the following statements about how to use of the parent-PMS?	Foreign subsidiaries Mean	SD	Domestic subsidiaries Mean	SD
You and/or your Japanese company's employees pay attention on the parent-PMS when exceptions to the parent-PMS happen.	3.043	1.473	3.131	1.560
Interactive Use				
The parent-company has paid attention to the day-to-day activities of your Japanese company through the parent-PMS.	4.931	1.565	4.486	1.632
You and/or your Japanese company's employees have paid day-to-day attention to the parent-PMS.	4.914	1.602	5.065	1.518
The parent-PMS enables continual challenge and debate of underlying data, assumption and action plan.	4.893	1.602	4.453	1.432
The parent-PMS enables discussion in meetings with the parent-company and other employees.	4.884	1.547	4.696	1.475
Formal meetings are frequently held with the participation of employees in both the parent-company and your Japanese company to discuss the parent-PMS.	4.850	1.708	3.936	1.226

Descriptive statistics on impact of parent-PMS on subsidiaries' decision making

To what extent does the parent-PMS influence your decision-making on the following items?	Foreign subsidiaries Mean	SD	Domestic subsidiaries Mean	SD
Budgeting decisions	5.124	1.404	5.542	1.280
Decisions about performance evaluation	4.721	1.809	3.336	1.813
Pricing decisions about products or services	4.718	1.793	3.542	1.783
Target setting decisions for employees	4.650	1.962	3.243	1.794
Incentive scheme decisions	4.585	1.877	3.631	1.755
Choosing target customer decisions	4.470	2.032	3.500	1.776

(Continued)

Descriptive statistics on impact of parent-PMS on subsidiaries' decision making

To what extent does the parent-PMS influence your decision-making on the following items?	Foreign subsidiaries Mean	SD	Domestic subsidiaries Mean	SD
Human resource decisions	4.423	1.752	3.453	1.806
Responsibility accounting decisions	4.372	1.953	3.173	1.721
Distribution channel decisions	4.206	2.132	3.360	1.765
Investment decisions	3.944	2.043	5.140	1.535
Production planning decisions	3.737	2.129	5.547	1.273
Supply chain management decisions	3.705	2.117	3.439	1.691
Making or buying decisions	3.677	2.081	3.472	1.672
R&D planning and control decisions	3.559	2.028	4.121	1.705

Appendix B

Descriptive statistics on comprehensive PMS

	Foreign subsidiaries Mean	SD	Cronbach' α	Domestic subsidiaries Mean	SD	Cronbach' α
COMP	5.068	1.244	.912	4.541	1.164	0.909
DUSE	4.171	1.040	.639	4.307	.980	0.651
IUSE	4.894	1.257	.842	4.527	1.047	0.766
INF-C	4.599	1.594	.883	3.367	1.594	0.921
INF-S	4.468	1.812	.896	3.460	1.621	0.923
INF-D	3.699	1.677	.865	4.570	1.126	0.787
AUTH-C	5.311	1.075	.795	3.416	1.611	0.906
AUTH-S	5.713	1.107	.781	4.886	1.740	0.931
AUTH-D	3.543	1.446	.814	5.174	1.234	0.825

Acknowledgment

This study was supported by the Tokai University Research Organization Grant.

References

Abernethy, M. A., Bouwens, J., and Van Lent, L. (2004). Determinants of control system design in divisionalized firms. *The Accounting Review*, 79(3), 545–570.

Abernethy, M. A., Bouwens, J., and Van Lent, L. (2010). Leadership and control system design. *Management Accounting Research*, 21(1), 2–16.

Anthony, R. N. and Govindarajan, V. (2007). *Management Control Systems* (12th edition). McGraw-Hill.

Asada, T. (2010). Performance management of group companies. In Tani, T., Kobayashi, Y., and Ogura, N. (eds.). *Performance Management Accounting* Chuokeizai-Sha Holdings, Inc., Tokyo, 255–280.

Asada, T., Oura, K., Hirai, H., and Horii, S. (2020). Comparative study on budgetary management for domestic and overseas subsidiaries. *The Journal of Cost Accounting Research*, 44(1), 156–168.

Bartlett, C. A. and Ghoshal, S (1989). *Managing across Borders: The Transnational Solution*. Harvard Business School Press.

Burchell, S., Clubb, C., Hopwood, A., and Hughes, J. (1980). The roles of accounting in organizations and society. *Accounting, Organization and Society*, 5(1), 5–27.

Burns, W. J. and Waterhouse, J. H. (1975). Budgetary control and organization structure. *Journal of Accounting Research*, 13(2), 177–203.

Busco, C., Giovannoni, E., and Scapens, R. W. (2008). Managing the tensions in integrating global organisations: The role of performance management systems. *Management Accounting Research*, 19(2), 103–125.

Chenhall, R. H. (2003). Management control systems design within its organizational context: Findings from contingency-based research and directions for the future. *Accounting, Organizations and Society*, 28(2), 127–168.

Chenhall, R. H. (2005). Integrative strategic performance measurement systems, strategic alignment of manufacturing, learning and strategic outcomes: An exploratory study. *Accounting, Organizations and Society*, 30(5), 395–422.

Chenhall, R. H. (2007). Theorizing contingencies in management control systems research. In C. S Chapman, A. G. Hopwood, and M. D. Shields (eds.). *Handbook of Management Accounting Research*. Oxford, UK: Elsevier, pp. 163–205.

Dossi, A. and Patelli, L. (2008). The decision-influencing use of performance measurement systems in relationships between headquarters and subsidiaries. *Management Accounting Research*, 19(2), 126–148.

Dossi, A. and Patelli, L. (2010). You learn from what you measure: Financial and non-financial performance measures in multinational companies. *Long Range Planning*, 43(4), 498–526.

Guenther, T. W. and Heinicke, A. (2019). Relationships among types of use, levels of sophistication, and organizational outcomes of performance measurement systems: The crucial role of design choices. *Management Accounting Research*, 42, 1–25.

Henri, J. F. (2006). Organizational culture and performance measurement systems. *Accounting, Organization and Society*, 31(1), 77–103.

Kaplan, R. S. and Norton, D. P. (2001). *The Strategy-Focused Organization*. Harvard Business School Press.

Kimura, I. ed. (2005). *Management Accounting for Group Companies*. Zeimu Keiri Kyokai Co, Tokyo.

Koufteros, X., Verghese, A. J., and Lucianetti, L. (2014). The effect of performance measurement systems on firm performance: A cross-sectional and a longitudinal study. *Journal of Operations Management*, 32(6), 313–336.

Kubota, Y., Kondo, T., Ito, M., Nishi, T., and Nakagawa, Y. (2014). Management control packages for the tensions of organizational design in multinational corporations: A comparative case study. *The Journal of Cost Accounting Research*, 38(2), 39–51.

Lee, C. L. and Yang, H. J. (2011). Organization structure, competition and performance measurement systems and their joint effects on performance. *Management Accounting Research*, 22(2), 84–104.

Mahlendorf, M. D., Rehring, J., Schäffer, U., and Wyszomirski, E. (2012). Influencing foreign subsidiary decisions through headquarter performance measurement systems. *Management Decision*, 50(4), 688–717.

Matsuo, T. (2005). Group Management and Performance Measures. In I. Kimura, (ed.). *Management Accounting for Group Companies*. Zeimu Keiri Kyokai Co, Tokyo, pp. 65–86.

Nishii, T. (2018). The effects of distances on the development of performance management systems. *The Journal of Management Accounting, Japan*, 26(1), 3–21.

Nohria, N. and Ghoshal, S. (1997). *The Different Network: Organizing Multinational Corporations for Value Creation*. San Francisco: Joeesy-Bass.

Onitsuka, Y. (2019). The influences of parent-performance management systems on autonomous subsidiaries. *The Journal of Management Accounting, Japan*, 27(1), 109–124.

Quattrone, P. and Hopper, T. (2005). A "time–space odyssey": Management control systems in two multinational organisations. *Accounting, Organizations and Society*, 30(7), 735–764.

Simons, R. 2000. *Performance Measurement and Control Systems for Implementing Strategy*. Prentice Hall.

Smith, M. and Bititci, U. S. (2017). Interplay between performance measurement and management, employee engagement and performance. *International Journal of Operations and Production Management*, 37(9), 1207–1228.

Sonoda, T. (ed.) (2017). *Management Accounting for Corporate Groups*. Chuokeizai-Sha Holdings, Inc., Tokyo.

van Veen-Dirks, P. (2010). Different uses of performance measures: The evaluation versus reward of production managers. *Accounting, Organizations and Society*, 35(2), 141–164.

Yokota, E. (2017). From pure holding company to operating holding company: Balancing centrifugal and centripetal forces. In Sonoda, T. (ed.). *Management Accounting for Corporate Groups*. Chuokeizai-Sha Holdings, Inc., Tokyo, pp. 57–74.

Yori, M., Asada, T., and Tomo, M. (2012). Analysis of the management control system in holding companies: Its integrative functions in corporate governance. *Melco Journal of Management Accounting Research*, 5(1), 15–30.

© 2025 World Scientific Publishing Company
https://doi.org/10.1142/9789811295652_0011

Chapter 11

A Case Study on Enabling Control in Sustainability Management

Yan Li

Takushoku University, Tokyo, Japan

Abstract

This study aims to clarify the role of enabling control in sustainability management by examining a case study of Saraya Co, Ltd, a company known for its social evaluations in this area. The analysis shows that enabling control is an integral part of the company's sustainability efforts. Specifically, Saraya uses management controls to utilize the experience and values of employees involved in external sustainability activities and integrate them into the organization through personnel control and structural design. These management control practices enable the company to identify and address social issues beyond its core business, thereby enhancing its role in the social network for solving social problems. The study highlights the importance of increasing "global transparency" while providing employees with the "flexibility" to act beyond organizational logic. In addition, integrating external sustainability activities with business operations enables the pursuit of social value and organizational goals. However, in the early stages, there were barriers between global transparency and internal transparency, which were managed through management control practices such as the philosophy of top management and the use of communication tools by senior managers. The study suggests that enabling control has significant potential in sustainability management and contributes to the theoretical development of enabling control in response to contemporary organizational challenges.

1. Introduction

Sustainability management has become critical for contemporary business organizations. Accordingly, there has been a call to investigate the role of management accounting and management control (MC) in managing sustainability by addressing the sustainability perspective in the activities of business organizations (Gray, 2010; Milne, 1996).

This study suggests that enabling control (Adler and Borys, 1996; Ahrens and Chapman, 2004) can be relevant for exploring the role of MC in sustainability management. Research on enabling control suggests that MC can be designed and implemented to enhance employees' skills and capabilities and to leverage their capabilities, allowing them to pursue multiple goals simultaneously (Ahrens and Chapman, 2004; Wouters and Wilderom, 2008).

The skills, experience, and value of employees involved in sustainability activities have been identified as critical drivers of organizational sustainability management (Heggen *et al.*, 2018; Johnstone, 2019). In addition, sustainability is a concept that encompasses economic, societal, and ecological values and transcends organizational boundary (Dixon and Fallon, 1989). The pursuit of the value of sustainability therefore inevitably involves the challenge of managing multiple objectives that are often in tension (Norris and O'Dwyer, 2004).

The purpose of this study is to explore the role of enabling control in sustainability management through a case study of Saraya Corporation (hereafter referred to as Saraya), a company that is actively engaged in sustainability activities and has received considerable public recognition in Japan. In doing so, the findings from the company are expected to contribute to a deeper understanding of the role of enabling control in sustainability management, both in practice and in academia.

2. Literature Review

According to Adler and Borys (1996), formal procedures can be designed in either a coercive or an enabling way. The former is based on a fool-proofing and deskilling rationale, aiming to reduce reliance on employees' skills and capabilities; instead, the latter is based on a usability and upgrading rationale, aiming to enhance and leverage employees' skills and capabilities to enable them to deal more effectively with the inevitable contingencies. Ahrens and Chapman (2004) have adopted and developed this concept in MC research, stating that "formal control systems designed in this way can thus enable workers and operational management to pursue the objectives of efficiency and flexibility simultaneously" (p. 281).

There are four general characteristics of enabling control that distinguish it from coercive control: (1) internal transparency, meaning that employees understand the logic of their own work; (2) global transparency, whereby employees recognize the place of their work within the organization as a whole; (3) repair, by which employees are able to repair the system themselves when faced with unexpected events; (4) flexibility, referring to giving employees discretion over whether or not to release control systems (Adler and Borys, 1996; Ahrens and Chapman, 2004).

There is a growing body of empirical evidence on how the four characteristics are involved in a wide range of organizational activities, including the management of the relationship between headquarters and subsidiaries (Ahrens and Chapman, 2004; Goretzki *et al.*, 2018), the development and introduction of performance measurement systems (Jordan and Messner, 2012; Wouters and Wilderom, 2008), supply chain management (Free, 2007), new product development (Jørgensen and Messner, 2009), information systems integration (Chapman and Kihn, 2009), knowledge management (Wouters and Roijmans, 2011), strategising (Li, 2011), and so forth.

These studies argue that enabling control plays a role in utilizing the skills and capabilities of employees, such as experience and professionalism (Wouters and Wilderom, 2008), creativity (Adler and Chen, 2011), and local knowledge (Goretzki *et al.*, 2018). Furthermore, by enhancing and leveraging these skills and capabilities of employees in operations, control systems with the four characteristics introduced above enable them to manage multiple goals that are often in tension with each other, such as efficiency and flexibility (Ahrens and Chapman, 2004; Jørgensen and Messner, 2010), creativity and control (Adler and Chen, 2011), and local and global objectives (Goretzki *et al.*, 2018).

This study suggests that these findings provide insight into the relevance of enabling control in sustainability management. First, the skills and capabilities of employees involved in sustainability activities are critical to an organization's sustainability initiatives. For example, through a comparative analysis of two companies in the same industry with advanced and less advanced sustainability activities, Heggen et al. (2018) found that one factor explaining the difference between the two companies is the presence or absence of employees with expertise in sustainability activities. Second, sustainability is originally a concept that encompasses economic, societal, and environmental values (Dixon and Fallon, 1989), and integrating this broad concept into business activities inevitably involves the challenge of pursuing multiple objectives that are often in tension. For instance, Norris and O'Dwyer (2004) illustrated that even among companies that were considered advanced in sustainability management, there was a conflict between formal control to achieve organizational goals and social control and self-control to integrate sustainability concerns.

Thus, the insight into the potential role of enabling control in sustainability management can be derived from two crucial roles that enabling control entails—the utilization of employees' skills and abilities in operational activities, and the pursuit of the dual goals of sustainability value and business purpose. Although at an early stage, emerging research attempts to examine the role of enabling control in sustainability management. Based on a literature review, Johnstone (2019) pointed to the potential of boundary spanners as an enabling control to utilize employees with sustainability skills and capabilities. By working outside the organization based on their skills, experience, and values, they can bring a sustainability perspective to the organization and have the potential to change the overall sustainability management system.

Some studies have examined the impact of enabling control on achieving multiple goals. Wijethilake et al. (2018), for example, found that the enabling use of MC positively moderates the correlation between environmental innovation strategies and organizational performance. Heggen and Sridharan (2021) also examined that the enabling use of diagnostic eco-controls positively impacts environmental performance, but the impact of the enabling use of interactive eco-controls is unknown. They also claimed that an enabling approach may come at a trade-off and that providing employees with too much freedom and flexibility may result in inefficiencies, resource wastage, and ultimately a decline in performance (p. 6).

Due to the lack of consensus, limited empirical evidence, and insufficient critical examination of the characteristics of enabling control, there remains a lack of in-depth understanding of how enabling control can be implemented in corporate sustainability management. The purpose of this study is to contribute to this emerging body of research by exploring the role of enabling control in sustainability management through a case study. In doing so, the findings from the company are expected to contribute to a deeper understanding of the role of enabling control in sustainability management, both in practice and in academia.

3. Case Site and Data Collection

This chapter is based on a longitudinal case study of Saraya, a company that is actively engaged in sustainability activities and has received considerable public recognition in Japan. Since its establishment in 1952, Saraya has developed its business on the basis of environment, hygiene, and health. The company is actively involved in a range of sustainability initiatives, including biodiversity conservation in Borneo, sanitation support in Uganda and East Africa, climate change, and the marine plastic waste crisis.

The author conducted semi-structured interviews (24 in total, approximately 42 hours) with nine members of the company, including the president, and ten relevant individuals outside the organization between April 2018 and December 2021. Participatory observation was also conducted by attending lectures, conferences, and other events (29 times, approximately 49 hours in total). The analysis in this chapter is based on these data, as well as information gathered from the company's website and other published documents.

4. Case Analysis

Of the various sustainability activities undertaken by the company, this chapter focuses on biodiversity conservation in Borneo as it has had a significant impact on the company's subsequent initiatives (Saraya, 2010, 2016).

4.1. *Case background*

In the 1970s, when synthetic petroleum-based detergents were the norm, Saraya's palm oil-based detergent stood out as a product with a low environmental impact because it was made from vegetable palm oil. In the 1990s, palm oil-based detergents became popular with consumers as a synonym for natural detergents that were not only environmentally friendly but also gentle on the hands.

In 2004, however, Saraya was criticized in the media for using palm oil in its products. As demand for palm oil has risen with global population growth, oil palm plantations have expanded on the island of Borneo. It was considered a biodiversity hotspot, but in the forty years between the early 1970s and 2010, around 40% of the rainforest in the state of Sabah was lost due to the expansion of oil palm plantations. The expansion of the oil palm plantations and the loss of the rainforest have led to tensions between the wildlife and the local plantations. For example, Bornean elephants, displaced by the loss of natural rainforest, often invade plantations in search of food, leading to the destruction of oil palm fields. This causes social problems as plantation managers take serious action, including shooting.[1]

A Japanese TV program called "Tears of the Elephants" featured injured Bornean elephants that had been caught in traps set by farmers to prevent their invasion and the spread of palm oil plantations in August 2004, and the company had asked to appear on the program. The company's president felt responsible for the situation and decided to appear on the program to admit their unknowing and apologize, and that was the beginning of the Borneo Biodiversity Conservation Project.

In 2022, 18 years after the incident, the company is still involved in the project. Through this commitment, the company has not only addressed the social issue of biodiversity in Borneo but has also been able to integrate it into its business, as discussed further in this chapter. In all these efforts, it has been essential to utilize the skills and abilities of people both inside and outside the company. Drawing on the characteristics of enabling control, this section illustrates how enabling control is involved in the company's management of sustainability activities.

---

[1] Borneo Conservation Trust Japan Web site (https://www.bctj.jp/), accessed August 1, 2022.

4.2. *Outside activities to address the social problem*

The company stated that this media attention "triggered an awareness of environmental issues in raw material procurement in the supply chain that we were not aware of before" (Daishima, 2008). In other words, the media attention triggered the company's awareness of environmental issues in the supply chain in which it operates, i.e., global transparency. In its quest for this global transparency, the company has been involved in practices to address biodiversity issues in Borneo, starting with the recruitment of an employee with sustainability experience.

In 2004, the environmental problems in Borneo were largely unknown in Japan because palm oil was imported through trading companies. At the time, Saraya was a manufacturing company with fewer than 1,000 employees, and it did not have the experience or staff to be responsible for activities in relation to Borneo issues. The company therefore decided to recruit a researcher who was experienced in international cooperation activities to work on the issue and dispatch him to Borneo. The employee accepted Saraya's proposal because he felt it was in line with his experience and skills.

Flexibility, i.e., giving the employee discretion to do the work outside the organization without assigning a specific role, was an important factor for the employee in the carrying out of his activities in the field. The employee described his "mission" at the time as follows.

> At the time, nobody in the company knew anything about the problem. I thought it was necessary for me to do some research. But more than that, it was my mission to find experts, someone who knew the problem well, a mission I had set for myself.

Based on this understanding, and in the process of gathering information and knowledge on the issues, the employee found that palm oil plantations had spread across the island and were causing a variety of social problems, as the TV program had shown. At the same time, he realized that the oil palm industry was the basis of the economic life of the local people. For example, from the 1980s to the early 2000s, the oil palm industry in Malaysia created between 90,000 and 400,000 jobs, settled 110,000 households, and improved incomes and the quality of education (Basiron, 2008).

After the TV program broadcast, viewers and customers asked Saraya to stop using palm oil as a resource and to look for alternative raw materials. However, given the importance of oil palm plantations to the livelihoods of local people, the employee realized that stopping the use of palm oil and criticizing the farmers would not solve the underlying problems. Alongside a wealth of information gathered from local activities, he identified the Green Corridor Project, which had been initiated by the local research and administrative agency, as an approach to solving the underlying problem. The project aims to achieve human-animal coexistence by separating plantations and wildlife habitats, creating paths that allow wildlife free access to feeding and watering areas without destroying the plantation.

In order to involve as many stakeholders as possible in achieving the goal, the establishment of Not for Profit Organizations (NPOs) was seen as the ideal approach. However, due to the administrative agency's concern of local opposition and lack of funding, the project was stopped at the design stage without any steps being taken to establish the NPOs. This was then communicated within the organization by the employee, and the purpose of the project to address the root problem was agreed and supported by the top management. From there, Borneo Conservation Trust (BCT) and Borneo Conservation Trust Japan (BCTJ), two NPOs for the development of biodiversity conservation activities in Borneo, were established in 2006 and 2008 respectively, in collaboration with Saraya and related local institutions. Saraya has supported these activities by donating 1% of sales of palm oil-based products since 2007.

Although the employee was recruited for the incident shown earlier, he was still working for Saraya as an "external researcher" at the time of this research. As the job title suggests, his work involves Saraya's external sustainability efforts, with a focus on biodiversity conservation practices in Borneo. In parallel with the establishment of the NPOs, when the Roundtable on Sustainable Palm Oil (RSPO)—an international organization and regulation for sustainable palm oil—was not yet fully recognized in Japan, Saraya joined the RSPO as a board member in 2005. Consequently, the employee's work has expanded to include participation in the RSPO to raise awareness of sustainable palm oil. In recent years, the RSPO has received increasing attention in Japan. In April 2019, the

Japan Sustainable Palm Oil Network (JaSPON) was established in Japan, with Saraya as one of the founders, along with 18 related organizations. The employee, together with top management, has been continuously involved in these activities.

In this sense, Saraya's quest for global transparency on the issue of sustainability can be seen in its efforts to seek out and contribute to the social network on important social issues, such as biodiversity conservation. Recruiting people with sustainability experience and values from outside the company, and giving them the flexibility to carry out their activities based on their experience and values, rather than on the logic of the organization (such as restoring the company's image), is an important element in achieving global transparency. Structural segregation, which enables employees to work only on sustainability issues that are separate from the main business, has also been central to enabling employees to develop activities based on their own experiences and concerns.

This particular pattern of management control, aimed at utilizing the skills and capabilities of employees outside the organization, emerged in the incident of media attention, but has subsequently developed into the company's ongoing biodiversity conservation in Borneo and other sustainability activities. To date in 2022, in addition to biodiversity conservation activities in Borneo, the company is also involved in a range of sustainability activities. Accordingly, dozens of the company's employees work as specialist staff on these activities (according to interview data). As part of the activities of these dedicated employees, Saraya has established cooperation with 16 related organizations, including NPOs and various social institutions.[2]

4.3. *Inside activities to integrate sustainability into business*

In Saraya, sustainability activities outside the organization, initially aimed at addressing social problems, were gradually integrated into business activities. The activities of employees inside the organization, based on

---

[2] Saraya (2022) "Sustainability report."

internal transparency, i.e., employees' understanding of their own work, were crucial in this process.

The company has a long history of contributing to social issues through the development of environmental, hygiene, and health-related products. Founded in the 1950s during a dysentery epidemic in Japan, Saraya developed "Pearl Palm Soap," a product that could be used to sterilize and disinfect hands simultaneously. In the 1960s, when pollution in schools became a social problem, Saraya developed the "Kororo Gargle," a gargle machine that could be installed in schools and public places. And in the 1970s, the company continued to build on its heritage with the launch of "Palm Oil Detergent," which aimed to reduce the environmental impact of waste water, and "Hand Sanitor S," a pioneering alcohol-based hand sanitizer to prevent infection in medical settings. In the 1980s, the company also pioneered Japan's first refillable detergent pack to reduce the environmental impact of packaging waste.

The integration of the biodiversity-related activities in Borneo into the company's business activities were also in line with this tradition. As an RSPO board member, Saraya has been proactive in developing products and sourcing raw materials using certified oil. In 2009, soon after the certification scheme was launched, while other palm oil companies were reluctant to switch to certified oil, Saraya was keen to develop products using certified palm oil.[3] And indeed, in 2010, Saraya launched "Palm Oil Detergent Powder Neo," which was the first RSPO-certified product in Japan. In addition, in 2012 the company launched a new brand that is fully bio-processed, completely safe and less harmful to the environment, which was also made with segregated certified palm oils. And by 2019, Saraya has achieved that all products sold in Japan are made with RSPO-certified palm oil. As of June 2018, the company's use of RSPO-certified palm oil has reached 61%. This achievement, along with metrics including the target year and target range for 100% certified oil, has earned the company the highest marks compared to other companies using palm oil.[4]

---

[3] Nikkei Ecology (March 2009, p. 15).
[4] https://www.gpn.jp/assets/pdf/Palm_Oil_Scorecard_Japan2018-1.pdf, accessed on August 1, 2022.

Contributing to societal issues related to the environment, hygiene, and health has also required that the employees involved in the marketing activities to have specialized knowledge and skills. Since 1989, for example, the company's commercial hygiene business has introduced a food hygiene instructor system as part of its sales activities, which involves training food hygiene experts and sending them out to customers. Combined with socially responsible product development and specialized marketing, the company has developed its business as a value-added model for niche markets, rather than a low-cost model for the mass market (Saraya, 2010, 2016).

Integrating biodiversity activities in Borneo into marketing was also consistent with this strategy. In the 1990s, Saraya used TV commercials to promote the earth- and hand-friendly aspects of its laundry products. However, after the TV program aired, the company stopped advertising in the mass media and redirected advertising funds to support the activities in Borneo described above, while the marketing department took charge of the company's CSR. In 2006, after the Borneo activity won an award, Saraya resumed its advertising activities. However, instead of returning to TV commercials, they started Cause Related Marketing (CRM), which aims to attract consumers who want to make a contribution to social issues through their purchases. The CRM was designed to donate 1% of the sales of products containing palm oil to the Borneo biodiversity conservation project. Through the CRM, the social issues in Borneo became the story behind the products, and by linking the amount donated to sales rather than profit, the company's products gave meaning to the connection between consumer behavior and social issues. The range of products covered by the CRM has expanded from the palm oil detergent in 2007 to include more than 20 palm oil branded products and 19 other branded products.

In this sense, Saraya has progressively integrated its external sustainability activities into its product development and marketing. The basis for this integration is internal transparency, i.e., employees' understanding of the company's tradition of addressing social issues through their business and the business model that aims to create value in the niche market. However, this could not be achieved in a short period of time without tensions, particularly between external and internal activities. As described in

4.4. *The presence of organizational barrier and its management*

Structural segregation, which is critical to providing flexibility and utilizing the skills of employees outside the organization, has resulted in employees inside the organization not fully sharing, at least in the early stages. The employee, who had worked for a long time as a social entrepreneur in Uganda and was later recruited to run Saraya's sustainability activities in Uganda, claimed that it was difficult to communicate with the head office about their activities in Uganda in the early stages (Tajima, 2020). The company president also stated that there may have been a feeling among some employees that "if there was money to do things in Borneo, the money should have been in employee bonuses" (Saraya, 2016, p. 187).

These lines of evidence suggest that there was an organizational barrier (Gond et al., 2012) between employees working externally on sustainability activities and those working in the main business. One reason for this was the lack of company-wide information sharing. The activities of employees engaged in sustainability activities outside the organization were not frequently communicated to the whole company. In fact, the employee involved in the Borneo activities described above felt that he and his activities were not fully known to the majority of the organizational members until the activity won an external award (according to interviews).

Another reason was the different perception of the relationship between sustainability and business. While employees outside the organization engage in sustainability activities that address social issues themselves, employees within the company have a long tradition of contributing to social issues through the business. In the short term, therefore, there is little connection between the two perspectives and, at worst, they can be perceived as being in tension with each other. Activities such as elephant rescue in Borneo and the establishment of NPOs were not directly linked to the business and its performance. In fact, the amount the company has spent so far on the Borneo biodiversity project is more than 100 times the amount it had originally earmarked as an appropriate donation to the NPO (Saraya, 2010; Takahashi, 2018).

In the case company, although it took a long time, it was crucial to build an identity as a socially responsible company through a gradual process of managing the organizational barrier. An important initiative for building the identity was the renewal of the company's philosophy. From its inception, Saraya's corporate philosophy was "Natural Saraya," which meant contributing to social issues through its business, as exemplified by its palm oil detergent. However, through its activities in Borneo and other places, Saraya has recognized the social networks around significant social issues, such as biodiversity conservation. Its corporate philosophy was updated in 2012 to "Connecting Life," reflecting the company's role and contribution as part of the social network for building a sustainable society. The president of the company explained the significance of the new corporate philosophy as follows.

> Connecting Life is similar to the previous philosophy, but expresses a more proactive attitude than "Natural Saraya." Product development and social contribution are all things that the philosophy calls for. In a nutshell, the philosophy is about connecting and protecting the lives of all living beings, not just humans. (Saraya, 2016, pp. 19–20)

Another practice in building a corporate identity is the acquisition of various forms of social recognition. In the context of increasing societal demands for sustainable management, the company's activities have received significant public recognition. For example, the company received the "1st Japan SDGs Award" from the Ministry of Foreign Affairs in 2017 and the "Best Practice Award for Sustainable Palm Oil Procurement" from the World Wide Fund for Nature Japan in 2018.

The educational value of the company's work has also been acknowledged, with an SDGs study site in primary and secondary schools as an example of advanced practice.[5] Such external recognition is described as an "internal communication tool." A senior manager in the CSR

---

[5] https://sdgs.edutown.jp/, accessed on August 1, 2022.

department explained why the company actively applies for, and aims to win, awards from external bodies.

> Winning awards is an internal communication tool. Even if we tell our employees that we are doing something for society, they don't really understand it. But if we tell our employees that we have won an award or received praise from a third party, they and their families are likely to get the perception that our company is doing well.

Achieving social approval is also recognized as a factor that increases employees' sense of belonging and satisfaction (Saraya, 2016). It also aligns with business objectives in terms of fundraising and recruitment.[6]

5. Discussion and Conclusion

Drawing on a case study, the purpose of this study is to explore the role of enabling control in sustainability management. The characteristics of enabling control were found in the journey of sustainability management in the case site. Media attention prompted the company to seek global transparency—an understanding of the social issues in the supply chain within which it does business. A particular pattern of personnel control (Merchant and Van der Stede, 2007), i.e., recruiting people with experience and concern for social issues and providing them with flexibility, was central to achieving this global transparency. Flexibility, in this context, meant that employees were able to work on the basis of their experience and values rather than on the basis of corporate objectives. Management control through structural design (Malmi and Brown, 2008), structural segregation in this case, was crucial in providing the flexibility that enabled the employees to focus on their external work on social problems. These findings are partly consistent with previous research on the role of enabling control, which involves designing organizational structures to pursue dual goals (Jørgensen and Messner, 2009).

Subsequently, by identifying the root cause of social problems and the social network around them, and by participating in the social network,

---

[6] Article published in *Nihon Keizai Shimbun*, August 27, 2008.

employees' activities outside the organization have deepened and broadened global transparency. Although it has taken time, external sustainability activities have gradually been integrated into the business, particularly in procurement, product development and marketing. Internal transparency—the understanding by employees within the organization that their tradition of contributing to social problems through business, and the business model that aimed to add value in the niche market—was the basis for the integration. These findings support previous research showing that employee activities with high internal transparency lead to innovation, such as new product development (Jørgensen and Messner, 2010). In addition, previous research has argued that employees' external activities with flexibility could lead to a decline in performance (Heggen and Sridharan, 2021). The results of this study suggest that a broader perspective, both temporal and spatial, is needed to evaluate the performance of employees' activities with flexibility.

The integration of sustainability activities outside the organization into the business, however, has not been without its challenges. Under structural segregation, there was an organizational barrier between external and internal activities, at least in the early stages. This was due to a lack of company-wide information sharing and a different perspective on social problems—external activities focused on the social problem itself, while internal employees were aware of the link between the social problem and business activities. The presence of this organizational barrier could be explained by Adler and Borys' (1996) suggestion that in order to increase internal transparency, "it is important not to overload users with unnecessary system information ... layered access is key" (p. 72). Wouters and Wilderom (2008) also found that when the internal transparency of employees with expertise increases, conflicts arise over the allocation of company-wide resources. The results of this study also support this aspect of the conflict between global and internal transparency, at least for a period of time.

In managing the organizational barrier, a more indirect and long-term perspective was taken to build an organizational identity as a socially responsible company. The management control exercised by top and senior management, including the renewal of the corporate philosophy and the acquisition of third-party recognition, was central to this process.

These findings diverge from previous literature on the role of top management, which found that top and head office management interventions may reduce employees' perceptions of the enabling nature of the control system (Ahrens and Chapman, 2004; Jordan and Messner, 2012).

Overall, the previous research argues that enabling control plays a role in utilizing the skills and capabilities of employees and that control systems with the four characteristics enable the organization to manage multiple goals that are often in tension with each other. The results of this study suggest that the role of enabling control can be relevant in managing sustainability. In terms of utilizing employees' skills and abilities, this study found that the experience and value of employees who have been involved in external activities have influenced the way in which the company contributes to solving social problems. This study also found that the tradition and knowledge of employees within the organization is critical to integrating sustainability activities into the business. By utilizing the skills and abilities of employees both inside and outside the organization, the company was able to pursue a dual objective of addressing the social problem itself and achieving its business objectives.

References

Adler, P. S. and Borys, B. (1996). Two types of bureaucracy: Enabling and coercive. *Administrative Science Quarterly*, 41(1), 61–89.

Ahrens, T. and Chapman, C. S. (2004). Accounting for flexibility and efficiency: A field study of management control systems in a restaurant chain. *Contemporary Accounting Research*, 21(2), 271–301.

Basiron, Y. (2008). Malaysia's oil palm–Hallmark of sustainable development. *Global Oils & Fats Business Magazine*, 5(4), 1–7.

Chapman, C. S. and Kihn, L.-A. (2009). Information system integration, enabling control and performance. *Accounting, Organizations and Society*, 34(2), 151–169.

Daishima, Y. (2008). Messages that resonate come from the day-to-day activities of the business). *Brain*, 48(11), 47–49 (in Japanese).

Dixon, J. A. and Fallon, L. A. (1989). The concept of sustainability: Origins, extensions, and usefulness for policy. *Society & Natural Resources*, 2(1), 73–84.

Free, C. (2007). Supply-chain accounting practices in the UK retail sector: Enabling or coercing collaboration? *Contemporary Accounting Research*, 24(3), 897–933.

Goretzki, L., Strauss, E., and Wiegmann, L. (2018). Exploring the roles of vernacular accounting systems in the development of "enabling" global accounting and control systems. *Contemporary Accounting Research*, 35(4), 1888–1916.

Gray, R. (2010). Is accounting for sustainability actually accounting for sustainability ... and how would we know? An exploration of narratives of organisations and the planet. *Accounting Organizations and Society*, 35(1), 47–62.

Heggen, C., Sridharan, V. G., and Subramaniam, N. (2018). To the letter vs the spirit: A case analysis of contrasting environmental management responses. *Accounting, Auditing & Accountability Journal*, 31(2), 478–502.

Heggen, C. and Sridharan, V. G. (2021). The effects of an enabling approach to eco-control on firms' environmental performance: A research note. *Management Accounting Research*, 50, 100724.

Johnstone, L. (2019). Theorising and conceptualising the sustainability control system for effective sustainability management. *Journal of Management Control*, 30(1), 25–64.

Jordan, S. and Messner, M. (2012). Enabling control and the problem of incomplete performance indicators. *Accounting, Organizations and Society*, 37(8), 544–564.

Jørgensen, B. and Messner, M. (2009). Management control in new product development: The dynamics of managing flexibility and efficiency. *Journal of Management Accounting Research*, 21(1), 99–124.

Li, Y. (2011). The role of management accounting in strategizing: A case study from developing new business domain. *Melco Journal of Management Accounting Research*, 4(1), 23–40 (in Japanese).

Malmi, T. and Brown, D. A. (2008). Management control systems as a package — Opportunities, challenges and research directions. *Management Accounting Research*, 19(4), 287–300.

Merchant, K. A. and Van der Stede, W. A. (2007). *Management control Systems: Performance Measurement, Evaluation and Incentives*. Pearson Education.

Milne, M. J. (1996). On sustainability: The environment and management accounting. *Management Accounting Research*, 7(1), 135–161.

Norris, G. and O'Dwyer, B. (2004). Motivating socially responsive decision making: The operation of management controls in a socially responsive organisation. *The British Accounting Review*, 36(2), 173–196.

Saraya, Y. (2010). *What the Smallest Elephant in the World Has Taught Us*. Toyo Keizai Inc. (in Japanese).

Saraya, Y. (2016). *The Businesses of the Future Will Do Well With "Good Sounding" Practices*. Toyo Keizai Inc. (in Japanese).

Tajima, T. (2020). *The African Continent of Passion — The Full Story of the Saraya's "Disinfectant Dissemination Project"*. Gentosha Media Consulting (in Japanese).

Takahashi, A. (2018). Saraya and the 17 SDGs for a changing world, *Food Chemical*, October, 58–63 (in Japanese).

Wijethilake, C., Munir, R., and Appuhami, R. (2018). Environmental innovation strategy and organizational performance: Enabling and controlling uses of management control systems. *Journal of Business Ethics*, 151(4), 1139–1160.

Wouters, M. and Roijmans, D. (2011). Using prototypes to induce experimentation and knowledge integration in the development of enabling accounting information. *Contemporary Accounting Research*, 28(2), 708–736.

Wouters, M. and Wilderom, C. (2008). Developing performance-measurement systems as enabling formalization: A longitudinal field study of a logistics department. *Accounting, Organizations and Society*, 33(4), 488–516.

© 2025 World Scientific Publishing Company
https://doi.org/10.1142/9789811295652_0012

Chapter 12

Establishment and Operation of Management Systems for Sustainability Development

Asako Kimura

Kansai University, Suita, Japan

Abstract

This chapter explores management systems for embedding sustainability development in management. Sustainability development encompasses a range of issues, including the environment and human rights, but this chapter focuses on management systems to address gender disparity. For Japanese companies, gender disparity is essential in terms of human rights considerations and organizational productivity. It describes examples of Japanese companies establishing and operating the management system.

1. Introduction: Background of Japan

1.1. *Gender disparity*

In sustainability development, companies must manage various environmental and social issues. Among these issues, social efforts from Japanese companies especially diversity, are considered inferior to Western companies. A report by the World Economic Forum (2023) showed that Japan's

Gender Gap Index (GGI) in 2023 ranked 125th out of 146 countries. The GGI evaluates four aspects: economy, politics, education, and health, with a value of one indicating full equality. Education and health were close to one at 0.997 (47th) and 0.973 (59th), respectively. In contrast, politics and economy were low at 0.057 (138th) and 0.561 (123rd), which are low values compared to the rest of the world. The politics evaluation covers the gender ratio of members of the National Assembly, the gender ratio of cabinet ministers, and the gender ratio of tenure of the heads of the executive branch over the past 50 years.

The economic evaluation covers the gender ratio of labor participation, the gender gap in wages for the same work, the gender ratio of estimated labor income, the gender ratio of managers, and the gender ratio of professional and technical personnel.

Differences between men and women in the economy are also evident in employment patterns and wage differentials. According to the Ministry of Health, Labor and Welfare (2023), in 2022, the average wages for full-time employees and regular workers will be 2,764,000 JPY for women and 3,536,000 JPY for men, and for non-regular employees and regular workers, 1,989,000 JPY for women and 2,475,000 JPY for men. These differences in average wages can be attributed to differences in the ratio of female managers and the length of service. In companies with 100 or more employees, the percentage of women in 2022 will be was 24.1% for section chiefs, 13.9% for section managers, and 8.2% for department heads (Ministry of Health, Labor and Welfare, 2023). The Japan Institute for Labor Policy and Training (2023), the percentage of women in management positions in 2021 was 41.4% in the United States (US), 37.8% in France, 36.5% in the United Kingdom, 29.2% in Germany, and 13.2% in Japan.

Additionally, the average length of service for the general workforce in 2022 was 13.7 years for men and 9.8 years for women (Ministry of Health, Labor and Welfare, 2023). Furthermore, the employment rate for women aged 25-29 peaked at 87.7%, declined to 80.6% for those aged 30-34 and 78.9% for those aged 35-39, and then rose again to 81.5% for those aged 40-44 and 81.9% for those aged 45-49 (Ministry of Health, Labor and Welfare, 2023). This trend occurred mainly due to women's marrying and bearing children. According to the Ministry of Health,

Labor and Welfare (2023), the highest number of regular female staff and employees was in the 25-29 age group, and the employment rate increased after age 40, mainly due to non-regular employment. After childbirth, women resume work when their children enter elementary school; however, they tend to choose non-regular employment.

1.2. Women's Advancement Promotion Act (WAPA)

One cause of the wage gap between men and women in Japan and differences in work patterns and job titles is that women resign from their full-time positions when life events occur. To correct this disparity, in 2015, the Japanese government enacted the "Act on the Promotion of Women's Active Engagement in Professional Life," also known as the WAPA. This law aims to reform the male-centered corporate society, promote women's empowerment in their professional lives, and realize a vibrant society.

Even before this law was enacted, the government made several proposals. In 2003 the Gender Equality Bureau Cabinet Office stated that it "expects the percentage of women in leadership positions in all sectors of society to be at least 30% by 2020." Later, in 2013, Prime Minister Abe stated that he expected all listed companies to actively promote women in executive and managerial positions to achieve the government's goal. The Japan Business Federation has also launched a training course for female managers. However, the gender gap remained large.

In 2014, Prime Minister Abe revised the "Japan Revitalization Strategy" and made promoting female advancement one of the action plans. Under this strategy, in 2015, the WAPA was enacted. This law requires companies to assess women's advancement status, analyze issues, and formulate and publish an action plan. Companies must use the analysis to determine the percentage of female workers, the difference in the average length of service between men and women, and the percentage of women in management positions. The action plan must include a planning period, numerical targets, and specific details of the initiatives and their implementation dates. Moreover, the Financial Services Agency requires that security reports include sustainability information beginning in the fiscal year ending March 31, 2023. The report must disclose the ratio of female managers, the percentage of male employees taking childcare leave, the wage gap between men and women, and the company's approach and initiatives regarding sustainability. Thus, management's consideration of women's work styles has become indispensable in Japanese society.

2. Literature Review

Most diversity literature in accounting examines the association between female directors and firm performance. Post and Byron (2015) examined 140 prior studies between 1997 and 2014. They found that firms with a higher percentage of women directors on their boards were positively correlated with profits (e.g., ROA, ROE), but not with market value (e.g., book-to-market ratio, Tobin's Q). Post and Byron (2015) interpreted female directors' knowledge, experience, and values as influencing board decision-making and enhancing their ability to generate profits. Carter et al. (2010), analyzed the relationship between gender and ethnic diversity on US corporate boards and financial performance. They found a significant positive relationship between the number of female directors and ROA. However, there was no significant relationship with Tobin's Q. This trend is similar to the results shown by Post and Byron (2015).

Previous studies covering different countries have shown that the relationship between female directors and financial performance in Norway is particularly interesting. For example, since 2005, Norway has required that 40% of the boards of directors of listed companies be women. Ahern and Dittmar (2012) showed that after this law was implemented, Tobin's Q in Norwegian listed companies dropped significantly compared to the pre-enactment level. They interpreted this as a result of companies appointing young, inexperienced women as directors. In other words, the results show skepticism about increasing the number of female directors by law without adequate preparation.

Furthermore, Miyazaki (2021) randomly selected and examined 200 listed Japanese companies from 2019 to 2020 after the WAPA went into effect. He found that the percentage of female directors on boards was positively correlated with ROE, ROA, and Tobin's Q. Miyazaki (2021) analyzed one year of data before and after the appointment of female directors, revealing — a positive relationship between financial performance and an increase in the number of female directors. This finding suggests that firms with improved financial performance will likely increase the number of female directors. In other words, it is unclear whether the presence of female directors in Japan truly affects financial performance. Miyazaki (2021) also analyzed the relationship between the background of female directors and financial performance, showing that appointments from within the company positively correlate with ROE and Tobin's Q. Moreover, Matsumoto (2019) investigated the correlation between the proportion of female directors and the financial performance of Japanese firms from 2007 to 2013, before the enforcement of WAPA. Controlling for industry, they found no positive correlation between the ratio of female directors and financial performance. Therefore, no positive relationship between female directors and financial performance has been identified for Japanese firms before and after implementing the WAPA.

Prior studies have shown that women are more ethical and less likely to engage in immoral behavior than men (Betz *et al.*, 1989; Kaplan *et al.*, 2009). Gull *et al.* (2018) based their hypothesis on this argument, finding that female directors with business education and financial expertise may inhibit managers from manipulating profits. Furthermore, Yamamoto (2018) suggested that in firms with internal systems that consider work styles and firms with high retention rates of newly graduated women, higher ratios of women to full-time employees and women to managerial positions can increase productivity and profitability. In other words, while the presence of female directors has not politively affected financial performance in Japanese corporate society, looking at individual firms, there are cases where female directors are helpful in organizational management decision-making.

Many Japanese companies are still based on the lifetime employment system; thus, training internal human resources to become directors is essential to increase the number of female directors. However, in Japan, where the number of female managers is lower than that of the rest of the world; in this environment, it is unclear how to train women as candidates for board positions. This study examines a case study of a Japanese company that implements good practices regarding the development of female employees.

3. Research Method

This study identifies how firms construct and operate management systems to develop female employees. It is preferable to employ a case study to discuss what management systems were built, when, and why (Merchant and Van der Stede, 2006). This study considers the case of the Japanese airline FlyAir (tentative name). In the airline industry, female human resources are limited to flight attendant work with few opportunities for promotion (Smith *et al.*, 2021). However, FlyAir advanced a system for women's work before enforcing WAPA and is considered one company that demonstrates good practices.

This study examines FlyAir using publicly available documents, including integrated reports. Additionally, interviews were conducted for 1.5 hours with the Environmental, Social and Governance (ESG) Promotion Office, 1 hour with the Human Resources Department, and 1 hour with the Integrated Planning Department.

4. Case Study

4.1. *FlyAir overview and awareness of issues*

FlyAir is a major airline company in Japan that is mainly engaged in the air transportation business. The ratio of male-to-female employees is approximately 50%; however, the distribution of human resources is uneven, with many male pilots and many female flight attendants. FlyAir made a top-down management decision in 2014 to address this issue and issued a diversity declaration, announcing goals and measures for promoting female employees to all group employees.

In 2014, FlyAir announced the goal of increasing the ratio of female managers in the FlyAir Group from 14% to 20% by the end of FY2023, and the ratio of female organizational managers in section managers and above from 10% to 15% or more. As a result, as of FY2021, the company achieved a ratio of 21.9% of female managers, 2 years ahead of the plan, and once again set a target of 30% by 2030. FlyAir has successfully planned and executed its goal of increasing the ratio of female managers.

As of 2023, one of the six full-time directors was a female employee of FlyAir. Thus, FlyAir can be considered a company that has successfully developed female talent within the company, therefore, this study examines how the company established a management system to develop female managers.

4.2. *Management system for human resource development*

FlyAir's management system for human resource development began with its diversity declaration in 2014. The company established a department to promote the advancement of women, which was managed primarily by female employees. The department was later expanded to an LGBTQ-inclusive diversity department, run by both men and women.

According to the 2018 Integrated Report, FlyAir promotes ESG management that includes social issues, including women's success and environmental and governance issues. In 2021, the company positioned the ESG strategy as one of the three pillars of its management strategy. Promoting women's empowerment is one of FlyAir's fundamental policies.

FlyAir institutionalized measures to "create a comfortable work environment" and "measures for employee growth," aiming to promote women's empowerment (the goal of the Diversity Declaration) and utilize human resources, including men and employees of overseas group companies. The company implemented systems such as flextime, telework, workcation, and bleisure, intending to transform its employees' work styles. In the integrated report, the number of teleworkers and the number of people who use the Workcation and Bleisure systems are indicators of the results of diversity promotion. The company also has a childcare leave system, a nursing care leave system, and a leave system for accompanying a spouse on relocation. The Human Resources Department is also designing a system to make it easier for male employees to take childcare leave, enabling-more people to use this system without difficulty.

FlyAir is also improving productivity and work style transformation, using total hours worked, annual leave take-up rate, and average monthly overtime hours as performance indicators. The company is promoting the development of human resources by balancing the improvement of work comfort and productivity. Furthermore, the company has established various study groups for employee growth, offering study sessions tailored to different ranks and life events, such as leadership education, study sessions for female leaders, and study sessions focusing on issues after maternity leave. Moreover, volunteer employees also hold voluntary study sessions, which the integrated report describes as being for "learning and practicing" rather than "going to receive education." Additionally, the company shares materials explaining the work of each department and has employees who perform and explain their work; thus employees can think autonomously about career development.

4.3. *Management system Key Performance Indicators (KPIs)*

FlyAir has positioned various systems and workshops for human resource development in its ESG strategy. FlyAir has also formulated a business strategy as one of its management strategies and has set targets for financial indicators. FlyAir has set specific targets for financial indicators such as operating margin and ROIC, which the company must achieve while at the same time implementing various measures to develop human resources.

FlyAir sets ESG-related target values for each department and subsidiary, for example, a 20% ratio of female managers. These targets are not set uniformly; they are allocated according to the situation of each department so that 20% can be achieved as a whole. Furthermore, the target value for total annual hours worked is company-wide — all departments and subsidiaries are required to achieve this target. The company has also implemented various systems designed to reduce the number of annual hours employees work while by improving individual productivity to maintain company-wide productivity. Productivity per hour has traditionally been a KPI; thus improving productivity through changes in how employees work is likely to be accepted by employees.

In addition to standard performance measures, FlyAir's directors set individual goals for the economy, society, and environment, designed to be linked to their compensation. Directors are responsible for the profitability of the departments they are in charge of and for society and the environment.

5. Discussion and Conclusion

This study examined establishing and operating a management system for corporate sustainability development, particularly from the human resource development perspective. In Japan, a significant gender gap exists in average wages, and the number of female managers and directors is lower than that of their male counterparts. Previous studies of Japanese firms found no clear evidence of a positive impact of female directors on financial performance (Miyazaki, 2021; Matsumoto, 2019); however, prior studies suggest that female directors impact accounting profits (Carter *et al.*, 2010; Post and Byron, 2015). For example, Post and Byron (2015) interpreted accounting gains as a result of good managerial decision-making when women directors bring new knowledge and opinions to the board.

Gull *et al.* (2018) showed that business education in higher education may prevent women directors from manipulating organizational profits, and business education may influence the success of female employees. In Japan, Miyazaki (2021) also showed that female directors promoted from within the company were positively related to accounting profits, suggesting that fostering female employees within the company affects profitability. In Japan, lifetime employment is assumed, and a significant economic disparity exists between men and women; thus, promoting women's empowerment can lead to organizational growth.

Nonetheless, in a corporate society like Japan, where male-dominated work styles have been established, it is difficult to establish a management system that considers diversity, including women. As Gond *et al.* (2012) indicated, when sustainability thinking is introduced into an existing management control system, the sustainability control system tends to be constructed independently. In other words, the management control and sustainability control systems are decoupled, neglecting the sustainability control system.

At FlyAir, the ESG strategy and business strategies are developed separately. The company introduced various systems to change employees' work styles while implementing, measures to improve productivity. By setting KPIs linked to productivity as nonfinancial indicators, the company realized diverse work styles while maintaining company-wide productivity. The company also created a comfortable working environment for both men and women, providing opportunities for study sessions and helpful materials at various life stages. This situation enabled women to continue working in various departments for many years.

Thus, the company has achieved its goal for the percentage of female managers.

FlyAir's management system for work style is independent of its sustainability control system, however it sets nonfinancial indicators tied to productivity as organizational goals. A sustainability control system that develops employees helps improve profitability by contributing to increased productivity and, is consistent with a traditional management control system that emphasizes profitability. Conversely, the ratio of female managers, one of the performance indicators in the sustainability control system, is set as a realistic target value tailored to the situation of each section and subsidiary. This ensures that managers in each section can achieve the organization's goals while respecting individual career development choices. For employees who value productivity per hour, it is easier to accept working within the target hours for their career development. This paper concludes that the FlyAir case can be managed to achieve sustainability development by adding a sustainability control system to the conventional management control system and balancing each.

Acknowledgements

This work was supported by Japan Society for the Promotion of Science (JSPS) KAKENHI grant number 23K01687 and the Kansai University Fund for Supporting Young Scholars, 2019 — "Research on the development of management control systems that contribute to SDGs." The author is grateful for the constructive comments provided on this study by the volume editors of Vol. 21, including Professor Eri Yokota.

References

Ahern, K. R. and Dittmar, A. K. (2012). The changing of the boards: The impact on firm valuation of mandated female board representation. *Quarterly Journal of Economics*, 127(1), 137–197.

Betz, M., O'Connell, L., and Shepard, J. M. (1989). Gender differences in proclivity for unethical behavior. *Journal of Business Ethics*, 8, 321–324.

Carter, D.A., D'Souza, F., Simkins, B. J., and Simpson, W. G. (2010). The gender and ethnic diversity of US boards and board committees and firm financial performance. Corporate governance. *An International Review*, 18, 396–414.

Durden, D. (2008). Towards a socially responsible management control system. *Accounting, Auditing & Accountability Journal*, 21(5), 671–694.

Gull, A. A., Nekhili, M., Nagati, H., and Chtioui, T. (2018). Beyond gender diversity: How specific attributes of female directors affect earnings management. *The British Accounting Review*, 50(3), 255–274.

Gond, J. P., Grubnic, S., Herzig, C., and Moon, J. (2012). Configuring management control systems: Theorizing the integration of strategy and sustainability. *Management Accounting Research*, 23(3), 205–223.

Japan Institute for Labour Policy and Training (2023). *Databook of International Labour Statistics* (in Japanese).

Kaplan, S., Pany, K., Samuels, J., and Zhang J. (2009). An examination of the association between gender and reporting intentions for fraudulent financial reporting. *Journal of Business Ethics*, 87, 15–30.

Matsumoto, M. (2020). An empirical analysis of the effects of introducing female directors in Japanese firms: Does the introduction of female directors contribute to improved firm performance? *SangyoKeiri*, 80(2), 78–93 (in Japanese).

Merchant, K. A. and Van der Stede, W. A. (2006). Field-based research in accounting: Accomplishments and prospects. *Behavioral Research in Accounting*, 18(1), 117–134.

Ministry of Health, Labor and Welfare (2023). *Basic Survey on Wage Structure 2023* (in Japanese).

Miyazaki, M. (2021). The relationship between female directors and financial performance: An empirical study on Japanese firms. *Journal of Atomi University Faculty of Management*, 32, 1–18 (in Japanese).

Post, C. and Byron, K. (2015). Women on boards and firm financial performance: A meta-analysis. *The Academy of Management Journal*, 58(5), 1546–1571.

Serafeim, G. (2020). Social-impact efforts that create real value: They must be woven into your strategy and differentiate your company. *Harvard Business Review* (September–October).

Smith, W. E., Cohen, S., Kimbu A. N., and Jong, A. (2021), Reshaping gender in ailine employment. *Annals of Tourism Research*, 89, 1–14.

World Economic Forum (2023). *Global Gender Gap Report 2023*.

Yamamoto, I. (2018). Firm performance and the promotion of women's participation and advancement: Evidence from Japanese firm panel data, *Hitotsubashi Business Review*, 66(1), 30–43, (in Japanese).

© 2025 World Scientific Publishing Company
https://doi.org/10.1142/9789811295652_bmatter

Index

A
absorptive capacity, 108, 110, 117, 130, 135
Act on the Promotion of Women's Active Engagement in Professional Life, 213
AI, 127
Ameba Management, 165
Anglo-Saxon, 88
archival data, 146, 154

B
balance, 152
bootlegging, 148, 152
broker, 134
budgeting, 32, 34–37, 40–43, 45–47
budget management, 17
budget system, 161, 164, 169–170
business intelligence (BI), 127
business performance evaluation, 160

C
15% culture, 152
case study, 93
codification, 128
codification strategy, 128
combination, 129, 134

combinative capabilities, 130, 134
controller, 2

D
decode, 130
de-codification strategy, 130
decontextualization, 128
diagnostic, 173, 177, 180, 184–185
diagnostically, 178
digitalization, 124
digital transformation, 123
dynamic tension, 149, 152

E
enabling control, 194–196, 206
enterprise resource planning (ERP), 95, 125
ESG, 217–219
experiential learning capability, 108, 110, 116–117
explicit knowledge, 128, 132
externalization, 129, 134

F
fit, 93
fixed compensation system, 161

flexibility, 195, 199, 206
formal controls, 144

G
Gender Gap Index (GGI), 212
global grading system, 164
global transparency, 195, 199, 206

H
hourly profitability, 131
human resource evaluation, 160
human resource management (HRM), 160–164, 167–171

I
implementation, 93
informal controls, 142, 144, 152
interactive, 173, 180, 184–186
interactive control systems, 145
interactively, 178
internalization, 129, 134
internal transparency, 195, 202, 207

J
Japanese management accounting, 68
job-based pay system, 161
job costing, 52

K
key performance indicators (KPIs), 163–166, 169–170
knowledge, 134
knowledge brokers, 130
knowledge combinations, 126
knowledge conversion, 129, 134
knowledge creation, 125, 129
knowledge integration, 126
knowledge management, 125
knowledge sharing, 123
knowledge transfer, 126

L
lean manufacturing, 68
levers of control, 145, 152

M
3M Company, 142, 146, 152
management accounting capabilities, 106, 114, 117
management accounting studies, 141
management accounting systems, 143
management by objectives (MBO), 32, 34–36, 38, 40, 42–43, 45, 47, 166
Management control (MC), 2, 124
Management control package, 71
Management control systems as a package, 24
management control systems (MCS), 123, 174, 178
management control tools (MCT), 32, 34–36, 41–42, 45, 47
medium-term management plan, 32, 34, 36–37, 39, 41–42, 45, 47
medium-term plans, 7
Micro Profit Centers (MPC), 54, 68

O
open-book management, 165
operations orientation and group dynamics, 92
organizational change, 153
organizational culture, 130
organizational resources, 149
organizational transformation, 132

P
path dependence, 128
performance evaluation system, 163
performance management, 19
performance management systems (PMS), 173–178, 180, 184–186
personalization strategy, 128
philosophy-based management system, 165
PMI, 162, 172
product orientation and bureaucratic dynamics, 91

Q
QCA, 56

R
15% rule, 142
reporting line, 165, 168
resource-based theory, 125
return on invested capital (ROIC), 88

S
seniority-based pay system, 161
seniority system, 166
simplification, 128
Six Sigma, 142, 149, 152
socialization, 129
standard costing, 53
strategy, 6
stretch goals, 148
subsidiary, 173–180, 183–186
sustainability management, 194, 196, 206

T
tacit knowledge, 128, 132
target costing, 68
tension, 142, 152
tight management control, 145
Total Quality Management (TQM), 93
Toyota Production System, 68

V
Value-based management, 88
variable compensation system, 161
VBM sophistication, 91

W
WAPA, 213, 215

www.ingramcontent.com/pod-product-compliance
Lightning Source LLC
LaVergne TN
LVHW012321090525
810667LV00002B/18